3.11への文化からの応答
24人のクリエーター・文化人へのインタビュー

3.11への文化からの応答
Commitment to 3.11

24人のクリエーター・文化人へのインタビュー
Response to Disaster through Culture and Creativity in Japan

グイド・フェリッリ
Guido Ferilli

Guido Ferilli

目次 | Contents

グイド・フェリッリ | Guido Ferilli —— 009
3.11への文化からの応答——24人のクリエーター・文化人へのインタビュー
Commitment to 3.11
Response to Disaster through Culture and Creativity in Japan

今村有策 | Yusaku Imamura —— 054
3.11への芸術文化からの応答
The Response of Art and Culture to 3.11

[インタビュー | Interviews]

荒川靖彦 | Yasuhiko Arakawa	061
荒木 猛 | Takeshi Araki	070
遠藤一郎 | Ichiro Endo	076
逢坂恵理子 | Eriko Osaka	083
大友良英 | Yoshihide Otomo	091
甲斐賢治 | Kenji Kai	100
加藤種男 | Taneo Kato	110
假屋崎省吾 | Shogo Kariyazaki	121
黒瀬陽平 | Yohei Kurose	126
後藤和子 | Kazuko Goto	135
小山薫堂 | Kundo Koyama	141
近藤誠一 | Seiichi Kondo	148
橘 正紀 | Masaki Tachibana	162
タニノクロウ | Kuro Tanino	170
Chim↑Pom | Chim↑Pom	178
津田大介 | Daisuke Tsuda	185
中村政人 | Masato Nakamura	194
南條史生 | Fumio Nanjo	203
福原義春 | Yoshiharu Fukuhara	210
藤原秀樹 | Hideki Fujiwara	214
古谷誠章 | Nobuaki Furuya	222
山口真樹子 | Makiko Yamaguchi	227
山野真悟 | Shingo Yamano	232
山本高之 | Takayuki Yamamoto	237

Guido Ferilli

3.11への文化からの応答
24人のクリエーター・文化人へのインタビュー

グイド・フェリッリ

イントロダクション

3.11の地震により、日本は近年の歴史上もっとも困難な瞬間を経験することとなった。東北地方太平洋沖地震によってもたらされた破壊的な影響には、即時に経験されたものにとどまらず、さらなる困難を引き起こすであろう、将来的な混乱も含まれている。

3.11からまだ数年しか経過していないが、これまでに起こったことと今後起こることは、全ての人の日常生活の一部である。私の生活にとっても例外ではない。3.11当日、私はイタリアのボローニャにいた。妻と見たテレビに映し出されたイメージと友人や家族から伝えられたニュースは、これからも私たちの心の中に残り続けるであろう。3.11以前、最後に東京に滞在したのは2010年の10月、私が教鞭をとる大学の学生たちとの研修旅行のためであった。それは東京研修旅行の2年目であったが、東京での経験は常に私たちの期待を遥かに上回るもので、二度の東京研修旅行はともに大成功であったことを思い出す。

2011年5月5日 サン・バルトロメオとガエターノ教会祈祷所でのイベントの様子
Event at oratory of the Church of Saints Bartolomeo and Gaetano (Bologna, May 5th, 2011)
Photo: Guido Ferilli

記述することさえはばかられるほどの破壊的な地震のイメージを目の当たりにし、私はすぐさま何か助けになることをしたいと考えた。ボローニャ市民と、ボローニャに就労・就学している日本人コミュニティとの連帯に焦点を当てたイベントに参加、協力した。この大学とパスタソースで有名な街が、日本で起こっていることを理解し、確かな手助けを行うため日本と真剣に接触しようとしていた。私たちは募金集めのために出来る限りのことをし、もっとも微小な意思表示であっても助けになるのではと信じて日本の製品を購入した[1]。一方で私は、私の文化分野の研究者としての能力を活かす方法を模索していた。この悲劇的な出来事を文化や創造を通じて新陳代謝（メタボライズ）する、日本社会の許容力に焦点を置くというのが私の基本的なアイデアであった。この許容力については数えきれないほどの実例があり、またあらゆる形態の日本文化史の節目となっている。

2012年3月11日
コンヴェント・サン・フランチェスコ図書館でのイベントの様子
Library at the Convent of San Francesco (Bologna, March 11th, 2012)
Photo: Guido Ferilli

日本の近年の歴史上、第二次世界大戦と広島と長崎への二度の原爆投下以来、これほどのスケールでトラウマ的な損害を残した出来事は他にない。文化生産という側面から考えたとき、第二次世界大戦と原爆投下によってもたらされた影響はこの国独自のものであった。事実、第二次世界大戦に続く出来事は、伝統芸術（絵画、彫刻、ビジュアルアート）やサブカルチャー（マンガ、アニメ、映画）を通じて表現され、並外れた創造の系譜が発展することに直接的な影響を与えた。今日、サブカルチャーは日本の古典文化とともに日本の国家アイデンティティを特徴づけ、その国際的なソフトパワーを強化

するものとして、日本政府によっても認識されている。文化や創造産業の発展は、今では世界の国々にとっても優先議題であり、地域開発のエンジンとして競争力を高める戦略は、伝統的な工業ではなく、この文化産業を指していることが多くなってきている。破壊的な出来事のトラウマ的影響を新陳代謝するためには、新しい個人的・集団的な表現という形、つまり、芸術的・文化的生産とその消費が非常に重要な道具になりうることを、日本の歴史は教えてくれる。その例は、圧倒的な天変地異からよりよき社会のための状況構築まで、様々である。豊かな時代の芸術生産の成果は、文化や創造セクターという、国際的に重要であると認識される産業の発展でもある。

例えば今日、イタリアや世界の多くの国で、数世代にわたるマンガ、アニメ文化と自身との関連を認識しない人は少ないだろう。その作品テーマの多くは災害と結びついており、例えば宮崎駿の『未来少年コナン』や、『ゴジラ』、最近の例で言えば『東京マグニチュード8.0』、プレイステーションのゲーム『絶体絶命都市4』などがある。私の研究のアイデアは、このような出来事に対する一般市民とコミュニティの反応に、どのように文化や創造が貢献しているのかということを率先的に考えることであった。もし3.11が新たな日本文化の波を作り出すとするならば、テーマ（環境や自然資源の利用、エネルギー生産と利用、またライフスタイルや個人的、社会的な幸福）の重要さと実際性を考慮したとき、この惨事が一般にどのような影響を与えるのかも考えてみたかった。

日本に落ち着きを取り戻すために活動している多くの人たちの声を、日本と世界中の読者のために記録し、彼らに話を届けるという意味でも、当時起こっていたことを理解することは興味深い試みだと考えた。この考えは、トーキョーワンダーサイトの滞在プログラムとして私の提案が検討された決定的なポイントであったと信じているし、私の関心が受け入れられたことに非常に感謝している。この結果、2011年の10月から12月まで東京を訪れ、青山にあるトーキョーワンダーサイトに一ヶ月滞在することになった。
その時の様々な活動の調査結果は本章に記載されている。このテキストは、私が滞在中に学んだことを概述しているため、それ自体が関心の対象となるかもしれないが、ここで強調したいことは、私が集めた証言の重要性である。日

本の当時の行動が「冷静」で「整然」としていたと見られていたという事実は、日本社会を揺るがしたこの出来事に対処する尋常ではない繊細さと、創造性の証明となっている。全般的に、3.11後たった数ヶ月後には表現的な活動が実施され、それらは日本国民にとっても、国際社会全般、また近年多くの破壊的な自然災害を経験したイタリアにとっても、特に重要で興味深い思考のための糧となった。

本書に収められているインタビューは、2012年に四回に渡って日本を訪れた際に実施した四本のインタビューを除き、2011年の10月から12月にかけて実施された。四本のインタビューは英語で行われ、それ以外のインタビューは大岩希代子さんの不可欠なサポートにより日本語で実施された。その後全てのテキストはイタリア語に翻訳され、大岩さんと平文代さんにより日本語に翻訳された。最終的にインタビューを受けてくれた全ての人に内容確認をお願いし、また必要であれば内容を更新してもらうように頼んだ。加えて、インタビュー参加者にはテキストを補完する関連イメージの提供をお願いした。その後テキストは英語に翻訳され、私のテキスト部分は日本語に翻訳された。本書の売り上げによって得られる印税は全て、東北の文化活動の促進のために寄付される。

文化と創造性を通じ、トラウマに反応すること

日本文化の歴史を振り返った時、地震のようなトラウマ的出来事の最初のシンボルとしては、鯰が想起される。1592年まで遡ると、豊臣秀吉が京都所司代に送った手紙に、1586年の地震後に京都に伏見城を建設することに心配の意を表明している。鯰絵の普及とその大衆性は1855年までに遡ることができ、今日においても日本文化の中で地震を表象している[2]。トラウマ的出来事が歌舞伎で最初に表象されたのは、磐梯山の噴火に続く1888年であり、噴火によって大打撃を受けた福島地域の写真イメージに影響を受けたものであるが、ハッピーエンドで終わる劇的な恋愛物語の舞台装置となった[3]。『富嶽三十六景』(1830–1832)のシリーズで世界的に有名な『神奈川沖浪裏』を通じ、北斎は圧倒、支配の対象としてではない自然の力、彼の愛した自然の内包するリズムというテーマを伝えている[4]。

鯰と職人たち：鯰大尽の遊び
国際日本文化研究センター所蔵
Namazu (catfish) with artisans
Coutesy of the International Research-Center for Japanese Studies

08-001 音聞浅間幻灯画
地震火災版画張交帖
（Ishimoto Collection I）
BS:11
東京大学総合図書館所蔵
Print showing the actor Kikugoro V
Ishimoto Collection I
BS:11
Archive of the University of Tokyo General Library

葛飾北斎
富嶽三十六景
神奈川沖浪裏
千葉市美術館所蔵
Katsushika Hokusai,
Thirty-Six Views of Mt. Fuji: Under the Wave off the Coast of Kanagawa
Chiba City Museum, Chiba

ガイド・フェリッリ | 13

日本が地震や津波、台風や火山噴火のような自然災害や、戦争や火災のような人間によってもたらされた出来事の影響に対処しなければならないのは、今回が初めてではない。しかしながら、日本が他の国々と異なるのは、そのような出来事を文化生産や表現を通して解釈し、新陳代謝する能力ではないだろうか。新陳代謝という言葉は、時間と空間を超え、外傷的（非外傷的）な出来事を自身で参照する、広い意味での日本の文化的な物語の生態に言及している[5]。トラウマ的な出来事に関して言えば、日常的に目にすることができる言及は地震によって引き起こされたものであるが、日本はそれらと長くて複雑な関係がある。あらゆる要素が研究、分析されてきた別の例は、今日でも強烈な集団的記憶であり続けている、第二次世界大戦の影響である。第二次世界大戦の影響は広い範囲において豊かな文化生産の源となっており、社会の変化を反映するものとなっている。日本の文化的、創造的生産は直接的、間接的に第二次世界大戦に影響を受けているということができるだろう。詳細に検証すると、このような文化生産はエンターテイメントという名において再発するトレンドの結果としてではなく、むしろ社会の中で誘発される変化やこのような出来事に対する社会そのものの表現であり、芸術的表現の結果ではないだろうか。日本は、芸術生産を通じ、上記出来事を新陳代謝するユニークな能力を示した国であり、新しい形の考えを通じてそれを行った。この考えは、この国の物語を特徴づけ、文化生産や科学、テクノロジーといったあらゆる形態へと実を結んでいる。

広い意味でいうと、19世紀中頃以降の西欧への開国が「カルチャーショック」に寄与しているのではないだろうか。この群島と西洋社会との出会いにおける新陳代謝は、複雑でダイナミックな創造過程であり、社会的、経済的、文化的な進化を意味していた。これは、近代に到達するための座標の再構築と再定義を決定づけたが、19世紀後半のアドルフォ・ファルサーリやフェリーチェ・ベアトの写真は西洋化が浸透していない日本を映し出した。日本の伝統と儒教の価値観をベースにした勤勉、倹約、忠誠、学びのおかげで、伝統を破壊しない創造的な回復や発達が達成された[6]。
「環太平洋火山帯」に沿っているという地理的な位置のせいで、日本は地震に脆弱である。この特徴は地震に対処する技術と建築の発達をもたらした。日本において、建築は元来「耐震」や「免震」という言葉に代表されるよ

うに、地震に対応するために方向づけられてきたが、それは地震の揺れに慣れている日本人のための建築であったため、この日本のアプローチを理解できない日本に居住する外国人が、近代建築において技術的解決策の発展を促すために思考しデザインしてきたものである。大工（伝統的な日本の建築職人）という言葉は西洋の工事技術と思想を新陳代謝した、伝統的日本建築技術の進化の始まりを代表している。内装デザインでさえも地震の影響に耐えうるように発達してきた。1923年に起こった関東大震災後の復興も、社会と風景における変化の加速と同時に起こり、公共インフラの復旧だけにとどまらない、現代的な街を再構築（復興）する機会であった[7]。

この時点から、地震により大きな関心が払われるようになり、1960年9月1日には「防災の日」が設定された。「ヨーロッパ風」[8]に都市を現代化し、経済的、産業的進化を遂げ世界的な舞台に仲間入りした日本と日本社会、というイメージを現代化するための機会ともなった。建築と都市デザインはその後、第二次世界大戦以後の再建にも影響を受けたが、その傾向は1970年に開催された大阪万博で最高潮を極めた。万博において、日本は「メタボリズム」運動が作り出した都市開発の哲学を提案した。「単純に古いものの再構築や復活ではなく、確固とした実験性と新しさの追求として伝統を上手

日本万国博覧会（テーマ館）
大阪府より提供
Theme Pavilion at EXPO'70
Osaka Prefectural Government

ガイド・フェリッリ | 15

く取り入れる」とした「メタボリズム」は日本のモダニズムの新しいスタイルとして60年代に始まった[9]。90年代のバブル経済と社会の変化、また大阪万博のコンセプトの再生産に焦点を当てた2005年の愛知万博の失望的な結果により「メタボリズム」運動は、社会変化の再解釈という点においてその限界を指し示した。そして、本書の南條史生のインタビューによると、建築やインフラにおける機動性、エネルギー、情報など「ソフト」の追求に標準を合わせる、新しい思考である「新メタボリズム」を提案する必要性も示した。

大阪万博はアジアにおける最初の世界博覧会であり、日本にとってもその経済的、科学的、文化的進化を全世界に向けて示す初めての機会であった。お祭り広場に設置された岡本太郎の『太陽の塔』は万博を圧倒した芸術的シンボルである。岡本自身がテレビ番組で「芸術は爆発だ」とコメントしたが、アーティストが核兵器のトラウマと芸術を結びつけていたことがわかる。「新世代」のアーティストであるヤノベケンジは、第二次世界大戦後のマンガとアニメを読んで育ち、岡本太郎の人生に大きく影響を受けた。ヤノベは、1997年にチェルノブイリ原子力発電所を訪れた際に着用した黄色い放射能防御服『アトムスーツ』(1997)で知られており、この作品と他の多くの作品は、2011年に岡本太郎生誕百周年を記念して開催された岡本太郎記念館での展覧会で展示された。『トらやん』『サン・チャイルド』『サン・チャイルド島』に加え、最近、ヤノベが岡本太郎の『太陽の塔』に侵入した際のビデオも展示された。

岡本太郎記念館
ヤノベケンジ：サン・チャイルド
Kenji Yanobe, *Sun Child* (Taro Okamoto Memorial Museum)
©Yanobe Kenji
Photo: Guido Ferilli
(November 2011)

ビジュアルアート、マンガ、アニメ、おもちゃ、サイエンスフィクション、映画、ロボット(「人型ロボット」のデザイン)、ビデオゲームは全て、日本文化の表現形態であり、自然または人為的なトラウマ的出来事や社会の変化を反映させようとする試みにおける、日本の歴史的な物語から着想されてきた。創成期から、マンガはリアル、象徴、虚構という多様なテーマによって特徴づけられてきた。マンガには、12世紀のマンガ以前のアーティストで僧侶でもある鳥羽僧正(1053–1140)から、遊里の「浮世」を表す浮世絵や春画、17世紀から19世紀の妖怪絵、マンガにとってかわられた19世紀後半の「ポンチ絵」の登場までを含む、技術と内容進化の長い歴史がある。19世紀の変わり目と二度の世界大戦の間には、マンガ表現は軍事プロパガンダと関係したテーマを含んでいた。しかしながら、今日世界から関心を集めるマンガやサブカルチャー、古典芸術によって表現される長期的な文化、創造産業が実際に始まったのは、第二次世界大戦後になってからである。

次世代のアーティストに影響を与えている巨匠は、間違いなく手塚治虫(1928–89)である。爆撃や破壊という個人的な戦争体験とともに、国内外コミックや映画、演劇、ディズニー映画を通し、戦争プロパガンダと第二次世界大戦の破壊への内省を提供するという、手塚の作家としての特徴や創造性が形成されていった。

イタリアと同様に日本においても、第二次世界大戦後、1950年代にテレビが登場するまで検閲されていた映画が、アメリカから日本に到着し、民主化と現代化のための説得力のある手段となっていた。日本は一方で、60年代から80年代にかけて産業、技術、経済発展、消費主義からなる資本主義発展の時代に突入した。広島と長崎への原爆投下と核兵器テストによる大量破壊という戦争による敗北の灰から、マンガやアートなどの文化、創造的表現が新たに生まれたのであった。これらのトラウマ的出来事が、日本が新しい物語を再構築することに影響を与えているとしたら、冷戦、ベトナム戦争、70年代初頭の平和運動、70年代の石油危機、経済ブーム、バブル経済、冷戦の終わり、大きな物語とポストモダニズム衰退と続く出来事も、文化生産における物語に影響を与えた[10]。

原子爆弾によって引き起こされた第二次世界大戦の破壊と荒廃というテーマは、20世紀後半の文化生産に共通するものであり、それは様々な発展のための要素を決定し、また大戦後から現在までに起こった国内外の出来事の偶発によっても影響を受けた。第二次世界大戦後のトラウマに関係する文化、創造生産の物語をたどることはこのテキストの目的ではないが、例えば、黒沢明の『七人の侍』が第二次世界大戦後の日本の状況を伝え[11]、また『夢』が核の惨事を予期していたとすれば、『鉄腕アトム』は核エネルギー利用を表し、同時期の『ゴジラ』はその利用の酷い結果を描写している。ゴジラや汚染問題に関係するヘドラのような怪獣映画は、若手の映画監督・塚本晋也に影響を与えた。塚本は産業社会における個人の疎外を扱った『鉄男』と日本のサイバーパンク発展の生みの親である。このような怪獣映画は、ウルトラマンやウルトラマンセブンが、太陽光を再生することで地球侵略を試みる怪獣たちと戦うのとは対比的である[12]。

黒澤明「夢」(1990)
Akira Kurosawa,
Dreams (1990)
Courtesy of Kurosawa
Production Co.

過去数十年に渡り『AKIRA』『宇宙戦艦ヤマト』『機動戦士ガンダム』『新世紀エヴァンゲリオン』などのアニメや映画、また多くのSF映画で、核に関連したイメージが扱われてきた。しかし、私が若かった頃個人的に最も魅力を感じたアニメ主人公は、鈴川鉄久原作の『アストロガンガー』である。地球人の博士の父親と、宇宙人である母のもとに生まれた子どもの物語であり、主人公は「生きている」特別な金属によって作られているロボットと融合しており、海底火山のエネルギーが主人公を形成、再生することができる。この子どもは、人間の感情と容姿を持つロボットとともに、酸素を吸い取ることで世界破壊を望む宇宙侵略者と戦う。実寸と同じスケールで作られたガンダムが

18 | グイド・フェリッリ

アストロガンガー
ガンガーと星カンタロー
Astroganga, Ganga and Hoshi Kantaro
©ichi

2010年にお台場で展示され（数百メートル離れた、小さくて完璧な「自由の女神」の模倣を置き換えているように見えた）、2009年に神戸で、鉄人28号が実寸サイズのロボットとして展示されたように、アストロガンガーが日本の他の場所でも見られることを期待している[13]。

鉄人28号 モニュメント
神戸市
Tetsujin 28-go (Kobe)
©HIKARI PRODUCTION/
KOBE TETSUJIN
PROJECT2014

アカデミー賞受賞監督である宮崎駿によって作られた映画は、ヨーロッパを舞台にしたシナリオであってもしばしばトラウマに言及している。たとえば、『未来少年コナン』(1978)、『風の谷のナウシカ』(1984)、『天空の城ラピュタ』(1986)、『となりのトトロ』(1988)、『紅の豚』(1992)、『もののけ姫』(1997)、『千と千尋の神隠し』(2001)、『ハウルの動く城』(2004)は、日本と海外で監督の成功を決定づけた映画だが、多様で幅広い観客に、戦争、軍事目的のテクノロジー、ファシズム、人間と自然の関係というテーマについて日本の視点を提供した。『崖の上のポニョ』(2009)では、海と波のイメージが産業化された日本の環境問題を予感させた。

マンガ、アニメ、ドラマ、映画が、西洋の歴史に人間の物語と自然災害を組み込み、しばしば日本国外に舞台を設定していることは、日本が継続的に内容を強化し、歴史的、現代的、未来的に物語を昇華させるという、幅広い意味合いがある。日本の文化、創造産業が世界を征服したという考えは国際的な新聞や近年の科学論文でも目にすることができる。今日では、前述したように、イタリアや世界の多くの国で、自然や人為的な災害というテーマと結びついた、数世代にわたるマンガやアニメ、ビデオゲーム文化と自身との関連を認識しない人は少ないだろう。

1950年から1982年の間に、芸術家で夫婦でもある丸木位里と丸木俊によって制作された『原爆の図』は、日本人、アメリカ人、韓国人にもたらされた苦しみを伝える、普遍的な反核兵器、反戦争のメッセージである。アーティスト・会田誠（1965–）は、太平洋戦争の問題をテーマにした作品で、彼の国際的な経験とともに、比較的継続的な平和と経済振興を享受し、戦争を個人的に体験していないが[14]、国内的に再定義し直す必要性を感じる世代の意見を、多層なイメージを通して表現する。しかし、ここでいう平和は、1995年に兵庫県南部で起こった阪神・淡路大震災によって劇的に中断さ

会田誠
2011年3月13日あたりの幻視…（「みんなといっしょ」シリーズより）
2012
模造紙、油性マーカー、水彩絵具
217×157cm
©AIDA Makoto
Courtesy Mizuma Art Gallery

AIDA Makoto
Optical Illusion around 13th March, 2011 (from "Minna to Issho" series)
2012
paper, marker pen, watercolor
217×157cm
©AIDA Makoto
Courtesy Mizuma Art Gallery

れた。当時この震災は、1923年の地震に次ぐ二番目に酷い地震であり、都市の非物質的な再建にとって、文化による回復が重要な実践であると認識された震災でもあった[15]。大きな関心を集める近年の例は2000年に始まった「大地の芸術祭 越後妻有アートトリエンナーレ」である。2004年に、新潟県中越地震がこの美しい越後妻有の土地を直撃したが、近隣の若者ボランティアや世界中のアーティストたちの貢献も少なからずあり、この街は復興した。今日、このトリエンナーレと中間期間に実施される様々なフェスティバルは、文化や芸術を通じてコミュニティを構築する美しい例となっている。

村上隆
五百羅漢図(一部),
2012
100メートルに及ぶ巨大な作品で3.11の震災からインスピレーションを受け、約300人のスタッフにより制作され、2012年カタールで展示された。

Takashi Murakami, The 500 Arhats (detail) (2012) This 100-meter painting was inspired by the natural disaster of 3.11 and made by around 300 people. It was exhibited in Qatar in 2012.
©2012 Takashi Murakami/Kaikai Kiki Co., Ltd. All Rights Reserved.
Photo: GION

第二次世界大戦後のトラウマと文化生産を結びつけた、もっとも最近の成功例は、アーティスト・村上隆によって示されている。彼は原爆によってもたらされたトラウマをアニメやマンガ、オタク文化の発展を通して探求し、2001年にはポストモダンのマニフェストである「スーパーフラット」、2005年にはニューヨークのジャパン・ソサエティーで開催された『Little Boy: The Arts of Japan's Exploding Pop Culture』の展覧会と出版にたどり着いた。村上の作品は、サブカルチャーとオタク文化の驚くべき発展という原点を無視することなく、20世紀後半の日本の歴史を文化と芸術生産を通じ再定義し、新陳代謝するものとして捉えることができるだろう。例えば、エンターテイメントとアートを融合することで生じる結果を再考するなど、「スーパーフラット」というテーマを通じ、村上は日本の現代美術の意味を見つけ出そうとしている[16]。村上のマニフェストは思想家・東浩紀にも提示されている。東は別の出版物上で、デジ

ガイド・フェリッリ | 21

タル世代の次世代、現在のプロデューサーや消費者の新しい消費行動に期待しながら、オタク物語の消費の進化と、日本の現代社会の中でオタクのアイデンティティがデジタルテクノロジーによって構築され、またいかに浸透しているかを記述している[17]。日本文化が国際的に認識され浸透している例は、2000年代の初頭までには、グローバルな規模を強調するために「クールジャパン」と呼ばれていた。「クールジャパン」は知識経済に向かう先進諸国の進化というコンテクストにおいては、窓口であり、コンテンツ普及であり、東洋、ヨーロッパ、アメリカで広まってきている生産様式である。

今日、私たちが日本文化として認識しているものが90年代以降、具体的にはバブル経済の間に、圧倒的に、そして反循環的な形で爆発したのは偶然ではないだろう。経済成長と経済の達成を強調する産業社会から環境保護や文化政策を優先する——それが経済成長を最大化することと衝突したとしても——ポスト産業、ポストモダン社会への転換は、他の先進諸国、産業化が進んだ国においても見られる傾向であった[18]。富の蓄積と結びついた大量生産、大量消費のモデルが危機に陥っているのである。自国文化と西洋文化を貪欲に吸収してきた日本社会は、単純な蓄積や消費は人生そのものに到達する手段として、もはや十分ではないと認識している[19]。国内総生産が世界の第三位であるテクノロジーの国、日本は(ブラジル人バンド、パト・フはミュージックビデオ『Made in Japan』でメードインジャパンを賞賛した)世界に開き、自然や人為的な災害に対する優れて創造的な回復力を示すことで、国家をその最上の形で示している。古典芸術に加えて、現在は日本政府でさえ国家アイデンティティの特徴だと認識するサブカルチャー文化や創造性を通し、日本の姿を発信している。その結果はノーベル賞、アカデミー賞、ピューリツァー賞、チャイコフスキー国際コンクール、プリツカー賞、ベニスビエンナーレ賞、世界数学オリンピック、ローザンヌ国際バレエコンクールなどの国際的な賞や、パリのジャパンエキスポやロサンゼルスのアニメ・エキスポなどの達成によっても明らかで、グローバル化を牽引する文化リーダーの一国として貢献している。この状況は現代進行中であるが、「チャレンジ」のための環境は整っている。コンテンツ経済において、日本は世界で、アメリカに次いで一流の国々の一つであると考えるには十分であり、そして今後何年にも渡ってその立場を維持し、強めていくことになるだろう[20]。

3.11に対するコミュニティの対応

トーキョーワンダーサイトでの滞在中、その時間の全てはリサーチと、情報と意見の交換、人々の反応を理解することに費やした。3.11というトラウマ的な出来事に文化や創造がどのように反応するのかが基本的なアイデアであったが、地震の発生から間もない段階で、その証拠となるシグナルを拾い上げることができるのか確信はなかった。全ての人、全てのことが重要だった。一方、見物者や調査員としてではなく、東北に行く必要も感じていた。当時東京では、アートや文化、クリエティビティに関連する多数のイベントに出席していた。東北産の食品が提供されるレストランにも通い、可能な限り東北の製品を購入した。それが私にできる最低限のことだったからだ。結局、私はコミュニケーションするためにそこにいたのではないだろうか。たとえそれが私なりの小さな方法であっても、連絡先を開拓し、多くの人と話し、口コミ的な人間関係を作り、光、エネルギー、浄化、平静さを示す言葉を探していた。

2011年の秋は多数のイベントが開催された時期であり、それらは日本の状況、特に文化と創造に関して様々な視点を与えてくれた。多くの驚くべきイベントに参加したが、その一部を記載すると、「Tokyo Creative Weeks」(カオス*イグザイル、シンポジウムTOKYO-FUKUSHIMA!、FUTURE SKETCH東京会議、東京事典、アーティスト・イン・児童館)、TOKYO DESIGNERS WEEK、六本木アートカレッジ、横浜トリエンナーレ、アートイベント・デザインフェスタ、森美術館での『メタボリズムの未来都市』展、岡本太郎記念館でのヤノベケンジの作品を展示した展覧会、トーキョーワンダーサイトでのオープンスタジオと展覧会、日本ハーバード・クラブでの会議、TEDxTokyo、東京中のアートギャラリーでの展覧会、その国際母体(ACEI)よりもはるかに多い600人以上の会員の会員を有する、文化経済学会の二十周年会議、などがある。

以前東京を訪れた時に、学生と一緒にデザインフェスタギャラリーを訪れた。ギャラリーは都市の心臓部・原宿にあり、アーティストにとっては美しい国際的な滞在場所である。今回、ギャラリーディレクターに会った時、国際的イベントであるデザインフェスタを見に行くようにとアドバイスしてくれた。この国際的なイベントは年二回開催され、おおよそ6500名のアーティストが参加し、

6万人以上の人が訪れる。2013年5月の実施時には、1万人のアーティストが参加していた。世界最大ではないにしても、アジアで最も巨大なアートイベントといえる。このイベントが、一年に二度も開催されるということを再度強調したい。素晴らしいイベントで、2011年には多くのアーティストが3.11に関連した作品を制作し始めていた。東北から参加しているアーティストもいれば、東北をボランティアとして訪れるアーティスト、距離を保ちながら当時の社会状況を批判しているアーティストもいた。彼らを通じて、最初の、最も直接的な3.11の影響といえる事例に出会うことができた。例えば、福島の原子炉に似た頭の先端がまるで燃えているかのように赤いロボット人形。私はその単純さと自然さに驚き、感動した。このイベントは多くの人を巻き込み、彼らの多くは最近芸術大学を卒業した若者か、単純にアートとクリエティビティを通し何かを表現する想いがある人たちだ。さらにいえば、アマチュアアーティストのためのオンラインのギャラリーART-Meterは、芸術的能力がある人なら誰でも表現することができ、ソーシャルウェブというプラットフォーム上での購入を通じ、作品が評価される方法である。ART-Meterのディレクターは3.11後、アーティストの中に生まれている変化と、東北地域のためにイニシアチブを進めたいというこのコミュニティの欲求に気づくことができた。

横浜トリエンナーレも国内外のアーティストの参加という点と、来場者数、そして3.11を反映した国内外作家の作品を展示したという意味では、並外れた偉業であった。

全てのイベントにおいて、3.11との関連を見つけることができた。例えば、東京デザイナーズウィークでも3.11との関連を見つけることができ、そこではChim↑Pomの作品を観ることになった。日本社会の中で思考停止に陥っている感覚に気づき、それを克服するため、芸術的創造性を通じすぐさま反応する必要性を表現する、活動的なアーティストグループである。日本の大学生のための作品展示場所にアーティストのための展示場所も設置されており、そこでChim↑Pomの『Real Times』がスクリーンで上映されていた。

カオス*ラウンジにも同様のことが言える。彼らの活動を知る機会に、若手アーティストの梅沢和木の作品にも出会うことができた。オタクコミュニティの様態を変える活動をしている彼は、新しい冷戦後世代のアーティストに属している。

この他にも数えきれない多くの例があるが、津波と、福島の原発に破壊をもたらした今回のマグニチュード9の地震は、単純に過去の経験と比較することができないものだ。

今回福島で起こったことは、過去の経験とは異なっている。今回の出来事は、単に明確な手法と長期的なプログラムを用い、破壊された地域を再興するということにとどまらず、実施される解決策を尊重するとともに、今後長期に渡って継続していく状況をマネージメントする必要がある問題だからである。福島の原子力発電所は日本の特異な歴史的時期である、驚異的な産業経済成長時に建築された。日本社会は当時、極端な繁栄と並外れた国際的知名度という時を生きていた。戦争後の経験と結びついた、トラウマ的であり煩わしい記憶である、核エネルギーを支配する能力は、解放であり、原材料の主要な輸入国である日本にとっては、願ってもない機会であった。福島原子力発電所建設のための技術はアメリカから輸入され、国際的に認識された技術進化のレベルは、その危険性をコントロールできると想定していた。不幸にも、全ては予測可能でプログラム制御できるものではないと、自然は教えてくれている。また、日本社会と、当時日本を動かしていた政治家や人々の考え方も、原発の建設を機に変わってしまったことを、歴史は私たちに教えてくれる。つまり、このような点において、以前には不測で、想像できなかった状況に日本政府が立ち向かう困難さを、少なくとも今回もたらされたレベルの損害とダメージや、不確定とその期間という点において、理解することができるだろう[21]。

変改の兆しはインタビューによってもうかがい知ることができる。漁業や農業などの日常的な暮らしの感覚を変容させる富の蓄積やコスト削減や、無条件に生産と消費を増やす傾向ではなく、自然との根源的な関係を見つける必要性、愛情や、人間関係に関連した人生の価値がより感じられたということができるだろう。親しい友人が話してくれたことを思い出している。東京ではエネルギー供給力への考慮という理由で、一般家庭と公共施設での電気使用量が制限されていたが、それは同時に、以前は理由なく大量エネルギーが無駄にされていたことに気づかされたと彼女は話していた。1997年、人間の持続不可能な開発による影響を緩和するために、京都議定書が締

結された。人類がこれと類似した状況を経験するのは、今回が初めてではない。1979年3月28日にペンシルベニア州で起こったスリーマイル島原子力発電所事故（第一原子炉は2034年まで運転）そして、1986年のチェルノブイリ（ここでの問題は、破壊され、不安定な原子炉に新しい防御箱を完成させることだ）が過去に起こっており、このような種類のエネルギー源や、それがコミュニティにもたらす結果への対処が、いかに複雑かを物語っている。

日本において、文化的回復と文化芸術を通してコミュニティの構築を促進する文化政策の発展は強い特権である。態度や口調はそれぞれ異なっていても、全てのインタビュー参加者は、変化や、応答しようとする意欲というテーマを強調していた。彼らはともに、寛容さや回復力を好む住民の意見や反応の多様性をともに尊敬し、代表しているかのようだった。若い世代の住民に向けた構想を大事にするために、幅広い範囲の有形、無形遺産を時間的また物理的に支援する計画を提供する政府の能力は、文化の役割が肯定的に評価されるという明確な考えを与えていることは間違いない。

東北地域におけるアーティストの存在意義は何度も指摘されてきている。アーティストは技術者のように何をすべきかを指し示したりせず、「人々が何を必要としているかを問う」からである。日常や将来の生活の新しい解釈の発見をサポートするために、アーティストは表現や芸術的実践を通し、地域住民とともに変化を思考することができるのだ。例えば、アーティスト滞在施設を作るためのビル修復ケースは、短期的なプロジェクトとして構想され、利用目的は地域住民の要望に応じて変更される。芸術に特化した3331 Arts Chiyodaのような施設は、東京都千代田区に位置することで、アーティストや地元地域にとっての拠点になり、また東北のアーティストや創造的な人々と東京や世界を結びつける手段となる。

活動を再開させたいと願う人々の強さや連帯、強い想いのおかげで、私は当時、地震によってもたらされたダメージや、回復活動の最初のサインを目撃することができた。また、世界中からの多くのボランティアが地域住民に感謝によって迎えられたことも知った。大船渡では、「ボランティアのみんな、ありがとう」と英語で書かれたポスターが店や家の前に貼られていた。これらの活動を目にすることができたのは、アーティストの遠藤一郎さんによるところが大き

い。遠藤さん（私は彼をこう呼び、彼は私をぐーさんと呼ぶ）のおかげで多くの人に出会い、ビルにペイントする活動や、人々とのピクニック、希望のメッセージが書かれた凧揚げなどの活動を通し、出会う人々の中にある回復力や寛容さを高める彼の活動を目にすることができた[22]。遠藤さんには、国際交流基金が主催したFUTURE SKETCH Tokyo会議で出会った。そこでは、ジャーナリストの津田大介さんにも出会った。彼はソーシャルメディアの利用により、3.11に関連するあふれる情報を、秩序にのっとり総合的な方法で伝達する、オルタナティブな方法を発見した。

この彼の実践は、私が出会った他のアーティストのやり方とは異なるが、創造性やアート、音楽、詩、生け花、演劇、個人的な肉体を通し、社会に起こった出来事と変化を反映させたいという欲望に関していえば、全て共通している。

せんだいメディアテークが示すように、物理的な位置やインフラは、それらが象徴すること／象徴されることによって重要である。せんだいメディアテークは2012年のヴェネチア・ビエンナーレ国際建築展で「福島に触発された」日本館で、金獅子賞を受賞した建築家・伊東豊雄が設計した[23]。物理的な場所は、家族にとっては家であり、コミュニティにとっては文化的、歴史的な遺産として、基点となるものである。伝統的な祭りや、民俗芸術や、「きりこ（切り紙）」の利用なども、出来事を記憶し、次世代に伝えるという点において、様々な形態の無形遺産文化もまた重要である。伝統は、距離を拡大するものとしてではなく、人々やコミュニティ、異なる地域間に新しい関係を生み出す出発点として、互いの違いを強調する機会にもなっている。全ての人と全てのことが重要であり、「絆」という言葉はトラウマを呼び起こす「津波」のような言葉よりもはるかに強い。

公的、私的な団体が企画する祭りのようなイベントや、インターネットを通して瞬間を共有し、情報を発信することで生まれる、社会的一体感は非常に重要な手段である。また、住民が反応できるように刺激し、共有財産としての過去と現在の物語を繋ぐブリッジを作るためにも重要である。東北における身体的な存在を必要としない、他の表現の形態も当然大切な要素となっていた。この短い文章を書きながら、2011年以降、何人かのマンガ家は証言を集めるために東北を実際に訪れ、3.11に言及した少なくとも66作のマンガが

出版され(3.11のまっただ中、もしくは3.11後の状況やエピソードを扱ったものから、東北を舞台にした話まで)、また3.11を扱った9作の映画、それから41作のドキュメンタリーも制作され、2013年には「After 3.11 Film Festival」が実施された。

個人的な経験を伝える心と強さをもった人たちの声に、耳を傾けていただけたら幸いだ。

註:
1. この態度は過去28年間にヨーロッパで出会った日本人から学んだものである。可能なかぎり日本産製品を購入することは、彼らにとっては当たり前のことであると話してくれた。多くの場合、日本産製品の金額は類似商品に比べると割高であるため、単に経済的な問題としてではなく、日本に属しているという鮮やかで実際的な感覚を得るための欲望である。
2. 災害史は語るNo.139、天正の大地震、伊藤和明、防災情報新聞、防災情報機構NPO法人、防災情報新聞社、2009, http://www.bosaijoho.jp/reading/item_1574.html (アクセス 2012.12.27)。
災害史に学ぶ　内陸直下型地震編、中央防災会議「災害教訓の継承に関する専門調査会」編、内閣府(防災担当)災害予防担当, March 2011, 27ページ。
3. 第3章 救済と情報メディア、中央防災会議、内閣府防災担当、93、94ページ、http://www.bousai.go.jp/kyoiku/kyokun/kyoukunnokeishou/rep/1888-bandaisanFUNKA/index.html (アクセス 2012.12.27)
4. Calza G.C., *Ukiyoe, il mondo fluttuante*, Electa, 2004, pag. 207
5. 本テキストは、外傷的出来事との関係性についての情報を提供するが、またそれは日本社会の二次的な要素にも転換することができる。
例えば、冷酷で、勝ち目がないというヤクザのイメージは北野武によって「パロディ」へと昇華され、よりソフトで複合的なイメージに変換された。最も成功したドラマの一つである『ごくせん』は、ヤクザの孫であり、血の気が多い学生たちのクラスを管理しなければならない、若く賢い先生の物語を伝える。別の物語である『任侠ヘルパー』は大幹部の意向によりやむにやまれず社会奉仕をする若いヤクザのグループの物語を伝えている。映画とドラマで有名な『電車男』は、型通りなオタクのイメージを一歩進めている、もしくは異なる解釈を加えている。なぜなら、後にテレビドラマ化されたこの映画は、内向き、不器用、マンガやアニメに狂信的であるというオタクの性質をすべて兼ね備えた男と、彼と全く正反対の、美しく、見かけが全ての上流階級出身女性の「エルメス」との恋愛物語だからである。このドラマは、型通りのオタクのイメージから脱却する必要性も含め、オタクの捉え方を変えた。上記の理由によって、社会的、文化的な歴史物語性の複雑さを文脈化しない限り、文化や創造産業を通して日本社会を定義するのは非常に難しいが、同時に魅力的でもあると考える。
6. Elise K. Tipton, *Modern Japan: A Social and Political History* (Nissan Institute Routledge Japanese Studies Series), first published 2002 by Routledge, London.
7. David W. Edgington, *Reconstructing Kobe: The Geography of Crisis and Opportunity*, UBC Press, The University of British Columbia, 2010.
8. Shimpei Goto, *General Plan for the Reconstruction of the Imperial Capital*, in Rem Koolhaas and Hans Ulrich Obrist, (Eds) Project Japan: Metabolism Talks..., (Taschen), 2011
9. Rem Koolhaas and Hans Ulrich Obrist, (Eds) *Project Japan: Metabolism Talks...*, (Taschen), 2011, p.19.
10. Lyotard, Jean-Francois, *La condition postmoderne, Rapport sur le sovoir*, Paris, Éditions de Minuit, 1979 (Italian translation, *La condizione postmoderna. Rapporto sul sapere*, Milano, Feltrinelli, 1981).
11. 村を守るための戦いを生き延びた侍が、農業という仕事に生き甲斐を感じている農民たちを観察するなかで、戦に勝ったにも関わらず、侍たちが敗者で農家たちが勝者であることを実感させる、本映画の最終シーンは有名である。このシーンは戦後日本社会の状況を集約するメッセージとしても受け取れる。

12. これらのマンガシリーズやテレビ番組、キャラクター玩具は、広範囲で多様なコンテンツと意味の生産の起源となっている。他に例をみない、怪獣や宇宙人、ヒーローのイラスト図解を考えてみてほしい。

13. アニメ、マンガキャラクターの実寸サイズの再生産は、日本では数年に渡って進行中であり、無形遺産を再物質化する過程と考えることができる。結果論になるが、『鉄人28号』は横山光輝による原作、イラストで、第二次世界大戦中の神戸空襲によってもたらされた破壊にひらめきを得て制作された。1994年の阪神・淡路大震災から15年後、神戸市が18メートルにもなる鉄人28号の銅像を、まるで街を守るシンボルであるかのように建築した。最新の実寸サイズのマンガキャラクターはエヴァンゲリオンである。これは80メートルにも及ぶロボットで、現在はまだ頭部のみしか完成していない。2010年には箱根市で、エヴァンゲリオンのバーチャルなイメージを携帯電話を使って見ることができるアプリが開発された。何千人もの人々が、スマートフォン上でエヴァンゲリオンを見るためにこの地域を訪れたのだ。この日本人のロボットへの情熱は高まっており、ロボット工学と人型ロボットという分野の高度な技術発展と同時期に起こっている。東京で毎年開催される国際ロボット展(IREX)は世界中からの展示ブースを誇り、その発展を見ることができる。加えて、高等専門学校生を対象にしたコンテスト(1988年から開催)、海外学生を対象にしたコンテスト(1990年から開催)、日本の大学生を対象にコンテスト(1991から開催)、アジアの大学生を対象にしたコンテスト(2002年から開催)等、数々のロボットコンテストも開催されている。

14. 会田誠・片岡真実・山下裕二・デヴィッド・エリオット(2012)、『会田誠作品集 天才でごめんなさい』、森美術館/青幻舎

15. Shin Nakagawa, Koichi Suwa, *A cultural approach to recovery assistance following urban disasters*, City, Culture and Society (2010) 1: 27–36.

16. 村上隆(2000)、『SUPER FLAT』、マドラ出版、25ページ
アートの意味を商品化することは、ビジネス論理をアート市場に持ち込むという大きなリスクを負っている。しかしながら、村上はこの方法により、日本文化に特徴的な作法を含み込んだ、広範囲の現代アート生産とその情報発信システムを展開させてきた。有限会社カイカイキキの支社は日本とアメリカに所在し、生産能力とアーティスティックな創造性を促進、拡大してきている。彼の取り組みはまた、新しい世代の日本人アーティストの成長を促し、現代アートの国内市場促進にも貢献している。

17. Azuma Hiroki, *Otaku: Japan's database animals*. Minneapolis: University of Minnesota Press, 2009.
Ito Mizuko, Okabe Daisuke and Tsuji Izumi, (Eds) *Fandom Unbound: Otaku Culture in a Connected World*, Yale University Press, 2012.
文化や創造産業におけるデジタルテクノロジーの「影響」にとって、Cultural Human Resources Council's (CHRC)のCultural HR Study 2010によると、「デジタル津波」が、文化産業の創造的連鎖の全ての段階に浸透しているとされている。東の研究は新しいテクノロジーに接触し、莫大な量の情報とデータに遭遇した、全ての人、世界の全市民の寓話のように思える。コンテンツのシステマティックな非物質化が生み出すデータは非営利サイト(Wikipedia)、もしくは営利サイト(有名で普及しているものを列挙すると、Google, Youtube, ツイッターなど)に見られ、私たちはこの過程にようやく気づきだした。

本テキストの目的からはそれるが、日本の話に戻っていく、二つの事例について触れたいと思う。その一つは個人的で、映画字幕と関連している。イタリアで目にすることができるテレビや映画は、全てがイタリア語に吹き替えられている。世界への視点という点から、「ゆがんだイタリア中心主義」を生み出していることがある(善玉や悪玉の吹き替えにも地域方言が使われる意味を考えてみてほしい)。加えて、英国に私が留学していた時に発見したのは、オリジナル言語の中に存在する「真実」だけではなく、字幕には母国語を弱体化させずに、第二外国語をより簡単に学ぶための二次的な影響があるという事実である。私は15年前のことを現在話しているが、メディアコンテンツ(例えば、映画やテレビ)をオリジナル言語と字幕で拡散している国と、第二外国語を操るヨーロッパ市民の地図を比べた時、そこに「奇妙な」偶然を発見する。今日イタリアには日本のアニメや映画、ドラマのために字幕生産を行う、80のオンラインコミュニティがある。このコミュニティは古典的な意味におけるビジネスのために存在しているのではない。というのも、全ては基本的に「楽しみ」という目的のために作られていて、新しいコンテンツの創造に「別の、異なる」方法で参加することなのである。日本のコンテンツ開発において、この新しい形態の能動的な参加は、2000年以降実験されてきており、その例としては、ケイタイ小説がある。ケイタイ小説は、著者が、携帯電話やソーシャルメディア上で執筆し、100万部以上の出版になる場合もある。そのうちのいくつかは、Yoshiの『Deep Love』、マンガやテレビ、映画に脚色された美嘉の『恋空』シリーズのように、ベストセラーになったものもある。このような形態の進化は、リレー小説と呼ばれ、小説家コミュニティが複数で執筆する形式をとっている。これらはシンプルな例であるが、

彼らはテクノロジーがどのように個々のスキル発達を加速させるのかを理解している。それはもう一方で、巨大なデジタル環境の中で新しいコンテンツを生み出すことにもなり、セマンティックウェブやデジタル・ヒューマニティーズの最前線で反映されている。

18. Inglehart, Ronald, *Globalization and Postmodern Values*, The Washington Quarterly, Volume 23, Number 1, Winter 2000, pp. 215-228 (Article).

19. 宮崎駿の『千と千尋の神隠し』(2001)の登場人物である「カオナシ」は、強力な道具としてのお金を使い食料を貪欲に貪り、結果的に支配的で、エゴイスティックな、孤立した孤独な巨大怪物になる。この登場人物は一方で、社会的な関係性を再解釈する必要と、もう一方で、金銭やその蓄積のみを中心にする欠乏感も要約している。この考え方をここで展開することはできないが、新しいハイブリッド形態の贈与経済が新たに登場してきている知識経済の世界で、「少なくあること」という考えは、認識分野の蓄積と市場取引に関わってくるのだろう。

20. 日本のエンターテインメントとメディアのコンテンツ産業は、アメリカに次いで世界で2番目の位置にあり、この状況は今後も数年間続いていくものと思われる。プライスウォーターハウスクーパースが2012年に発表した、「Global entertainment and media outlook 2012-2016: The End of the digital beginning」によると、エンターテインメントとメディアの以下の分野（インターネット接続費、インターネット広告、テレビ購読とライセンス費、テレビ広告、映画エンターテインメント、ビデオゲーム、音楽、消費者雑誌、出版、新聞出版、ラジオ、家庭外広告、消費、教育本出版、B2B）の成長が続いていくことが予想されている。

21. 原子力発電所の運転期間を、40年間から100年間まで延長する試みがあるのは周知の事実だ。加えて、原子炉を石棺で覆う埋葬の手法は、高いコストがかかる解体という手法に対する別の方法であり、最近より大きな関心を集めている。別の要素としては、100年と言わないまでも、数十年単位の物理的場所の永続性の問題がある。遺物であり、この「重大な遺産」の例は原子力発電所であり、緊急的で長期的な保存と関心を必要とする。この要素は興味深い。なぜなら、物理的遺産の多くはユネスコの世界遺産になる一方で、それらが今日まで生き残るのは偶然の産物であり、放棄されたり、重要だと考慮されていない場所も存在し、ベネチアの例のように転換に伴う財政が不足している場合もありうる。原子力発電所に関して言えば、環境に対する危険性のためには、高度な技術やエンジニアデザイン、人間のテクノロジー発達の印は、保存されるか（より極度の注意を伴い解体されるか）すべきである。イタリア人がこの「重大な遺産」に関わらないと決めたのは、物理的な遺産との何千年にも渡る経験が地域で共有されているためであり、この長期的な要素を無意識に自覚しているからかもしれない。（ローマのコロシアムのケースでいうと、キリスト教者の迫害というトラウマ的な出来事と結びついている。）さらに、このような国民投票を通じた決断は、チェルノブイリや3.11がイタリア国民に大きな影響を与えたことを物語っている。

22. 「未来へ」と黄色で車体に書かれた遠藤さんの車に乗って東北に向かった。この車には、旅行中に出会った人々が自由に希望のメッセージや、元気になるような願いごとを書くことができた。東北への旅の途中、遠藤さんは、3.11後、東北の人々に送るポストカードを準備していたところ、郵便で送るのではなく、直接彼らに届けようと決めたことを話してくれた。そして、その時以降、東北住民に出会うために、東北に人々を運ぶために活動してきている。私は彼や彼の友人、日本テレビ局のスタッフ、それから何よりも現地で出会った人々とあの場所にいることができたことを感謝している。遠藤さんが多くの都市を紹介するなかで、「この地域はすごい破壊を受けた」といった後、自分自身の言葉を訂正しながら、以前に比べたら大きな進歩があり、彼自身も驚いていると発言したことが私は嬉しかった。

23. このテキストを書き終えた時点で、伊東豊雄が日本人としては6人目となる、プリツカー賞を受賞したことを知った。

Commitment to 3.11
Response to Disaster through Culture and Creativity in Japan

Guido Ferilli

With the occurrence of the Great East Japan Earthquake on March 11th, 2011 ("3.11"), Japan went through one of the most difficult moments in its recent history. The catastrophic effects caused in the Tohoku area by the Pacific offshore earthquake and tsunami consist not only of those immediate ones experienced at the time, but also future complications which are very likely to cause later difficulties for the population.

Only a few years have passed since 3.11, but what has happened and what will happen now and in the future are part of everyone's life, mine included. I was in Bologna, Italy, on 3.11 and the images that my wife and I saw on television, as well as the news that came from friends and family, will always remain in our minds. The last time I was in Tokyo was in October 2010, giving a study tour with a group of my students from the university where I teach. It was the second year that I had brought students to visit Tokyo and both journeys had been a success mainly because our expectations were always widely surpassed by the experience of being in the city. Seeing those indescribable images of the earthquake made me immediately want to do something that might be of some help. In Bologna I participated in several events for establishing solidarity organized by the local Bolognese and Japanese communities. There were moments when the city of *Alma Mater Studiorum* and the famous pasta sauce engaged in earnest contact with Japan in order to understand what was happening and to lend concrete help. We gave what we could to raise funds and bought Japanese products because we believed that even the most infinitesimal gesture could be helpful.[1]

In the meantime, I thought that it could be interesting to find a way to apply my skills as a researcher in cultural fields. My basic idea is to focus on the capacity of Japanese society to metabolize the traumatic events through culture and creativity. The examples of such are numerous and punctuate the narrative of all forms of cultural production in the country. In Japan's recent history there had not been an event of such scale and traumatic consequence since World War Two and the two atomic bombings of Hiroshima and Nagasaki. The repercussions that resulted from both events were unique in terms of cultural production. In fact, the events following World War Two directly provoked the development of an extraordinary vein of creativity that has been expressed through both traditional arts (painting, sculpture, visual arts) and also other forms of culture (manga, anime, video games, cinema) that are now recognized, even by the Japanese government, as elements which along with historical Japanese culture characterize Japan's national identity and strengthen its soft power internationally. The development of cultural and creative industries is now a priority on the agendas of many governments around the world and the strategies being implemented to enhance competitiveness increasingly refer to these sectors, rather than to those of the industrial period, as resources for local development. The history of Japan teaches us that artistic and cultural production (as well as consumption) was a very important tool for metabolizing the traumatic effects of catastrophic events into forms of renewed individual and collective expression. Such forms ranged from absolute catastrophism to the creation of conditions for a better society. The effect of this fertile period of artistic production is also the development of an industry linked to the cultural and creative sectors, which is now recognized as one of the most important in the world.

Today, for example, it is almost impossible to find in Italy (as in many other countries in the world) a person who does not recognize him/herself in a few generations of manga or anime, of which many were related to the theme of disasters, from Hayao Miyazaki's *Future Boy Conan* to *Godzilla*, and more recently, to the *Tokyo Magnitude 8.0*, *Hakuryu Legend* and *Disaster Report 4* (a PlayStation video game). My idea was to proactively survey how culture and creativity were contributing to the reaction to these events by private citizens and community, and how this has had an effect in general, taking into consideration the importance and actuality of these themes (in the environment, use of natural resources, production and use of energy, but also lifestyle and personal and social wellbeing, etc.), and if the scale of this event may cause a renewed Japanese cultural wave.

Therefore, I thought that attempting to understand what was happening at that time could make an interesting endeavour to document and deliver to Japanese readers, as well as to readers around the world, interested in listening to the voices of so many people working to return some form of serenity to the country. I believe this was a decisive factor that allowed my proposal to be considered for the residency research program at Tokyo Wonder Site (TWS) in Tokyo, and I am grateful for their interest in my project. This allowed me to travel to Tokyo between October and December 2011, where I was hosted for a month by TWS at its location in Aoyama.

The findings of these activities are described in the following pages. The interviews themselves reveal the way in which the country, often seen as "inflexible" and "ordered," demonstrates instead an extraordinary sensitivity and creativity in responding to an event that has shaken Japanese society. At large, it has done so with expressive forms and activities which were realized only a few months after 3.11 and which can be important and interesting food for thought for Japanese citizens, as well as for the global community in general, and in particular for Italy, which in recent decades has also experienced many devastating natural disasters.

The interviews were carried out between October and December 2011, with the exception of four interviews completed in 2012 during my subsequent four trips to Japan. Four interviews were conducted in English, while all others were conducted in Japanese thanks to the indispensable help of Kiyoko Oiwa. All texts were later translated into Italian for reading and sorting, and then translated back into Japanese by Kiyoko Oiwa and Fumiyo Taira. Finally, the texts were sent to each person to ask them to verify the accuracy of the interview and to update the content if necessary and submit relative images as complimentary additions to the texts. The texts were then translated into English, while my text was translated into Japanese. All royalties raised from the sale of this book will be donated to the promotion of cultural activities in Tohoku.

Responding to Trauma through Culture and Creativity

If we look back at Japanese cultural history, perhaps the first evidence of a traumatic event such as an earthquake being represented through comprehensible symbols dates back to 1592, when it was described as a catfish (*Namazu*) in a letter sent by Hideyoshi Toyotomi to the government office, in which concerns were expressed about the construction of Fushimi Castle in Kyoto after the earthquake of 1586. The diffusion of pictorial representation of the earthquake catfish (*Namazu-e*) and its popularity dates back to 1855 and also today this symbol continues to represent the earthquake in Japanese culture.[2]

The first representation in Kabuki of such a traumatic event occurred in 1888, with the *mise en scene* of a dramatic love story with a happy ending, inspired by photographic images of the Fukushima area which was devastated following the eruption of Mt. Bandai.[3] Around the same time, in the world-famous picture *The Great Wave off Kanagawa* from the series *Thirty-six Views of Mount Fuji* (1830-1832) Hokusai conveys his concept of the forces of nature, not to overwhelm or dominate, but to love and indulge in the inner rhythm of its power.[4]

Japan was not unique in having to deal with the effects of these events, not only the natural ones, such as earthquakes, tsunamis, typhoons, and volcanic eruptions, but also those caused by man, such as wars and fires. However, what I believe distinguishes Japan from other countries is its ability to interpret and metabolize these events through all forms of cultural production and expression. With the term metabolism I refer in a broad sense to the ecology of the cultural narrative of Japan, self-reflecting the effect of traumatic (and non-traumatic) events, over time and space.[5] With regards to the traumatic events, Japan has a long and complex relationship with them, although the references that we find on a more regular basis are those caused by earthquakes. An example of a traumatic event which was man-made and has been studied and analysed in all its aspects is that of World War Two and its effects, which are still vivid in the collective memory. These events have been the source of an extensively rich cultural production that reflects on these events and the changes they induce in the society.

It could be argued that most of the cultural and creative production of Japan is directly or indirectly influenced by these events. Upon closer examination, such cultural production has not been the result of a reoccurring trend in the name of entertainment but, on the contrary, the result of artistic expression as a means to reflect changes induced in society and the expression and reaction of the society itself to these events. Japan is the country that through its artistic production has been able to demonstrate its unique ability to metabolize these events, and has done so through new forms of thought which have characterized the narrative of the country and have come to fruition in all forms of cultural production, as well as in science and technology. In a broader sense, the opening of Japan to the West from the mid-nineteenth century onwards could have attributed to a "cultural shock." The metabolization of the contact of the archipelago with the West was its social, economic and cultural evolution in a complex dynamic creative process that has determined a reworking and redefinition of the coordinates of reference, to arrive at modernity, whereas the photography of Adolfo Farsari and Felice Beato from the late nineteenth century portrayed a country not yet pervaded by Westernism. We see a process of creative resilience (and development) that has not destroyed its traditions but, on the contrary, has been reached thanks to Japanese customs and the Confucian values of hard work, frugality, loyalty and learning.[6]

It is a fact that the geographical position of the country along the Pacific Rim of Fire makes it particularly susceptible to earthquakes. This characteristic has led to the development of technologies and architecture to cope with these events. Architecture that was initially oriented by Japanese to counter earthquakes (known as *taishin* and also *menshin*) was then designed and conceived not so much for the local Japanese, who were accustomed to the tremors of earthquakes, but for and by foreigners living in the country who did not fully comprehend the Japanese approach to these events and wanted to develop modern technological solutions. The term *daiku* (traditional Japanese architectural carpenter) represents the beginning of the evolution of the traditional Japanese architecture technique that metabolized Western technique and philosophy of construction. The reconstruction of Tokyo after the Great Kanto Earthquake of 1923 coincided with the acceleration of changes in society and the landscape, leading to the rebuilding (*fukko*) of a modern city, including but not exclusive to the reconstruction (*fukkyu*) of public infrastructure.[7] Even the internal design of houses has been developed over time to withstand the effects of earthquakes.

From this point onwards earthquakes were given greater attention and on September 1st, 1960, National Disaster Prevention Day was established. It was also an opportunity to modernize the city in an European–style order[8] and the image of Japan and Japanese society as having entered the international arena of economic and industrial progress. Architecture and urban design were also influenced later by postwar reconstruction, which culminated with the Osaka Expo of 1970, where Japan proposed a philosophy of urban development, "Metabolism," coined by the eponymous movement in architecture. This movement started in the 1960's and was best described by Hans Ulrich Obrist "as a new style of Japanese modernism by assimilating tradition [...] with profound sense of experimentation and a search for the new, rather than simply a recombination and resurrection of the old."[9] The bursting of the bubble economy in the early 1990's and the prolonged economic stagnation and subsequent changes in society, as well as the disappointing results of the Expo Aichi 2005 that focused on the reproduction of the concepts of the Osaka Expo, revealed the limits of the movement to interpret social change and to propose a new form of thought, a "New Metabolism," oriented towards the search for "soft" forms in architecture, as well as in the infrastructure for mobility, energy, and information (see the interview with Fumio Nanjo in this book).

The Osaka Expo, the first World Fair in Asia, was also the first time Japan showed off its economic, scientific and cultural progress to the entire world, and the *Tower of Sun* by Taro Okamoto in the Festival Plaza is the artistic symbol that dominated the Expo. The artist himself expressed a way to combine the nuclear trauma with art when he stated in a television program that "Art Is Explosion." Kenji Yanobe, an artist from the generation following Okamoto's, grew up reading and watching postwar manga and anime, and was greatly influenced by Okamoto's life. He is famous for his yellow hazmat suit, *Atom Suit* (1997), which he wore during his visit to the nuclear power plant at Chernobyl in 1997, and many other works which were exhibited in the Taro Okamoto Memorial Museum in 2011 on the centenary of the birth of Okamoto. In addition to *Torayan*, *Sun Child*, and *Sun Child Island*, the artist exhibited a video of his recent incursion into Okamoto's *Tower of the Sun*.

The visual arts, manga, anime, toys, science fiction, cinema, robots (and humanoid robot design), as well as video games, are all forms of expression in Japanese culture that have been able to draw inspiration from natural and man-made traumatic events and from Japan's historical narrative in attempts to reflect changes in society. From its beginning, the production of manga has been characterized by the variety of its themes, both real, symbolic and imaginary. It has a long history of evolution of technique and content, starting with the twelfth-century proto-manga artist-priest Toba Sojo (Toba-e, 1053-1140) and passing through the seventeenth to nineteenth centuries and their *ukiyo* prints depicting the entertainment quarters of the "floating world", *shunga* (literally "spring pictures," erotic prints) and *yokai* prints, before arriving at the *ponchi-e* in the second half of the nineteenth century, which were then replaced by manga. At the turn of the twentieth century and during both World Wars they contained themes related to militarist propaganda. But it was not until after World War Two that the long wave of cultural and creative production, which still grips the world's attention today, actually started.

The master who inspired future generations of artists is certainly Osamu Tezuka (1928-89). The personal experience of the World Wars, the bombings and the destruction, together with local and imported comics, theatre, national and international cinema, and Disney, all contributed to form a character and creative talent which offers reflection on war propaganda and the devastation of World War Two. Just as in Italy, in Japan the films which were censored before the end of World War Two were American imports. These were then diffused also with the arrival of television in the late 1950's, and were one of the most direct means of democratization and modernization. Meanwhile, Japan was entering the arena of capitalist development in industry, technology, economic development, and consumerism from the 1960's through to the 1980's. Manga, art and other forms of cultural and creative expression were reborn out of the ashes of defeat in war, the mass destruction of the atomic bombs on Hiroshima and Nagasaki, and the postwar U.S. nuclear tests. If these are the traumatic events which inspired Japan to rebuild a renewed narrative, other events that have influenced the narrative expressed in cultural production included the Cold War, the Vietnam War and the peace movements during the 1960's and 1970's, the oil crisis of the 1970's, the economic boom period, the bubble economy, and the end of the Cold War that followed the grand narratives' decline and postmodernism.[10]

The theme of wartime destruction and the devastation caused by the atomic bombs, however, is the common thread that can be found in the cultural production of the second half of the twentieth century, determining the various strands of development and also affected by the contingency of national and international events from the postwar period to date. To trace the narrative of the whole cultural and creative production of Japan after World War Two and connected to trauma, as mentioned in the introduction, is not the purpose of this text. For example, if Akira Kurosawa with *The Seven Samurai* depicts the conditions in Japan after the end of World War Two[11] and *Dreams* the prediction of nuclear disaster, Astro Boy represents the use of nuclear power and Godzilla (from the same period) portrays the devastating effects of the use of nuclear weapons. Godzilla and other monsters in the genre (*kaiju eiga*) such as Hedorah (related to the problem of pollution) were the inspiration for the young Shinya Tsukamoto, the creator of *Tetsuo: The Iron Man* (and the development of the cyberpunk movement in Japan), which expresses problems related to the alienation of the individual in the industrial society. These monsters contrast with the giants Ultraman and Ultraseven, who fight invading monsters through the regeneration of sunlight.[12]

We find nuclear imagery in many movies and anime such as *Akira*, *Space Battleship Yamato*, *Mobile Suit Gundam*, and *Neon Genesis Evangelion*, and in many science fiction movies over the past decades. In recent decades we also notice a process of re-materialization of these characters around Japan. One example is the full-scale model of the robot Gundam, built and exhibited in Odaiba in Tokyo in 2010, which seemed to almost replace the small-scale imitation of the Statue of Liberty located just a few hundred meters away. Another example in this vein is the 1:1 model of the robot Tetsujin 28-go, built in Kobe in 2009.[13] However, one of the most appealing anime to me, espccially as a child, was *Astroganga* by Tetsuhisa Suzukawa. This is the story of a child born from a human scientist father and alien mother, who is assimilated inside a robot, created by a special living metal alien which shapes and regenerates him thanks to the heat provided by an active submarine volcano. The child, together with his human-like robot (it has human feelings and appearance), fights against alien invaders who want to destroy the world by taking all the oxygen. I hope that a 1:1 version of Astroganga will also one day be materialized somewhere in Japan, just like the version of Gundam mentioned above.

The anime of the Academy Award-winner Hayao Miyazaki often refer to trauma, even when set in European scenarios. For example, *Future Boy Conan* (1978), *Nausicaä of the Valley of the Wind* (1984), *Laputa: Castle in the Sky* (1986), *My Neighbor Totoro* (1988), *Porco Rosso* (1992), *Princess Mononoke* (1997), *Spirited Away* (2001), and *Howl's Moving Castle* (2004) have brought success for the director, both in Japan and internationally, offering to a wide and varied audience a Japanese point of view on such themes as war, military technology, fascism, and the relationship between man and nature, to name but a few. With *Ponyo* (2009), on the other hand, the imagery of the sea and the waves prefigure the environmental problems of industrialized Japan.

Japanese manga, anime, TV drama and films are often set outside of Japan, with narratives that braid Western history with the narrative of human and natural disasters, a fact which Japan continuously enriches with content, useful for enhancing the broader significance of the sublimation of its historical, contemporary and futuristic narrative.

While *The Hiroshima Panels*, created over the period of 1950 to 1982 by the artists (and married couple) Iri and Toshi Maruki, have a universal anti-nuclear and anti-war message that also transmits the suffering caused to Japanese, Americans and Koreans, the artist Makoto Aida (b. 1965), with his works on the subject of the Pacific War and his international experience, expresses through various layers of images the perspective of a generation that has not personally experienced that period[14] but still feels the need to reinterpret it, in a national context, of relative persistent peace and economic prosperity—a peace that was dramatically interrupted in 1995 with the Great Hanshin-Awaji Earthquake (or Kobe earthquake) in the southern part of Hyogo Prefecture. At the time the Great Hanshin-Awaji Earthquake was considered Japan's second worst earthquake in the twentieth century, after the quake of 1923, and recovery through culture began to be considered an important practice also for the "immaterial" reconstruction of the city.[15] A more recent example that has aroused great interest is the

Art Triennale Echigo-Tsumari, started in 2000. The Chuetsu earthquakes struck the beautiful natural area of Echigo-Tsumari in 2004 and the recovery has been successful not least thanks to young volunteers from the neighbouring villages and artists from all over the world. Today the Triennale and other festivals organized in the intermediate years are a beautiful example of community-building through culture and art.

The most successful recent attempt at connecting postwar trauma and creativity is that offered by the artist Takashi Murakami, who explores the trauma caused by the atomic bombings through anime, manga, and the development of *otaku* culture, arriving at his manifesto of postmodern "Super Flat" in 2001, and the *Little Boy: The Arts of Japan's Exploding Pop Culture* exhibition (and catalogue publication) at the Japan Society in New York in 2005. The work of Murakami can be seen as the reinterpretation and metabolization of Japanese history in the second half of the twentieth century through cultural and artistic production, without neglecting the origins of the astonishing development of *otaku* culture. Through the concept Super Flat, Murakami tries to find the meaning of contemporary Japanese art by, for example, rethinking the results obtained by the integration of layers of entertainment and art.[16] His manifesto is accompanied by the contribution of philosopher Hiroki Azuma, who describes also in other publications the evolution of *otaku* narrative consumption and the way its identity in contemporary Japan is built and pervaded by digital technologies, anticipating the future/present of producers/consumers in the digital age.[17] Examples of internationally diffused and recognized Japanese cultural production abound, which by the beginning of the 2000's was also being called "Cool Japan" in an attempt to highlight its global dimension: A window as well as platform for dissemination of content and modes of production that has reverberated also in Asia, Europe and America, in the context of the evolution of more advanced countries towards a knowledge economy.

I do not think it is a coincidence that Japanese culture as we know it today has exploded in a preponderant and countercyclical way from the 1990's onwards, namely, from the period of economic recession. It is a period during which such a phenomenon was also seen in other advanced (highly industrialized) countries, the transition from an industrial society that emphasizes above all economic growth and economic achievement to a post-industrial (postmodern) society that gives priority to the protection of environment and cultural issues, even when these goals conflict with maximizing economic growth.[18] It is the model of mass production and consumption which is in crisis. Japanese society, which has absorbed both its own culture as well as Western culture voraciously, realizes that simple accumulation (or consumption) is no longer sufficient to achieve its own life, its own self.[19] The technological Japan (that same *Made in Japan* praised by the Brazilian band Pato Fu in their 2007 song and video) gave the best of itself as it opened to the world and demonstrated an extraordinary creative resilience to natural and man-made adversities. And it has done so with a culture and creativity that has been expressed through the traditional arts, but also through the popular cultures which are now recognized even by the Japanese government as elements that characterize national identity, along with Japan's traditional culture. The results are also expressed by Japan's international awards, by the achievements of the Japan Expo in Paris, and the Anime Expo in Los Angeles, and in the ability to contribute actively to being one of the cultural leaders in the globalized world. As said, even though it still seems a situation in progress, the "challenge" already appears to be in place. It suffices to say that Japan is one of the leading countries in the world in the content economy and in the coming years will continue to maintain and strengthen its position.[20]

Community Responses to 3.11

During my residency at TWS, all my available time was dedicated to conducting research, also understood as exchange of information, opinions, and reactions of people. Although I had my basic idea to develop, which concerned the reactions to the traumatic events of 3.11 through culture and creativity, I was still unsure that evident signals could be picked up as such within such a short period time after the earthquake. Everyone and everything was important. In the meanwhile, I felt the need to go to Tohoku, but not as a spectator or investigator. At that time in Tokyo, I followed and attended many events related to art, culture and creativity. I went to the restaurants where they served products from Tohoku, as I was used to buying products from that area as often as I could. It was the least that I could do. After all, I was there to communicate: To create contacts and links, to discuss with everyone, forming a kind of word of mouth between people, to search for words that could offer light, energy, clarifications, and serenity, albeit of course in my own small way.

Autumn 2011 was also a season of events that offered various perspectives on the whole situation of Japan, in particular with regards to culture and creativity. I attended so many surprising events: Tokyo Creative Week (during which I attended a CHAOS*EXILE event, Symposium TOKYO-FUKUSHIMA!, FUTURE SKETCH: Tokyo Conference, Tokyo Jiten, Artist in Jidokan), Tokyo Designers Week, Roppongi Art College, Yokohama Triennale 2011, Design Festa, the Metabolism exhibition at the Mori Art Museum, an exhibition by Kenji Yanobe at Taro Okamoto Memorial Museum, open studios and exhibitions at Tokyo Wonder Site, meetings at the Harvard Club of Japan, TEDxTokyo, exhibitions at art galleries throughout the city, and the twentieth anniversary of the Japanese Association for Cultural Economics, which today has more than 600 members and far greater than the same international organization (ACEI), to name but a few.

During my previous visits to Tokyo, I had visited and also brought my students to visit Design Festa Gallery, a beautiful international space for artists in Harajuku, in the heart of the city. When I met the director of the gallery during my residency in Tokyo in 2011, he advised me to also visit the biannual Design Festa art event. At that time, this international event hosted around 6,500 artists and received more than 60,000 visitors (whereas for the May 2013 edition they predicted more than 10,000 artists). It is the biggest art event in Asia, if not in the world. I found in 2011 many artists beginning to produce works related to 3.11. Some artists came from that area, others arrived as volunteers, and still others were keeping their distance and criticizing what was happening. Through them I came into contact with the first, most direct, example of evidence of the effects of 3.11, a puppet robot with a head similar to the Fukushima Nuclear Power Plant, red on the top, as if he were on fire. The simplicity and spontaneity surprised and moved me. The event brings together many artists, in many cases young people who have just graduated from art school or university, or others who simply desired to express themselves through art and creativity.

Moreover, even the online Gallery ART-Meter, dedicated to amateur artists, is a means allowing anyone with artistic abilities to express themselves, and be appreciated, through the purchase of their work via the web platform. The ART-Meter director was able to notice the post-3.11 changes in the artists and also the desire of his community to promote initiatives for the Tohoku area.

Extraordinary too were the achievements of the Yokohama Triennale 2011, in terms of the participation of national and international artists, the number of visitors to the event, and the change in some of the works from Japanese and foreign artists, reflecting 3.11.

In all these events I have found a link with 3.11. For example, also at Tokyo Designers Week I saw the video *REAL TIMES* by Chim ↑ Pom, a group of young active artists expressing their need to react immediately through their artistic creativity and overcome the sense of immobility that they perceived in society. I also came into contact with the artist group CHAOS*LOUNGE and their activities, including the artworks related to 3.11 by Kazuki Umezawa, a young artist belonging to the new post-Cold War generation of artists attempting to evolve the mold of the *otaku* community. There are numerous other examples but above all I believe what happened during 3.11 is simply not comparable to past experiences since the earthquake (magnitude 9.0) caused the tsunami and damaged the Fukushima Nuclear Power Plant.

What happened in Fukushima is not "just" a matter of rebuilding a devastated territory with a very clear long-term program. Fukushima Nuclear Power Plant was built during a very particular historical period in Japan, that of impressive industrial economic growth. At that time Japanese society was experiencing high levels of prosperity and exceptional international visibility, so the ability to dominate nuclear energy was a great opportunity for a country which was, and still is, a major importer of raw materials. The technology for the realization of Fukushima Nuclear Power Plant was so advanced that the risks were envisioned as controllable. Today nature teaches us that everything is not as predictable and programmable as we would like, and history also teaches us that Japanese society has changed since the construction of the power plant, as have the politicians and spirit that drove the country at that time. Perhaps in this way we can see the difficulties the government has now in tackling what was previously an unforeseen and unimagined scenario, at least to the extent of the harm and damage caused, as well as the uncertainty and duration.[21]

The signs of change can be perceived in the interviews, when they talk of the increased value placed on emotions and relationships, and the need to find an original relation with nature, rather than the current one of accumulation of resources and efficiency of cost—constant unconditional production and consumption—which risks deforming our sense of everyday practices such as fishing or agriculture. I am reminded of what a dear friend and colleague once told me when she said that while household electricity in Tokyo and certain public services was rationed after Fukushima in order to save power, she also noted how much energy was previously wasted. The fact remains that it is not the first time that the human race is going through a similar situation. Cases such as the Three Mile Island accident in Dauphin County, Pennsylvania, on March 28th, 1979 (where in fact the first reactor continues to operate until 2034) and then that of Chernobyl in 1986 (where the problem is that of completing a new protective encasement for the damaged, still not stabilized, reactor) have been in the past and up to today traumatic examples demonstrating the complexity of handling this type of energy source, as well as the consequences that may occur for the community when something goes wrong.

It is a strongly felt prerogative in Japan to develop cultural policies that promote cultural recovery and also encourage the community to build through arts and culture. The theme of change and willingness to respond is highlighted by all interviewees with manners and tones that are all very different, as if they together represent the diversity of opinions and reactions of the population, in favour of open-mindedness and resilience. Without doubt the government's ability to provide a plan of intervention on a vast range of tangible and intangible heritage, and initiatives addressed to younger age groups, gives a clear idea of how the role of culture in these times is being positively evaluated.

The presence of the artist in the Tohoku area has been pointed out many times mainly because an artist *asks* what the people need, rather than indicates what to do, as the technician does. The artist reflects on the changes, together with the inhabitants, through forms of expression and artistic practices that help people to find new interpretations of everyday and future life. The case of the restoration of a building into an artist residence is offered as a temporary intervention, for which its destination or use is dependent upon citizens' needs. Instead, when the space is dedicated to art, such as the 3331 Arts Chiyoda, located in Chiyoda (central Tokyo), it becomes a reference point for artists and the local community and also a means to connect artists and creative people from the Tohoku area with Tokyo and the rest of the world.

During those days I spent in Tohoku, I witnessed the damage caused by the earthquake and tsunami, as well as the first signs of recovery activities, thanks to the strength, solidarity and will of everyone to begin again. I also found many volunteers from all over the world, who were met with much gratitude by residents. In Ofunato, Iwate Prefecture, posters saying (in English) "Thank you, all hands volunteers" were hung up in shops and homes. It is thanks to an artist, Ichiro Endo, that I got the chance to meet so many people. Seeing how Endo-san (this is how I call him, and he calls me Gu-san), through activities such as releasing colors on buildings, holding picnics with groups of residents that extend from one place to another in the territory, and flying kites with messages of hope attached, helps to develop resilience and open-mindedness in the people he meets.[22] I met Endo-san at FUTURE SKETCH: Tokyo Conference, where I also met Daisuke Tsuda, a journalist who had discovered, through the use of social media, an alternative way to communicate the cloud of information related to 3.11 in an orderly and comprehensible fashion.

This is a different practice to that of other artists I met, but all are united by the desire to reflect on the events and the changes in society with their creativity through art, music, poetry, *ikebana* (flower arranging), theatre, physically going to Tohoku, or trying to find time during work breaks for initiatives of solidarity through art with a group of friends.

The physical location, the infrastructure, is important for what it represents, such as the Sendai Mediateque, designed by Toyo Ito, winner in 2012 of the Golden Lion at the Venice Biennale for the Japanese pavilion "inspired by Fukushima."[23] The physical site is a reference point for the family as a house, or for the community as cultural heritage, but the traditions, and all forms of expression of the intangible heritage are also important, such as traditional festivals, folk arts, and the use of *kiriko* (traditional paper cutouts), in addition to being a way to remember and pass on what happened to future generations. This traditional intangible heritage also becomes an occasion to highlight the differences as a starting point for creating new connections, rather than increasing distance between people, communities, and areas of the country. Everyone is important, everything is important, and the word *kizuna* (bonds) has become, since 3.11, stronger than the word evoking the trauma (tsunami).

Social cohesion is a very important means by which to share those traumatic moments following 3.11 and to disseminate information (through festivals and events organized by public and private bodies, but also through the Internet) and stimulate the population to react. Today it is especially important for building a bridge between past narratives, the present and the future as a common good, and all the other forms of expression that do not require a physical presence in Tohoku are also of great importance. While I am writing this short text, I have become aware of the fact that since 2011 there have been at least 66 manga that refer to 3.11 (dealing with episodes and circumstances that occurred during and after 3.11 or setting stories in Tohoku), as well as nine films, and 41 documentaries about 3.11. Some *mangaka* (manga artists) also went to the Tohoku area to collect testimonies. Moreover, in 2013 the After 3:11 Film Festival was organized in Tokyo. In order not to take anything else away from the rest of the book, I simply invite you to read the voices of those who had the strength and heart to tell their personal experience.

Notes:

1. This behaviour I learned from many Japanese who I have met in Europe over the past 28 years. They told me that it is normal for them to always choose a Japanese product when possible; it is not just an economic issue, since in many cases their prices are higher than similar products, but also the desire to retain a vivid and practical feeling of belonging to their country.

2. Kazuaki Ito, *Talks about disaster history No.139, Great Tensho Earthquake*, in Disaster Prevention Information newspaper, (Disaster Information Organization – NPO, Disaster Information Journal), 2009, http://www.bosaijoho.jp/reading/item_1574.html (accessed 12/27/2012)
Learning the history of disaster: Inland epicentral earthquake, Central Disaster Prevention Council: Expert Committee on the inheritance of disaster lessons learned, Cabinet Office (Disaster Management) Disaster Prevention Personnel, March 2011, p. 27

3. *Relief, Information and Media* (Chapter 3), Central Disaster Prevention Council: Cabinet Office Disaster Management, pp. 93-94, http://www.bousai.go.jp/jishin/chubou/kyoukun/rep/1888--bandaisanFUNKA/index.html (accessed 12/27/2012)

4. G.C. Calza, *Ukiyoe, il mondo fluttuante* (Electa), 2004, p. 207

5. This text provides information on the relationship with traumatic events, but it can be transposed into other secondary aspects of Japanese society. For example, the narrative of the Yakuza as a ruthless and

insurmountable mafia is transformed until it arrives at "parody" with Takeshi Kitano. One of the most successful TV dramas, *Gokusen*, tells the story of a smart young teacher, the granddaughter of the Oedo Yakuza family, who must deal with the problem of managing her "exuberant" class of students. Another TV drama, *Ninkyo Helper*, tells the story of a group of young Yakuza who are compelled by their leader to carry out social services. The famous *Densha Otoko* ("man on the train") is a step forward or re-interpretation of the "stereotypical" image of *otaku*, since the film, and later the TV drama, recounts the love story between an *otaku* (complete with all the usual characteristics of the category: introverted, clumsy, fanatical about manga and anime) and a girl, who is exactly the opposite, called Ms. Hermes, who is beautiful and from an upper-class family which deems appearance as the greatest of values. This has contributed to change the way *otaku* are seen, while also showing the need to exit certain stereotypes. For this reason, I think that it is difficult (and at the same time fascinating) to interpret Japanese society through culture and creative production so long as they are not contextualized into the complexity of the social and cultural historical narrative.

6. Elise K. Tipton, *Modern Japan: A Social and Political History* (Nissan Institute Routledge Japanese Studies Series), first published 2002 by Routledge

7. David W. Edgington, *Reconstructing Kobe: The Geography of Crisis and Opportunity* (UBC Press, The University of British Columbia), 2010.

8. Shimpei Goto, *General Plan for the Reconstruction of the Imperial Capital*, in Rem Koolhaas and Hans Ulrich Obrist (Eds), Project Japan: Metabolism Talks..., (Taschen), 2011

9. Rem Koolhaas and Hans Ulrich Obrist (Eds), *Project Japan: Metabolism Talks...*, (Taschen), 2011, p.19.

10. Jean-Francois Lyotard, *La condition postmoderne, Rapport sur le sovoir* (Éditions de Minuit), 1979 (Italian translation, *La condizione postmoderna. Rapporto sul sapere* [Feltrinelli], 1981).

11. The final scene of the film is famous. The samurai who have survived the battle defending the village observe the farmers who are happy and sustained by their work, and realize that despite having won the battle, they, the samurai, are the losers and the farmers the winners. It can be read as a message that summarizes the state of Japanese society after the war.

12. These series of manga, television and toy characters created a vast and diversified production of content and meaning. Just think of the extraordinary editions of *zukai* (illustrations of monsters, aliens and heroes).

13. The full-scale reproduction of anime and manga characters is a process of re-materialization of intangible heritage that has been underway for several years in Japan. In hindsight, the manga *Tetsujin 28-go*, written and illustrated by Mitsuteru Yokoyama, was inspired by the devastation caused by the bombing of the city of Kobe during World War Two, and this same city 15 years after the Great Hanshin-Awaji Earthquake of 1994 has built its 18-metre high statue, as if to protect the city. The latest manga/anime character to become a full-scale model is Evangelion. It is, however, a robot 80 meters high, so only the head has been built for now. In 2010, though, it was possible to see its virtual image via a mobile phone in a specific location in the city of Hakone. Thousands of people went to this location to see the image of Evangelion through their own smartphone. This growing passion of the Japanese for the robot is accompanied by the development of the most advanced technologies in the field of robotics and humanoid robots, shown every year at the International Robot Exhibition (IREX) in Tokyo, which boasts exhibits from all over the world. In addition, there are the well-known national robot contests among the students from colleges of technology (since 1988), between international students at universities (since 1990), and among students of Japanese universities (since 1991), and also a contest among students of Asian universities (since 2002).

14. Makoto Aida, Mami Kataoka, Yuji Yamashita, David Elliott, Makoto Aida *MONUMENT FOR NOTHING* (exhibition catalogue) (Mori Art Museum / SEIGENSHA Ltd.), 2012

15. Shin Nakagawa, Koichi Suwa, A cultural approach to recovery assistance following urban disasters, City, Culture and Society (2010), Volume 1, pp. 27–36.

16. Takashi Murakami, *Superflat* (MADRA Publishing), 2000, p. 25. In his practice of commodifying the cognitive value of art, Murakami has taken a significant risk in challenging the migration of business logic to the art market. However, in this way he has developed an extensive system of production and dissemination of contemporary art, within which are contained the distinctive codes of Japanese culture. With the branches of Kaikai Kiki Co., Ltd. in Japan and America, the artist has expanded his production capacities and promotion of his artistic creativity, encouraging also the growth of a new generation of Japanese artists and promoting the contemporary art market in Japan.

17. Hiroki Azuma, *Otaku: Japan's Database Animals*, translated by Jonathan E. Abel and Shion Kono (University of Minnesota Press), 2009. See also Ito Mizuko, Okabe Daisuke and Tsuji Izumi (ed.), *Fandom Unbound: Otaku Culture in a Connected World* (Yale University Press), 2012. Regarding the "effect" of digital technology in many cultural and creative sectors, the Cultural Human Resources Council's (CHRC) much anticipated Cultural HR Study 2010 identified the "digital tsunami" that is permeating all stages of the cultural sector's creative chain. The study by Azuma seems an allegory for every citizen of the world, first and foremost of all those who come into contact with new technologies and are faced with the enormous amount of information and data that the systematic dematerialization of content is producing for non-profit (for example, Wikipedia) or profit (Google, YouTube, Twitter, to name the most famous and "pervasive"). It is a process that we begin to glimpse today.
Going beyond the main object of this text, there are two examples which I would like to touch upon that lead back to Japan. The first is personal and is connected to film subtitling. In Italy, everything that appears on television and in the cinema has been dubbed into Italian. Aside from the fact that it can cause a sort of "distortive Italian-centric" view of the world (just think of the regional accents used to dub goodies and baddies), during my period of study in England I discovered not only the greatest "reality" of watching videos in the original language, but also the fact that the subtitles produced for me the "collateral" effect of learning a second language more easily (without undermining my native language). That was a long time ago. Today if we compare the geographical map of the citizens of European countries who know a second language with those of the countries that promote the spread of media contents (i.e., cinema, television) in the original language with subtitle we will find a "strange" coincidence.
Today in Italy there are more than 80 online communities that produce subtitles for Japanese anime, movies and dramas. It is not for business (in traditional terms) because everything is created mainly for the purpose of "fun," but it is "another and different" way to attend the creation of new content. This new form of active participation in the development of content in Japan has since 2000 been undergoing experimentation with the *keitai shosetsu* (cell phone novel), the novel that is written by authors through their phone and viewed online, but also published in hundreds of thousands of copies. Some became bestsellers, like Yoshi's *Deep Love* and Mika's *Koizora* series, or *Sky of Love: A Sad Love Story*, also adapted for manga, television, and film. The evolution of this practice is the *rirei-shosetsu*, namely the community of authors who collectively write the content of a novel.
These are simple examples but they do help us understand how technology can accelerate the development of individual skills, which in turn make it possible for them to produce new content in a meta-digital ecology that is reflected at the forefront of the semantic web and digital humanities.

18. Ronald Inglehart, *Globalization and Postmodern Values*, The Washington Quarterly, Volume 23, Number 1, Winter 2000, pp. 215-228 (article).

19. The character No-Face (Kaonashi) in the film *Spirited Away* (2001) by Hayao Miyazaki voraciously devours the food which he gained by using money as a powerful tool of persuasion and eventually becomes a giant horrible monster with egocentric behaviour, however isolated and lonely. This character seems to summarize, on the one hand, the need to redefine the meaning of social relationships and on the other, the need to overcome the concept of scarcity centered only on money and its accumulation. Although I cannot develop this thought here, in a world knowledge economy where significantly new forms of hybrid and gift economies are emerging, the concept of scarcity could be more related to the cognitive sphere of accumulation and market transactions.

20. The Japanese content industry (entertainment and media) now stands in second place, a position it will hold in the coming years. Entertainment and media sectors refers to: Internet access spending, Internet advertising, TV subscriptions and license fees, television advertising, filmed entertainment, video games, music, consumer magazine, publishing, newspaper publishing, radio, out-of-home advertising, consumer and

educational book publishing, and business-to-business. *Global entertainment and media outlook 2012-2016: The "End of the digital beginning"* (PricewaterhouseCoopers International Limited) (PwCIL), 2012.

21. Today efforts are being made to gradually extend the operation of the nuclear power plant, from 40 years to 100 years. In addition, entombment (the creation of a sarcophagus to leave at the site) is an alternative to dismantling and has recently attracted greater interest, given the increasing high costs of dismantling. Another aspect is the permanence as a physical site, generally that of decades if not hundreds of years. Its legacy could lend a different interpretation, namely that of "heavy heritage," a heritage that requires not only immediate but long-standing preservation and attention. The physical heritage sites that we know today have become in many cases UNESCO World Heritage sites. They may have survived to the present day by mere chance, or because they were abandoned or were not considered interesting, or due to lack of resources for transformation (as is the case with Venice). On the contrary, nuclear power plants, the expression of the most sophisticated technologies and engineering design, the expression of the technological development of mankind, must be preserved (or dismantled with extreme care) due to the possible danger they may have on the environment. I think, for example, that Italians have decided not to partake in this "heavy heritage" perhaps because they subconsciously realize this long-term aspect, having had a thousand years of experience with physical heritage sites (in some cases, such as the Coliseum in Rome, also connected to traumatic events such as the persecution of Christians) which happen to be still distributed throughout the country. Furthermore, the coincidence of making these decisions through referendums with the Chernobyl and 3.11 events has had such a tremendous impact on the Italian population that it has determined their rejection.

22. We made the journey to Tohoku in his yellow bus, on which the inscription "Go for Future" was written and on which all the people we met during the trip were free to write messages of hope or do something they found heartening. During the trip Endo told me that after 3.11 he prepared a postcard to send to the inhabitants of Tohoku but decided to take it to them personally instead of sending it to them. From that moment on he has continued to go regularly to find the inhabitants and bring people to Tohoku. I am very grateful to him that I could be there, as well as to his friends, and a group from a national TV station (Nihon Television), and even more to the people I met. I was also happy when Endo, introducing a place we visited, said "this area, you will see, has suffered a lot of damage," but then corrected himself, saying that he was very surprised at the great progress that had been made with respect to the previous time when he was there.

23. Upon finishing this text Toyo Ito received the Pritzker Architecture Prize, the sixth Japanese architect to win this prestigious award.

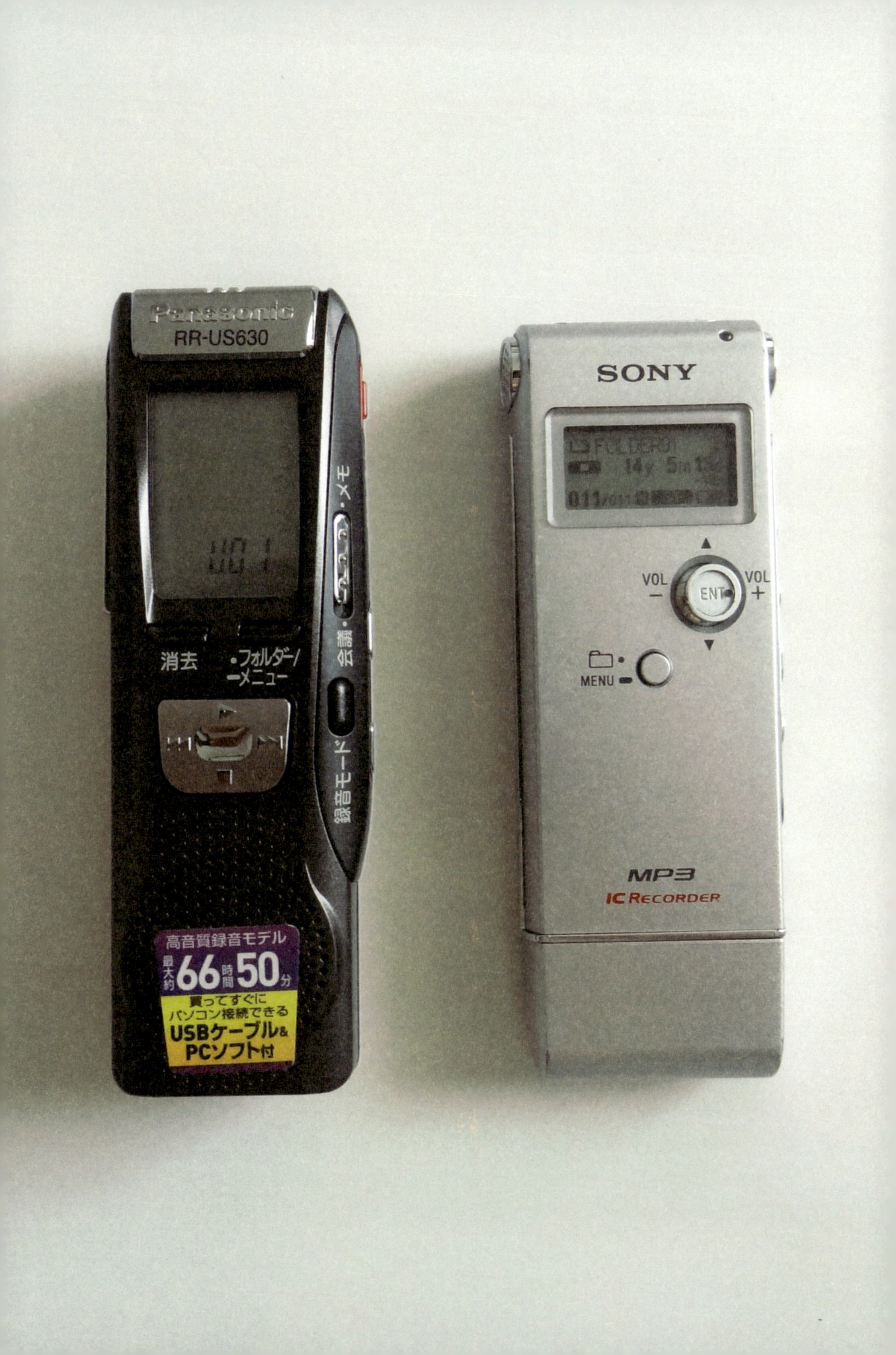
Panasonic
RR-US630
・メモ
会議・
消去
・フォルダー/
ーメニュー
録音モード
高音質録音モデル
最大約66時間50分
買ってすぐに
パソコン接続できる
USBケーブル&
PCソフト付
SONY
VOL
−
VOL
+
ENT
MENU
MP3
IC RECORDER

3.11への芸術文化からの応答

今村有策
トーキョーワンダーサイト館長

震災を受けて様々な反応があった。もちろん災害で芸術のあり方が変わるわけではない。しかし、今回の災害は社会のあり方と生き方を問い直される出来事であった。

渋谷の中心地に場所を持つトーキョーワンダーサイト（TWS）は、震災を受けて、急きょ予定のプログラムを休止し、文化における東北の現状と支援の情報発信地として対応可能なようにした。公園通りに面するTWSアートカフェには情報コーナーを置き、展示室はすぐに対応が始まった芸術文化による東北支援のプロジェクトに使ってもらえるようにした。TWSはちょうど10周年を迎えていたが、過去を振り返ってお祝いをするのではなく、この災害をどのように捉え、受け止めるべきかという対話を契機として我々の未来を考えることにした。定期的にアーティストが集まり、それぞれの震災への関わり方を紹介しながら、私たちが、今何を考えているか、どのように行動すべきかなどの意見を交換しあった。その対話のなかから生まれてきたプロジェクトを形にし、「NEXT10」というプログラムを行った。そこではアーティストたちの切実な心からの声が聞こえる稀有な機会となった。

アーティスト・イン・レジデンスには地震を経験したことのない国々のアーティストが滞在しており、また未曽有の災害を滞在先で経験するということから館内は不安と緊張感に包まれていた。いくつかの国は自国民を国外退避することに努力し、また、ある国は関西への一時避難を援助するなど、多様な対応がとられた。多くの滞在者が自国の指示に従い帰国する中で、自己判断に任されたアーティストと日本人滞在者をひとまず一時避難させるために名和晃平氏の助けを借りて、急きょ京都のSANDWICHに受け入れて頂いた。

その後、しばらくのレジデンスプログラム休止の後、本プロジェクトの推進者であるグイド・フェリッリ氏から当プロジェクトを行うために来日の打診があった。当館では、このプロジェクトの重要性を理解し、グイド氏の滞在を受け入れ、本プロジェクトがスタートした。TWSはこれまでのネットワークの中で、震

災へ積極的に対応する多くのクリエーターを紹介することとなった。

震災後4年を経てようやく出版の準備が整った。被災地では3年が過ぎ、いくつかの震災復興予算が終了する時期を迎えている。被災地ではいまだに多くの方々が仮設住宅に住んでおり、いまだ復興への道のりは遠い。4年目を迎える今、あの時に考えたこと、課題に取りかかれているかを改めて考え直す時がきているのではないだろうか。

災害で芸術のあり方が変わるわけではない。しかし、私たちの生き方、社会のあり方を問い直すこととなったことには違いない。あの時、芸術文化に携わる人々がどのように災害を受け止め、行動をしたのかを記録した、この貴重な資料が今を生きる私たちと次世代の人々に大切なものを伝えてくれることを祈念している。

The Response of Art and Culture to 3.11

Yusaku Imamura
Director, Tokyo Wonder Site

There was a wide array of responses to the 2011 Tohoku earthquake and tsunami. Of course, natural disaster does not change art itself, but the disaster certainly questioned our society and our ways of living.

Located in the center of Shibuya, Tokyo Wonder Site (TWS) canceled its scheduled events after the disaster, making its facilities available as a hub for information on the state of Tohoku culture and the support it needed. We set up an information booth in TWS Art Café facing Koen-dori Street and the gallery spaces were used by the cultural and artistic Tohoku aid projects that were initiated immediately following the disaster. It was our tenth anniversary year, but instead of celebrating the milestone by merely looking back on the past, we utilized the opportunity to take stock of our future through reflecting on how we faced and thought about the disaster. As artists regularly gathered at TWS to introduce their activities related to the disaster, we could exchange many opinions about what we were thinking and how we should act. We materialized the ideas stemming from the dialogue as the project Next 10, which became a rare opportunity to hear artists speaking from the heart.

As some of the artists in residence at that time had never experienced earthquakes in their home countries, let alone such an unprecedented disaster in a foreign country, our facilities were filled with anxiety and tension. There was a range of responses: some countries urged their nationals to evacuate from Japan, while others assisted their citizens in temporarily leaving for the Kansai region. Following the guidance of their governments, many resident artists decided to return to their home countries, though those who were left to make their own decisions joined Japanese peers in briefly evacuating to SANDWICH, an artist studio with residential facility, in Kyoto, with the help of the artist Kohei Nawa.

When we re-launched our residency program after a short suspension, Guido Ferilli contacted us inquiring if he could come to Japan to develop this project. We welcomed his proposal, understanding the importance of his project, which was launched upon his arrival. We were able to introduce Mr. Ferilli to a lot of creative professionals in TWS's existing network who were actively engaging in activities related to the disaster.

Four years have passed since the disaster and this documentation is finally ready to be published. After three years, some parts of the Great East Japan Earthquake Reconstruction Budget allocated to the region have now been spent, yet a large number of people still live in temporary housing and there is a long way to go before we will have achieved full reconstruction. As we enter the fourth year since the disaster, we have arrived at the point where we need to reexamine how we thought back then and whether or not we have been able to engage with the issues we discussed.

Natural disaster does not change art itself. However, it certainly questions the way we live and how our society operates. I hope this valuable publication, documenting how those of us who work in the art and culture field perceived the disaster and acted in its aftermath, will convey a vital message to people today and to future generations.

HTML5

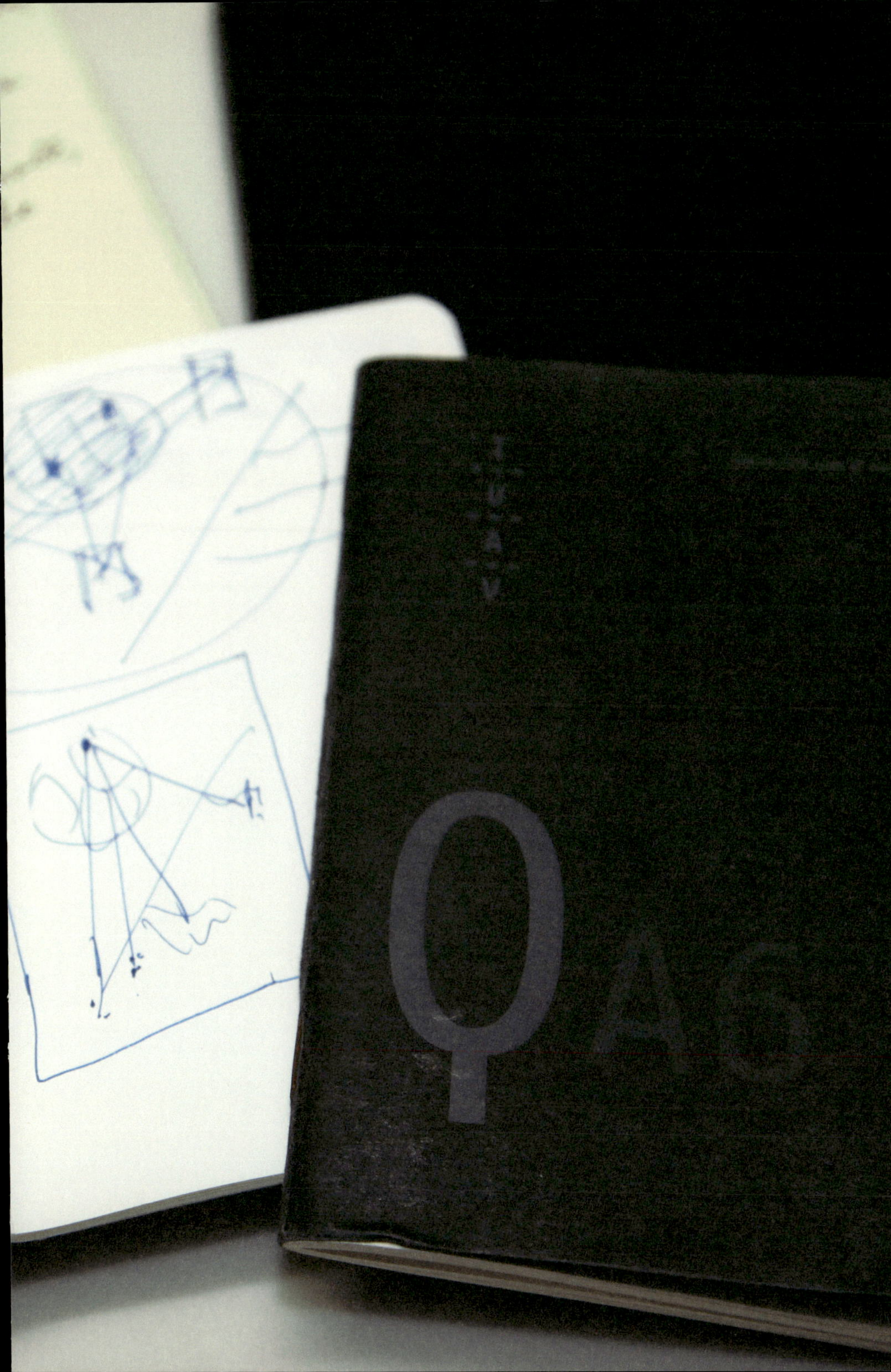

＊本書に収載する以下のインタビューは、2011年から2012年にかけて行われた。
名称等の記述は、当時を反映するものである。

*The interviews that follow in this book were conducted during 2011 and 2012.
Their content, including names, reflect the situation at that time.

荒川靖彦
Artists' Action for JAPAN 代表

3月11日の地震は、被災地のために力を合わせなくてはいけないという必然性を被災地以外の日本全域に伝えたと思います。

震災から3日後、自分は被災地のために何か具体的なことができないかと考え始めました。当時、色々な知り合いにすぐに何か出来ないかと問いかけ、3月26日から実際にチャリティー活動を始めました。メンバーが集まったきっかけはツイッターや口コミで、そのほとんどは美大や芸大の学生や卒業生でした。自分の場合は卒業生ですが芸術関係の友達がたくさんいたので、活動を呼びかけるとそれがだんだん外に広まっていって、他の美術大学にまで波及しました。

最初に自分たちがアートをやってきて、それを活かしてチャリティーか何かができないかというアイデアで呼びかけました。そうしたらその呼びかけの2日後には10人位、3日後には30人位が参加の意思を表明してくれました。もしかしたら、100人位集まって何かすぐに出来るんじゃないかという感触がありました。

でも、最初はアートを正式に展示する場所でとは考えていなくて、公共の場所のような所ならできるんじゃないかという考えでした。それで最初は、上野公園ではどうかと考えていました。上野公園なら単なる学生が企画した活動でも場所をかしてくれそうだなと。逆に展示をするような場所だったら同じようにはできないだろうなと考えていました。なので公園かどこか他の公共の場所で、大道芸の人が大道芸をやるような自由な発表のための場所が適当な場所だと考えていました。

これが3.11に対してのArtists' Action for Japan(AAfJ)の最初のリアクションと提案でした。このとき自分はまだ社会人になったばかりだったので、最初は本業との両立という面で簡単ではなかったですが、徐々に会社の内外で協力してくださる方に出会うことができました。

メンバーが集まりだした時に、ある会社の知り合いの方にこんな活動をしているんですよという話をしたんですね。そうしたらその方がこのチャリティー活動を

させてくれそうな色々な場所のインフォメーションを自分にくれたんです。自分はちょっと耳に入れておこうかなくらいで話したのですが、その方はたくさんの知り合いがいて「こういうことはすぐにやったほうがいいから会場を一緒に探してあげる」と言ってくれました。で、社会的な信用のある方たちがAAfJのアイデアに興味を示してくれて、どんどん話が進み、次々と会場が決まっていきました。これはAAfJにとっての転機でした。

一番最初は代官山ヒルサイドフォーラムでやり、そしてトーキョーワンダーサイト、六本木ヒルズ、東京ミッドタウン、銀座のワード資生堂でやりました。最初の代官山でのイベント後、他の場所も次々とすぐに決まりました。このように早く決まったのにはもう一つ理由があって、震災に対する配慮で、その時やっていたり予定されていた展示やイベントが自粛されたり、キャンセルになったりしたんですよね。でも自分たちの企画は配慮して中止しなければならないような内容ではなかったので、企業の方や会場の方がやってもいいのではないかと考えてくださり、個人や企業など多くの支持してくれる方が集まり、被災地の人達をサポートすることに結びつきました。

AAfJの活動内容を説明すると、まずその場で制作者がドローイングをし、それを壁に展示する。来てくださったお客さんは展示された作品を見て、いいと思ったのを買っていく。それが全部寄付にまわるという形です。それぞれの表現方法で全員が貢献できることが一番重要なことだったので、AAfJからは細かいスタイルの指定は行わず、各アーティストに可能な限り自由な方法で表現してもらうようにしました。

ワード資生堂開催風景
Event at Word Shiseido
©Artists' Action for JAPAN

六本木ヒルズ開催風景
Event at Roppongi Hills
©Artists' Action for JAPAN

東京ミッドタウン開催風景
Event at Tokyo Midtown
©Artists' Action for JAPAN

このような活動を始めるにあたって作品の金額を考えた時、まず最初に考えたのは、広い意味での社会参加を創り出すためにどれだけ多くの人を巻き込めるかということでした。多くの人に参加してもらいたいときに、千円以上の価格設定は関心を示してくれる人の数を減らしてしまうと考え、ドローイング1枚あたりの値段を千円+お気持ちとしました。なぜなら、より重要なのは参加するという感覚であったので、この価格設定はより皆の手に届きやすいと思ったからです。

一方で、通常のギャラリーが扱っている価格より低い値段を設定したら、ギャラリー市場との対立を引き起こしかねないとの不安もありました。でも、AAfJの

荒川靖彦 | 63

活動は美術界に対して何か特別なことをしようとしているわけではないと思い直し、アート制作への違った視点からのアプローチをし、結果的に、立場の違う様々な人の協力を集めることができました。

制作する上で、何人かのアーティストはとても重い内容を消化してドローイングを描いてくれました。一方で地震のこととは全く関係ない動物の絵とかを描いたアーティストもいました。しかし表向きには何の関係もない絵を描いたとしても、実はチャリティー活動に加わることで新しい絆を現実のものとしていました。

今回の活動で集まったお金は、全額日本赤十字に送りました。そこを最初に選んだのは、自分達に信用性が無かったので、誰もが知っていて信用性のある団体である必要があったからです。これはとても大切な要素でした。しかし今は自分たちの活動も拡大し、認識されたと思います。これまでのようにチャリティーを続けていくべきか、これからどういった形の活動をするのか、検討中です。震災後すぐの時期は、募金活動がベストだと感じました。交通手段は分断され、交通機関は止まっていて、現地へ行くことは困難な上、足手まといになる可能性がありました。現地の状況がよくわからず、そこで何が起こり、何が必要なのかわかりませんでした。美大を卒業したばかりの若いアーティストや僕らのやれることではこれがベストなアクションのように思えました。今は神戸でのイベントを終えたばかりで、自分の中で今後どういう風にしたらいいのか考えていて、他のメンバーもそのことについて考えていると思います。

自分には今回の活動で基本になる尺度があって、それはより多くの人を無理なく参加させること、何かで加担している人の数をできるだけ増やすことです。これが従うべき方針で、反対にアーティスト的な活動をするための方法は一人ひとりに任せています。つまり、3.11を思いながらどのように表現したいかは各アーティストに任せています。とにかく大切なのは、より多くの人を巻き込むことが出来るか、です。

AAfJでは大体10人くらいが毎回のイベントを企画するのに動いています。全員有機的な形で、毎回自分の意思で協力してもらい、縛りというのは設けていないので、新しい人が入ってくる可能性もあります。自分らが達成したい目標までは皆で頑張っています。そして、そのあとは自分の意思で次の目標に向かって続けていきたいか、それぞれが決めます。

現在、チャリティーで描かれた作品すべてを記録しています。ドローイングは売れてしまうけど、アーティスト、作品はデータとして自分たちが持っておき、それを

自分たちのウェブにアップロードします。というのは、被災地で暮らしている人たちに、「多くの人たちがあなたたちのことを思っていますよ」と伝えるのも目的のひとつだったからです。

AAfJの参加者はアーティストだけではなく、デザイナーや学生もいます。延べで、間違えなければ少し前のウェブに載っていたのは約7,300人でした。イベントは全部で10回以上、1会場につき2、3回、メンバーが集まれる週末や祝日にやっていました。具体的には3月から5月までは毎週末して、一度被災地にボランティアとワークショップに行きました。その後、夏の期間はお休みして、そして神戸でイベントを再開しました。夏の期間、私たちは完全にお休みしました。というのは、もう息が切れて……、要するに体力とお金が完全に尽きてしまったからです。

震災後自分の会社の仕事が止まっていましたが、また業務が通常に戻り、仕事によってこの活動に割ける時間が変わってくるので、今はどのように仕事とボランティア活動を両立するか考えなければなりません。大規模になりつつあるこの活動のためには、NPOにするのが有効であるとは感じています。とにかく基本目標は、どれだけ多くの人、何も出来ないと思っている人、やる気のない人を巻き込むことが出来るかであることが重要だと思います。時間と持続力を必要とする活動で、それをすることが特別なこととか、すごい大変なことだからやらないのではなく、普通のことだからみんな参加するというようにしたいのです。被災した方のために、自分たちの出来る事で参加するのは普通のことですから。

Yasuhiko Arakawa

Director, Artists' Action for Japan

I think the earthquake on March 11th communicated to the whole of Japan outside of the disaster zones the inevitability of working together for the afflicted areas.

Three days after, I began to wonder if I could do something concrete for the places hit by the disaster. Straightaway, I asked many acquaintances if there was something we could do and then from March 26th I actually started doing charity work. People were brought together through Twitter or word-of-mouth. Almost everyone was an art college student or graduate. I too am an art college graduate, so I have lots of friends connected to the arts. After calling in all these people it began to expand more and more outside of the group, and then it spread to other art universities.

We appealed to people with our idea about making art ourselves and then using that to do something charitable. Two days after the call-out we had reached about ten people, and by three days around 30 people had shown their intention to take part. We had the feeling that we could get around 100 people together and we could do something straightaway.

At first we weren't thinking about a place to exhibit the work formally; the idea was more to somehow do something in a public space. Initially we were thinking of Ueno Park, since there even students can rent spaces to do things. We thought that if it were a place for exhibiting work, then you wouldn't be able to do the same thing. So we thought what was suitable was a place like a park or other public place, a free place where street performers could put on a show.

This was Artists' Action for Japan (AAfJ) first response to 3.11. At this point I had only just started doing a proper job so it wasn't easy to do both my real work and this at the same time, but gradually I was able to meet people both inside and outside my company who would cooperate with me.

Once we had got the participants together, I told someone I knew at work about the project. He then gave me information about all kinds of places that would let us do charitable work. He knows lots of people and, though I just thought I'd let him know about the project, he told me that I should do it right away and even offered to look for places with me. After someone like this with social credibility had shown interest in AAfJ's idea, then things began to really move forward and one after the other the venues got fixed. This was a turning point for AAfJ.

The first event was at Daikanyama Hill Side Forum, after which we exhibited at Tokyo Wonder Site, Roppongi Hills, Tokyo Midtown, and Ginza's Word Shiseido. Following the event at Daikanyama, the other places very soon got decided.

There is another reason for why it moved so quickly and that was because the exhibitions and events planned at the venues had been canceled out of consideration for the situation in the wake of the disaster. But the event we were proposing was not the kind of project that needed to be canceled out of respect for the victims, so the corporations or people running the venues thought it would be fine for us to do it. Many individuals and corporations supported us, and this led to us being able to support the people in the disaster zones.

What AAfJ's activities actually involved was first of all, the creative team did a drawing and then this was exhibited at the venue, where the people who came to the event would see the artwork, and if they liked it they would buy it—and everything was then donated. Most important of all was that everyone was able to contribute to the cause through their own way of making art, so AAfJ gave no particular instructions as to the style, and just had each artist make their artworks in as free a way as possible.

When I thought about the pricing of the artworks as we were getting started, I first of all thought about how to involve lots of people in order to create social participation in a broad sense. I felt that around ¥1,000 per drawing was right but then when I wanted lots of people to take part, I thought that setting the price at more than ¥1,000 would reduce the number of people who would be interested. This is because I considered participation to be more important, so pricing things cheaply like this would make it easier to reach more people.

On the other hand, there was also the fear that if we priced things lower than at regular galleries, it would lead to a confrontation with the gallery market. But then I considered how AAfJ's activities are not attempting to do anything special in the art world, so our approach comes from a different perspective to producing art, and as a result we could get the cooperation of a range of people in different positions.

For producing the work, several of the artists did drawings that dealt with quite heavy themes. And on the other hand, there were also artists who drew things completely unrelated to the disaster, such as pictures of animals. However, ostensibly, even drawing pictures that were not related to the disaster nonetheless added to the charitable activity and thus created new bonds.

All the money that we collected through this work was given to the Japanese Red Cross. We chose the JRC first because we had no credibility ourselves and so we needed an organization that everyone knew and which was reliable. This was a very important part of it. However, today our activities have expanded and been recognized.

I am currently considering whether we should continue our charitable work the same way as we have up till now or what different form it should take in the future. I felt that in the period right after the disaster, the best thing to do was fundraising. The roads were blocked and so the means of transport were stopped, making it hard to reach the sites, hence we might just have been a nuisance if we had gone there. We didn't know about the state of the disaster zones, what was happening or what was needed. We thought this was the best kind of activity that young artists and recent art graduates could do. I've just now finished an event in Kobe and have been wondering about how to do things in the future, and the other members have also been thinking about it.

The rule that forms the basis of my activities is to make more people participate without much effort; somehow to broaden as much as possible the number of people taking part. This is the policy we should follow, but on the other hand, as for the means of doing artistic activities, I leave that up to each individual. In other words, I leave it up to each artist to work out how to express how he or she feels about 3.11. What's important is whether we can get more people involved.

In AAfJ there are usually around ten people for each event. Everyone takes part for definite periods, as per their intention each time, and there are no set commitments, which means new people can also join in. We all do our very best until we have reached the goals we want. And then everyone decides themselves whether to continue on to the next goal.

At present, we are recording all the artworks that are made for charity. Although they are sold off as drawings, the artworks are kept by the artists and then uploaded onto their websites. This is because one of our missions was to convey to those living in the areas hit by the disaster that lots of people are thinking of them.

The participants in AAfJ are not only artists but also designers and students. In total, unless there's been a mistake, around 7,300 individuals' work has been uploaded to the website as of a short time ago. We have held events over ten times, two or three times per venue, with the organizers getting together at weekends or national holidays. To be specific, we did the events every weekend from March until May, and we also once went to the areas hit by the disaster to volunteer and do workshops. After that, we took the summer period off, and then started again with an event in Kobe. We took a total break from activities for the summer. We'd run out of steam, and our bodies and wallets were completely exhausted.

After the earthquake, the company where I work shut down for a while, but once work had returned to normal, the time I could give for charitable activities changed, so now I have to consider how, in the future, I can keep doing a regular job alongside my volunteering. Since what I am doing is growing to be quite large in scale, I feel that it would now be workable to make it into a formal non-profit organization. At any rate, what's important is the fundamental goal of getting people involved who think they cannot do anything or aren't motivated. This activity needs time and sustainability, but it's not doing something that's special or something you cannot do because it's so difficult—it's something very ordinary, and that's why I want everyone to participate. Because doing what you can do for the victims of the earthquake is just a normal thing to do.

荒木 猛
Design Festa 代表

3.11以後、アーティストかどうかに関わらずすべての人、特に被害にあった地域の人たちは、生き延びることについて考えました。しばらくの間、僕らは前に進むためのモチベーションをなくしてしまっていました。ある人にとっては物質的なものだけではなく、家族や友人まですべてを失うという悲劇的な状況でした。3.11前に私たちは5月にイベントを企画していましたが、イベント開催に対する自粛ムードがあったので、開催するべきか非常に悩みました。しかし、開催するかの問合せや開催を希望する声をたくさんいただいたので、「デザインフェスタvol.33」の開催を決定したんです。原宿のギャラリーでのチャリティーイベントも企画しました。3.11以後、私たちを含めアーティスト達は、援助するということの本当の意味を理解しようと模索していたんだと思います。被災地に行く人もいれば、チャリティー活動をする人もいました。

震災後しばらくしてからですが、被災地のアーティスト達が自分たちの作品と創作活動の意味を考え始めたと感じています。地震について、家族について、そして人生の意味についてです。命が簡単に失われてしまった事実を受け

デザイン・フェスタ・ギャラリー原宿
Design Festa Gallery, Harajuku
©DESIGN FESTA

入れ、人生、家族、色んな人とのつながりの価値を考え直す必要がある。ツイッターやFacebookのようなソーシャル・ネットワークではこのような側面に対する議論がたくさんあります。ある人たちはアートは何の役にも立たないと言い、またある人たちは役に立つことがあると考え、作品を作り始めました。

震災から2、3ヵ月後、物理的な援助が行われると同時に、被災地の人たちが普段の生活を送る活力を得られるよう、精神面での援助が始まったように感じます。地域の復興ではなく、生きるための新しい自信を取り戻してもらうということです。被災地の近くに住む、靴のデザインをしている友人がいるのですが、彼は震災の2週間後、被災地を訪れてからここに来て、被災地の深刻な問題について話をしてくれました。4月下旬に再び彼が東京にチャリティーイベントに参加するために戻って来た時は、現地は少しずつ良くなってきていると言っていましたが、同時に復興のためにはもっと膨大な時間が必要なんだと実感せざると得ませんでした。

デザイン・フェスタ vol.34の様子
DESIGN FESTA vol. 34 (2011)
©Design Festa Ltd.

私たちデザインフェスタギャラリーの活動は、アーティストに表現する場所を提供することです。そこはアーティスト達の考えや、表現の意味を共有できるところなんです。記念館のような場所を欲しがる人もいますが、今のアーティストはより制作や表現の過程、その意味について考えているんです。

震災後「今どのように生活しているのか」、そして「どのように生きるか」がみんなの論点になりました。ある人たちは被災地の人たちのために作品を作った

デザイン・フェスタ
vol.34の様子
DESIGN FESTA vol. 34 (2011)
©Design Festa Ltd.

としても、実際はその人たちのためになってはいないと考えたり、一方で直接被災地に行かなければ意味がないとも考えました。ですから震災から2、3ヵ月は、被災地に行って働く人もいれば、東京に残りチャリティーオークションなどのイベントで寄付を募ることもしました。例の福島の私の友人も、以前は生活するために作品を作っていましたが、震災後は寄付を募るために制作活動を行っています。

今は福島の原発の問題に立ち向かう必要があって、そのためそれをテーマとした作品が増えています。建物の上の船が乗っているような写真作品など、津波をテーマとした作品は非常に多く見られます。東北地方からデザインフェスタギャラリーに来るアーティストも少しずつ増えていますが、彼ら自身、自分たちのためにアート作品を作るのか、他人のために作るのか、自問しています。

被災地のアーティストは、自分たちが伝えたい、自分たちの作品の新しい意味が何なのか理解しようとしていると思うんですね。少しずつですが、その理解が深められていると感じています。

デザイン・フェスタ
vol.34の様子
DESIGN FESTA vol.
34 (2011)
©Design Festa Ltd.

Takeshi Araki
President, Design Festa

Since 3.11, everyone, especially the people in the regions affected by the disaster, has thought about survival, regardless of whether they are artists or not. For a while we lost the motivation to move forward. For some people, this tragedy was not only a materialistic one but also one where they lost everything, including their family and friends.

Before 3.11 happened we had been planning an event in May, but because at the time a mood had descended on Japanese society calling for restraint from holding any events, I wasn't sure if we should go ahead. We eventually decided to host Design Festa 33 after receiving a lot of anticipatory inquiries about the event. We also organized a charitable event at our gallery in Harajuku. Many artists including us were trying to understand what aid really means; some of them went to the disaster areas and others engaged in charity work.

After some time I felt that artists from the disaster areas started to question the meaning of their creative activities and their existence as artists. They thought about the earthquake, family, and meaning of life. We need to accept the sudden loss of life and think about the values of life, family, and our relationships with different people. You can see lots of discussions on this topic on Twitter and Facebook. Some people argued that art is useless while others started creating artwork that believes in the role of art.

Two or three months after the disaster, we started to see a more spiritual approach to aid, concurrent with material support, enabling those who were affected to return to a normal life. The goal was to help people regain the confidence to live again rather than just to reconstruct. A shoe designer friend of mine visited me, and talked about his experiences visiting the areas and the serious issues he saw there two weeks after the disaster. When he came back to Tokyo in late April to participate in a charity event, he said that the areas were gradually recovering, though it also felt like an enormous amount of time will be needed to truly restore the devastated areas.

Design Festa's gallery activities aim to provide artists with a space to showcase their work, a place where artists share their thoughts as well as the meaning of their artistic expression. Some people want to have a place more like a static museum, but artists today are thinking about the process of producing work and expression, and what this means.

After the disaster, questions like "How do we live today?" and "How are we going to survive?" have been discussed by everyone. Some artists thought that even if they created work for the disaster's victims, it would be pointless for the people unless they directly visited the areas. So some decided to go to the disaster areas and work there for a few months, while others remained in Tokyo carrying out charity auction events. My friend based in Fukushima who I mentioned before now creates work to collect donations, whereas in the past he made artwork in order to make a living.

There is a necessity to tackle the issue of the Fukushima nuclear power plant and I see a growing number of artworks addressing this theme. I have also seen a lot of tsunami-themed work, like photography of ships left on top of buildings. The number of artists coming to Design Festa Gallery has been gradually increasing, and they are also questioning whether they are making art for themselves or for others.

In my opinion, artists from the devastated areas are trying to understand the new meaning of their art, and I can see that little by little they are deepening their understanding.

遠藤一郎
未来芸術家

一番最初に被災地を訪れた理由は、東北に帰れなくなった友達を送って行くためでした。また、何が起こっているか、ちゃんと自分の目で確かめることも必要だと思いました。そのとき出会った人がいて、また会いたいから行くことになる。東北をともかく、人が行き交うことで暖めないといけないと思った。それでこういう風に「未来へ号」に人を乗せて東北に行き来し始めたんですね。日本では「未来へ号」で車上生活もしていて、「未来号」は僕の活動をする場でもあり、生活の場でもある。バスには黄色地に紺色で「未来へ」と書いてあり、そのまわりには出会った人々の夢が描いてあります。それは、出会った軌跡でもあり、世の中にはこれだけの人が生きていて、前を向いて、未来へ向かって、夢をもっているんだという証明でもあります。

「未来へ号」は2006年、6年前からやり始めて、初めて東北に行った時には3号目のバンだったんですよ。3号で東北に行ったとき、すごいたくさん人がこの車に集まったんですね。どこでも人はだいたい集まってくるんだけど、東北もまた人が集まった。人が集まるとそれだけ色んなことが起こっていく。大船渡だったり、石巻だったり、福島だったり、だんだん起こっていく。東北の色んな所で、色んな人と出会って、つながりが出来上がっていくんです。これは必要なことだと思っています。今回行ったみたいに、何かが、何か行かなければならない用があって、「未来へ号」でそこに行くことによってどんどん可能性が広がって、そこに行く機会が増えていく。それは僕だけじゃなくて、そこに住んでいる現地の人達も含めての可能性でもある。「未来へ号」がそこに行くことによって祭りが興ったりとか、だから可能性が現地の人達にとっても広がっていったんです。

来年はもっと多くの人と多くの夢を乗せて東北に連れて行きたいです。僕はそれ以前も「未来へ号」が世の中に必要だなと思っていました。自分の使命みたいなものを感じています。今は世の中と共に東北地方に精力を傾けてます。自分がバスを運転してるわけだから、自分がやるしかない。それともう一つ別の理由があるんです。それは、被災地に最初に行った時、ただそこに居る

東北での活動（石巻）
Ishinomaki, Tohoku
(northeast Japan)
©遠藤一郎 / Ichiro Endo

だけで背筋に寒気が走るようなすごい寒さだったの。人がいなかったの。というより人が戻って来れない。津波に全部持っていかれて、たくさんの海岸沿いの所は瓦礫でいっぱいだから。今回行った被災地、陸前高田とか気仙沼とかはもちろん戻って来れないから人がいないけど、最初はどこもああいう感じだった。全体がもっともっとグレーだったの。みんな気仙沼に行った時、人がいなくて、ボロボロな状態で、すごいヒヤッという寒さを感じたと思うんだ。だから、これはただ単純に暖めなきゃいけないと思ったの。温かみが必要。温かみは色んな温かみ、人の心もね。暖めるためにはやっぱり動かないといけない、動きを作らないといけないと思ったの。で、そこには人がいた場所なわけだから、欲しい動きっていうのは人の動きだったの。本当に、ビジュアル的に人が歩くだったり、これも動きだし、人がそこで何かをしていくも動きだし。例えば、瓦礫撤去をしていくっていうのも動きだし、そこで人と人が出会う、これも動きだし。そういうのが全部摩擦なわけ。出会いだったりとか、実際そこで動いている、歩いているだったりとか、それがその場の摩擦になって温かみを生んでいく。

だから、自分に出来る限りより多くの人を連れて行ったり、多くの出会いを作り、自分だけじゃなくて、乗せていった人がそこで会話をすることも摩擦だし。そういう多くの人との出会い、被災地との出会いっていうのを生みたかった。これは自分のアーティスト活動としてのメインですね。これは、被災地を含めだけど、この全体の活動の基本となっていると言っていいです。

遠藤一郎 | 77

もし何か発見があったかというのであれば、全部見つけたし、発見した。例えば、ビジュアル的にボロボロになっているものも初めて見た。でもボロボロになってるものだけど、見方を変えたり、その変化に手助けをしたりすることで新しく何かを得るものだと思う。自分の活動は変わってないけど、3.11以後、自分の役割はより多くの人とか夢とか情報とか、そういうものを運ぶっていうこと。将来、自分の活動を大きく発展させるために、より大きなバスを使うと思う。

東北でも絵を描いてそこに色がつく。看板とかいろいろなものが津波に流されてしまって、人がいなくなってグレーになって、色がなくなってしまった。その色っていうのは見た目だけではなく、人の声も一つの色として、そういうのがなくなったとこに再び人を連れてって色をつける。

この活動っていうのは被災地を見ないと出来ないと思うけど、役に立つ可能性にあふれている。ここに通ってわかったけど、コミュニティを発展させるために何かをすることはとても重要。津波が起こる前は、地元の人たちにはすごく強いコミュニティと絆があって、でもそれが崩壊してバラバラの仮設住宅に移されてしまった。その仮設住宅のなかで、誰が住んでるのか知らないから外に出るのも話をするのも難しい。家にこもってしまうんですね。だから僕の移動で人が家から外に出て話したり、移動するように仕掛けてます。このバスで人を外に連れて行ったり、その人たちに色んな場所を見せたり、他の人たちと話をしたりする。これは摩擦を生み、人との信頼と社会とのつながりを発展させたい

東北での活動（やっぺし祭り）
Hachi-hen City Festival in Tohoku (northeast Japan)
©遠藤一郎 / Ichiro Endo

気持ちを大きくさせるんです。これは僕がしたいこと、そして分かってもらいたいことです。

将来したいことははっきりしていて、「未来へ号バスワールドツアー」です。このバスで、コミュニティがつながっていく色んなチャンスを作るために世界中を回りたい。今回バスに乗ってくれたから感じてくれたと思うけど、バスの中でもそうだし、バスの外でもまたそうだし、人との出会いとか新しい意味でのコミュニティを生んでいくの。これは自分の活動の一部で、石巻の仮設住宅の人達とバスで連れてきた人達と一緒にピクニックを計画したみたいに、このバスを使って人との出会いとか動きを仕掛けていきたいんですね。小さいコミュニティというのを移動させることによってまた別のコミュニティとつながっていく。人であったり、情報であったりそういうものの移動を少しずつ海外でも出来ると信じてます。海外ではタイ、インド、ロンドンに行って、現地の車で「未来へ号」を作ったの。これを世界中でやりたいんだよね。そうすれば一つになる。でもこれは僕の希望だし夢であるんだけれども、地球は一つの輪でつながれるはずなんだな。これから必要なのは、地球を一つの輪を結ぶことだと思っているし、だからそれを信じてます。

遠藤一郎と《未来へ号バス》
Endo Ichiro and *Go for Future Bus*
©遠藤一郎 / Ichiro Endo

Ichiro Endo

Future Artist

The reason why I visited the disaster zone for the first time was to drive my friend to the region as he didn't have any means of returning home. I also thought that it was important to see what was happening with my own eyes. I met people there at that time and I wanted to go back to see them again. Anyway, I thought we have to cheer up Tohoku by getting more people to go there. That is the initial reason why I started driving people to Tohoku in my "Go for Future" van.

In Japan, I live in my Go for Future van, which for me is a place both for living and creating art. The color of my van is yellow with "Go for Future" written in navy, surrounded by the dreams of the people I have met through my journey. These written dreams represent my history of meeting people and the proof that there are many people living in this world who have dreams for the future.

I started the Go for Future project six years ago in 2006. The van I drove to Tohoku for the first time was the third version and when I visited the region with this one, so many people came to gather round it. The van attracts a lot of people in general and Tohoku was no exception. When many people gathered round the van, a lot of things began to happen in Ofunato, Ishinomaki, and Fukushima. Meeting a lot of different people in different places in Tohoku creates connections between people, which I think is really necessary. Like this time, I had a reason to go to Tohoku in my Go for Future van, and the more I visit there, the more the possibilities open up. It is not just my own possibilities but the possibilities for those who live in the areas hit by the disaster. Through the Go for Future van, the possibilities for the people in the region expanded like creating a festival.

I want to bring more people and their dreams to the Tohoku region in 2012. Even before the disaster, I had felt the necessity for Go for Future in society. I think doing this is my mission. Now I am putting my energy into the Tohoku area on top of society in general. I drive the van and this is just what I have to do. Another reason for why I feel so strongly about Tohoku is that when I first visited the devastated areas, it was extremely cold and I was shivering. There were no people. People could not go back to the areas because the tsunami had taken away everything and the coastline was filled with rubble. Rikuzentakata and Kesennuma, the areas we visited that time, were so devastated that people could not return. But every place looked like that in the immediate aftermath of the earthquake. Everything looked gray. Those who visited Kesennuma must have felt a chill seeing the area completely wrecked and with no people around. I just thought we have to "warm up" the area. The place needs warmth—different types of warmth, including that of the heart. And to warm up the place, we have to move around and create movement. The areas used to have people, so they need the movement of people, say people literally just walking or doing some random actions. For example, an act of cleaning up rubble is also movement that lets people meet each other. All these activities create friction. Meeting other people, actually doing movement there like walking—all these activities create friction and eventually generate warmth.

Bringing as many people to Tohoku as possible, creating chances for people to meet each other, and engaging in conversations not just with me but with local people all creates friction. I wanted to create encounters between people and with the disaster areas. This is my main objective not only for my Tohoku-related project but also for all my work.

In terms of whether I found something, I found and discovered everything. For example, for the first time in my life I saw things that were, visually speaking, completely wrecked. We can gain something new from these destroyed things by looking at them from a different perspective and helping them to transform. Although the nature of my activities hasn't changed even after experiencing 3.11, I have realized that my role is to carry the dreams and information of many others. To broaden my artistic activity in the future, I think I will use a bigger bus.

Painting will add color to Tohoku. As everything was washed away, even the signboards, and the people also went away, the region has become gray and colorless. Color here implies not just a visual image, but also includes human voices. I want to add color by bringing people to the region.

I can't do this activity without being there physically and seeing the destruction. This project is filled with useful potential. Regular visits to the region made me realize that it is extremely important to do something related to building a community because before the disaster there was a strong sense of community and bonds among locals. Now everyone has been scattered into different temporary housing. People in temporary housing end up stuck in their houses because they have difficulty going out and talking to unfamiliar neighbors. With my van, I try to encourage people to go outside and move around. Driving people about, showing them different places, and talking to others, the project creates friction and makes them want to develop trust with others and connections with society. This is what I'm trying to do here and what I want people to understand.

I know what I want to do in the future and that's a "Go for Future: World Bus Tour." With this bus, I want to go around the globe with the aim of linking different communities together. Guido, you were on the bus with me so you have seen how the van creates relationships both inside and outside the van, and builds a community in a new sense. This van can connect people, like when I organized a picnic with people from temporary housing in Ishinomaki and those I had brought up from Tokyo. Through transporting a small community, it connects with another community. I believe that my activities transporting people and information are relevant in other countries as well. In the past I have created Go for Future vans in Thailand, India, and London using local cars. I want to do this all over the world because this will unite the world as one. This is my hope, my dream. The globe can be one big circle. What we need to do now is connect the world in a single loop. I really believe this.

逢坂恵理子

横浜美術館 館長
ヨコハマトリエンナーレ 2011総合ディレクター

3月11日に、「ヨコハマトリエンナーレ2011」のテーマとアーティストを発表する記者会見を午前中は横浜美術館で、午後は東京でやることになっていました。午後3時からの開始予定で、3.11東日本大震災発生時は、東京の有楽町にある日本外国人特派員協会のビルの20階にいました。会場には70人以上の記者がいましたが、もう皆立っていられないくらい大きく長く揺れました。エレベーターが全部止まったので、ビルの1階にいた50人ほどの記者は上がってくることが出来なくなり、記者会見を中止にせざるを得ませんでした。今後について検討した際、私はトリエンナーレを予定通り8月6日から実施すべきと主張しました。でも引き続いて起きた福島の原発事故のため、夏場の計画停電が懸念されました。横浜市からは開催延期と展覧会の内容変更の検討も出たほどでした。停電になるかもしれないがその予定がわからないということで、準備にとりかかれない状況が続きました。それでも地震後、アーティストから「横浜は大丈夫か?」、「展覧会は大丈夫か?」というたくさんのメールが届きました。そこで4月上旬に、アーティスティック・ディレクターの三木あき子さんに事情を説明してもらうため、海外のアーティストを訪ねてもらいました。そのうちに15%の節電で夏場の停電が回避できそうなことも分かったので、電気消費量をすべて計算して開館時間を短縮し、エスカレーターを止め、オフィスの電気を暗くし、ギャラリーは効率の良い電球に替えるなどの対策をたてました。

アーティスト達も、このような大変な時期だからこそトリエンナーレを開催することは大切だと賛同してくれ、4月半ばには横浜市長が「予定通り実施」を宣言して動き出しました。国内・国外共にアーティスト達は協力的でした。例えば、開催まで4か月ほどしかないのに、三木さんがオノ・ヨーコさんと会ったとき、彼女は予定していた作品ではなく悲惨な状況に直面している日本を励ます新作にしようと変更を決めてくれました。作品名は「TELEPHONE IN MAZE」。アクリルで出来た迷路の真ん中にある電話がオノ・ヨーコさんとの

ホットラインで、オノさんはどこにいても（ヨーロッパ・アメリカ・日本）不定期に直接電話をかけてきます。電話が鳴れば、迷路の近くにいた人が電話に出て、オノ・ヨーコさんと話せるという作品です。この作品は、困難な状況の後でも、対話やコミュニケーションが私たちを勇気づけ、励まし、希望へと導くことを示しています。美術館の外にはオノさんの大型のビルボード作品「DREAM」を設置しました。夢を描くことが難しい時期に、私たちは夢を持つことによって希望に向かい困難を乗り越えることが出来る。そうした思いがこの作品に込められています。

今回のトリエンナーレは「OUR MAGIC HOUR 世界はどこまで知ることができるか？」というタイトルのもと、改めて伝説や神話の神秘、世界や日常の不思議に着目しています。科学の限界を問うのではなく、人間の英知では理解できないものの存在や、疎外されたり忘れられた人間の本能や、無意識という領域の価値を再評価して、世界や人間を理解する新たな視点を問いかけています。

横浜美術館にはシュルレアリスムのコレクションが多くあります。ゲームやインターネットの普及で、現実と非現実の区別がなかなか分かりにくくなっている傾向があるためか、シュルレアリスムの作品に興味を持ってくださる若い方も増えています。シュルレアリスムは人間の無意識や夢ともつながっているので、オノさんのDREAMという言葉を掲げることは横浜美術館を会場とした今回のトリエンナーレにふさわしいとも考えました。

3.11後に考案されたもう一つの作品は、アーティスト・安部泰輔さんの作品「どこから来てどこへ行くのか」です。これは海上で船舶が交信するための文字旗の形をとった作品です。文字旗にはもともと「あなたと交信したい」という意味が含まれていますが、安部さんは旗のモチーフに、横浜美術館と福島県立博物館のコレクション作品を選びました。東日本大震災の被災地への思いを込めて、福島から出土した埴輪が縫い込まれています。旗は横浜の小学校の子供たちのマーチングバンドのパレードでも披露されました。

そしてジュン・グエン=ハツシバさんも3.11以降、作品を変更し「呼吸することは自由12,756.3:日本、希望と再生、1,789km」を制作しました。彼はお母さんが日本人でお父さんがベトナム人です。彼は横浜とホーチミン・シティの地図上に、桜の花をドローイングして走るルートを設定しました。横浜では実際に180人位の市民がGPSを装着してそのドローイングの通りに走りました。全

安部泰輔
《どこから来てどこへ行くのか》(2011)
ABE Taisuke, *Where did it come from and where did it go?* (2011)
Photo: KIOKU Keizo

部つなぐと1,789kmになります。寒い冬が過ぎると必ず春がやってきて桜が咲く、だから桜は日本の希望の象徴なんですね。東北の人たちにとって今は冬の状態かもしれないけれど、皆が手に手を取って協働することによって最後には花が咲く。また日本の文化では、特に桜の花を観賞し、春の訪れを祝うお花見への熱い思いもある、つまり日本の文化と皆が走ることをあわせた作品です。グエン＝ハツシバさんはベトナムのホーチミンに住んでいるので、この作品ではホーチミン市民も走りました。実際に横浜の地図とホーチミンの地図を重ね合わせていて、桜の幹の部分がメコン川なんですね。だからホーチミン市民と横浜市民のコラボレーションによって、日本の再生という希望の花を咲かせた作品です。

リヴァーネ・ノイエンシュワンダーさんも3.11後に、スクラブルのような作品の日本語バージョンを作ってくれました。荒木経惟＝アラーキーさんには生と死を象徴する作品をご出品いただきました。今回のトリエンナーレのタイトルは「OUR MAGIC HOUR」ですが、MAGIC HOURとは日没直前のすべてが輝く時間を指しています。彼は奥様が亡くなってから空の写真を撮り続けているのでその写真と愛猫の死に至る写真を展示しました。被災したおばあちゃんと孫娘に捧げる二つの椿の花を写した「被災花」は、凛とした美しい作品で、大学生のような若い人達がとても反応していました。

最後にもう一つ、カールステン・ニコライさんの8色のステッカー作品は、観客がステッカーを自由に壁に貼る作品です。ニコライさんの意向で子供には一部無料で提供しましたが、大人には1セット100円以上の募金をいただき、その総額を被災地のために寄付しました。たくさんの方が参加してくださり、外にある工事囲いの白い壁はカラフルなステッカーで埋めつくされました。

逢坂恵理子

3.11後は、多くの外国人が帰国したり、国内でも京都以西に多くの方が移動したように、皆が前述したアーティストのような積極的な反応をしてくれたわけではありません。ですから8月5日のトリエンナーレ開会式に招聘したアーティスト全員が来たいと言ってくれたこと、そして私たちが予想していた2倍以上の方々がこのトリエンナーレに来場してくださったことを、とても嬉しく、またありがたく思っています。

多くのアーティストが3.11の影響を受けました。私は日本は変わったと思います。自分の身の丈にあった生活とは何かを考え、原点をみつめ直したと思います。そして、違う考えや違う価値観をもっている人とも一緒に協力し合って生きていかなくてはいけないことを実感し始めた。私はそうした異なるものとの共存や多様性を教えてくれるのもアートだと思います。アートには一つの答えがなく、見方によっては様々な答えがあるものです。だからこそ、アートは人々が一緒に生活する上でも助けとなるものなのです。そして、アートを自分たちの生活から離れた少し贅沢なものとしてではなく、私たちの日常生活に必要なものとして受け入れてゆく人が少しずつ増えていくと思います。

言うほど簡単ではありませんが、私はアートのもっている力を、多くの人たちに様々なアプローチで伝えていきたいと思います。そのような意味で、今回のヨコハマトリエンナーレ2011は、私にとっても困難な道筋を経て、アーティストの力とアートの力を再確認できた貴重な機会となりました。

ジュン・グエン=ハツシバ
《呼吸は自由 12,756.3:
日本、希望と再生、1,789 km》(2011)
Jun NGUYEN-HATSUSHIBA, *Breathing is Free 12,756.3: JAPAN, Hopes & Recovery, 1,789km* (2011)
Courtesy of the artist and Mizuma Art Gallery

Eriko Osaka
Director, Yokohama Museum of Art
Director General, Yokohama Triennale 2011

On March 11th, we were planning to do a press conference for the Yokohama Triennale 2011 at the Yokohama Museum of Art in the morning and then in Tokyo in the afternoon. It was scheduled to start at three o'clock. When the 2011 Tohoku earthquake and tsunami happened, we were at the Foreign Correspondents' Club of Japan, on the twentieth floor of a building in Yurakucho in Tokyo. There were more than 70 journalists in the room, and the quake was so long and big that we were hardly able to stay standing. 50 journalists on the first floor could not come up because all the elevators had stopped. We had no choice but to cancel the press conference.

When discussing how to proceed in the future, I insisted that the Yokohama Triennale should happen as planned from August 6th. There was growing concern over the planned power outages in the summer due to the Fukushima nuclear power plant disaster. Yokohama City officials also suggested postponing and changing the content of the Triennale. Not knowing the schedule of the planned power outages, for a while we were unable to begin the preparations. We received a lot of emails after the disaster from the participating artists inquiring about the safety in Yokohama and at the Triennale. In order for us to respond to the concerns, we asked Akiko Miki, Artistic Director of the Triennale, to visit the participating overseas artists to explain the situation. In the meantime, we learned that by saving 15% of our energy consumption, we could avoid the summer power outage. We worked out countermeasures, including calculating our entire energy consumption, shortening the festival's opening hours, suspending the use of escalators, switching to dimmed office lights, and replacing existing light bulbs with more energy-efficient ones.

The participating artists agreed with us that it was important to hold the Triennale during this extraordinary time. We finally began preparing for the event after the mayor of Yokohama issued a statement in

April confirming that the festival would be held as planned. Both the international and domestic artists were very supportive. For example, when Miki met Yoko Ono, Ono decided to create a new work that aimed to cheer up Japan instead of showing an existing artwork, even though we only had four months left till the opening day. The name of the work was *Telephone in Maze*. It was a hotline phone connecting Ono directly with visitors and which was placed in the middle of a maze made from acrylic walls. Ono would randomly make a phone call from Europe, America, or Japan, and if a visitor was nearby, they could pick up and talk to her. This artwork indicates that dialogue and communication can encourage people and conduce hope even after experiencing extreme hardships. Outside the museum, we set up her large billboard work, *DREAM*, which is about how having a dream makes it possible for people to be hopeful and overcome hardships.

The 2011 Triennale was entitled "Our Magic Hour—How Much of the World Can We Know?" and focused on the mysteries of folklore or myth, and the wonder of the world and everyday life. Instead of questioning the limitations of science, the event reassessed what human wisdom cannot understand, as well as alienated and forgotten human nature, and the unconscious The festival posed new perspectives for understanding the world and humanity.

The Yokohama Museum of Art has an extensive collection of Surrealist works of art. Probably due to the popularization of video games and the Internet blurring the distinction between the real and the virtual, an increasing number of young people are interested in Surrealist art. Given that Surrealism is connected to the human unconscious and dreams, presenting Ono's *DREAM* was appropriate for the Triennale and its main venue, the Yokohama Museum of Art.

Another work conceived after 3.11 is *Where did it come from and where did it go?* by Taisuke Abe. This artwork features the signal flags used by ships to communicate with each other at sea. Signal flags originally signify the desire that "I want to communicate with you." And Abe also used some of the art from the collections of Yokohama Museum of Art and Fukushima Museum as motifs on the flags to express his sympathy and solidarity with the region affected by the 2011 Tohoku earthquake and tsunami. He also used the image of a *haniwa*[1] terra-cotta figure excavated in Fukushima and sewed it into the flag. A marching band

1. A type of terracotta figure found in ancient Japanese burial mounds.

comprised of elementary school children in Yokohama then showcased the flag during a parade.

Jun Nguyen-Hatsushiba also changed his exhibit after 3.11 to *Breathing is Free 12,756.3: JAPAN, Hopes & Recovery, 1,789km*. His mother is Japanese and his father is Vietnamese. Jun made a drawing of a cherry blossom flower on maps of Yokohama and Ho Chi Minh City, which functioned as a running route. In Yokohama, 180 citizens equipped with GPS devices actually ran along the route made by the drawing. The running route is 1,789km long if all the lines are combined.

Cherry blossoms represent hope in Japan because spring always arrives and the cherry blossom comes into bloom after the cold winter. Right now could be the winter for the people in Tohoku but flowers will bloom in the end if everyone works together. Additionally, we have a very strong emotional connection to *hanami*, the tradition of admiring and appreciating the flowers and celebrating the arrival of spring. Nguyen-Hatsushiba's work combines this Japanese culture with the collaborative act of running together. Nguyen-Hatsushiba lives in Ho Chi Minh City where citizens also took part and ran for the artwork. Superimposing the maps of Yokohama and Ho Chi Minh City, there was also a trunk of a cherry blossom tree representing the Mekong River. This collaboration between citizens of Yokohama and Ho Chi Minh City gave us hope for the rebirth of Japan.

Rivane Neuenschwander also created a Japanese version of her scrabble-like work after 3.11. Nobuyoshi Araki, a photography artist, showed work themed around life and death. The "magic hour" from the Triennale's title implies the hours right before sunset when everything shines. Since he lost his wife, Araki has been photographing the sky during this magic hour. He submitted pictures of the sky as well as photographs capturing his beloved, dying cat. Another work, *Hisaibana* (Flowers for Victims) capturing two camellia flowers and offered to two victims of the disaster, a grandmother and her granddaughter, is a dignified and beautiful work to which many young people responded strongly.

Finally, Carsten Nicolai's work using stickers in eight colors let audiences place a sticker on a wall freely. As Nicolai intended, stickers were partially provided to children free of charge, though a donation of more than ¥100 per set was collected from adults. All of the money was then donated to the disaster areas. A lot of people participated in the project and the white construction site wall outside the museum was filled with colorful stickers.

Since 3.11, not everyone responded positively like these artists; many foreigners left Japan and many people moved out west of Kyoto. For this reason, we are very grateful to all the artists we invited to the opening ceremony who expressed their willingness to attend, and for our visitors, more than double the number we anticipated would come to the Triennale.

Many artists were affected by 3.11. I think Japan has changed. Many people started to think about a lifestyle that is more grounded, and to reconsider origins. And people started realizing that they have to live side by side with those who have different ideas and values. I think art can teach people about diversity and the coexistence of different things. Art does not offer one answer; rather it offers multiple answers based on different perspectives. That is why art can help people to live together.

I also think there are growing numbers of people who accept art not as luxury objects far removed from their lifestyles, but as something indispensable for their daily life.

This is easier said than done, but I want to convey the power of art to a lot of people through a wide range of approaches. In this sense, the Yokohama Triennale 2011, though there were many difficulties, gave me the chance to confirm the power of artists and art.

大友良英
音楽家

　地震が起きたとき新宿代々木のレコーディングスタジオにいて、何曲かレコーディングをしていました。東京にいながらも揺れを感じたので、その後すぐにテレビで東北地方と福島のニュースを知ったんです。東京で感じた地震がすごく大きかったので、震源地は大きな被害が出てるに違いないと思いました。
　すぐに僕の家族が住んでいる福島市、それと福島の原子力発電所のことを思ったんですが、どこにもその情報は流れてなかったんです。津波の被害がすごすぎて内陸の福島市の情報はほとんど入らないし、原発に関しての公式発表もすぐにはなかったんです。その日の夜に原発から5キロ圏内の住民の避難についてラジオやテレビで知ることになって、やっぱりと思いました。
　当時、福島の人たちは放射線量を測る機械すら持ってなくて、何もすることが出来ませんでした。福島だけではありません、日本中、一般の人はだれも状況を判断できなかった。僕もすごく心配で福島に駆けつけたかったんですが、ガソリンもなく、そこへ行く道も崩壊していたのですぐに行くことは出来ませんでした。3月に予定されていたヨーロッパツアーのコンサートをすべてキャンセルし、とにかく東京に残りました。日本から離れることはできない、日本から離れたくないと強く思ったんです。
　それで、現状をよく把握するためインターネットで入手可能な情報を全部探しました。僕の二人いる兄弟は南フランスに住んでいるんですが、そのうちの一人が1週間後に帰国し、福島に入りました。彼は様々なサバイバル・スキルを持っていて、支援活動をしてました。わたしが福島に行くことが出来たのは、震災から1ヶ月後の4月11日でした。古い友人やネットで出会った人たちに会い、彼らに何が起こったのかを知るためにたくさん話をしました。彼らはみな心から血を流しているように見えました。非人道的な事態が今起こっているのに、そのことがほとんど伝わってない、そう思いました。放射線は目で見ることが出来ません。まったく感じないんです。空や山などすべての美しいものは前と変わらなく見えるのに、でももう3月11日以前と同じではなくなってしまいました。な

のに情報はほとんど入ってきませんでした。現地の人たちはどうしていいかわからずに絶望してる、それについて誰も発言出来ず、発信も出来ていない……そんな状況でした。

それで、何かをしなければいけないと考えたんです。でも、何かが分からなかった。福島で、詩人の和合亮一氏に会ったんですが、彼は震災以降、毎日福島の状況についてツイッターで詩を書き始めていました。彼と二晩話し、その次の晩もまたその次も友人達と話し合い、何をするか考え、また福島出身でわたしの大先輩にあたるパンクロッカーの遠藤ミチロウさんとも話し合いを重ね、そして、8月にフェスティバルの開催を決めたんです。震災の始めのころ、被災地の人々は緊要の必需品を必要としましたが、日を追っていくと何か心の支えとなるものを必要としました。でも、それだけではありません。フェスを開くことを発表すれば、当然賛否も起こります。そのなかで放射線の問題もあらわになるし、そこでフェスをやっていいかどうか議論になる。そうしたプロセスを全部見せる必要があると思ったんです。政府が隠しているなら、それと反対のことをやろうと。ミチロウさんのアイデアで開催は8月15日に決めました。終戦記念日です。僕たちは、この問題が日本の戦後の問題とつながってると直感したんです。でも、その時点で僕たちに明確なプランがあったわけではありません。

フェスティバルをやるために、ミチロウさん、和合さんと私が中心になり、福島の内外から数十人の人たちが集まって「プロジェクトFUKUSHIMA!」を立ち上げました。5月7日のことです。最初はDOMMUNE FUKUSHIMA!とい

16日記者会見
Press conference in 2011
Photo: k-osamu 菊池修 (Kikuchi Osamu)

うUstreemingテレビで番組をつくることから始めました。毎月2回、日曜日に放送しました。それと同時に、福島で行う野外フェスティバルの計画を進めました。

オーケストラ
FUKUSHIMA!
Orchestra
FUKUSHIMA!
Photo: k-ryosuke 菊池良助（Kikuchi Ryosuke）

僕らはまずは、放射能の専門家を探すことから始めました。ちょうど5月15日放送のNHK番組「ネットワークでつくる放射能汚染地図」が放送されました。これは本当に衝撃的な番組でした。それまで情報が出ていなかった福島の現状を伝えた、初めての番組なんです。そこで中心的な役割を果たしたのが、木村真三博士です。彼はチェルノブイリの研究もしてきた人で、3月11日以前は政府で働いていましたが、福島の調査を自由にやるために退職し、どこにも属さないやり方で科学的なリサーチを始めました。NHKはこのことを報道したんです。この放送を見た後すぐに彼とコンタクトを取り、協力してもらうことになりました。彼に会場を含め福島の状況を調べてもらい、そのプロセスを僕らは全て公開しました。賛否はもちろんありましたが、そのなかで現状を正しく把握し、議論することが僕らには必要だったんです。

フェス会場に選ばれた場所は、比較的放射線量の低い場所です。周りには人もたくさん暮らしています。それでも福島の外から人を招く以上は、充分に対策を練る必要がありました。僕たちは木村博士のアイデアで、フェスティバルの会場の地面に「シーツ」をかけることにしました。地面にあるセシウムが舞い上がらないようにするためです。シーツには「風呂敷」という日本の伝統的な生地を使いました。この生地は日本の人なら誰でも持っている、物を包むための

大友良英 | 93

もので、約1m四方の布です。これを全国から大量に集め、何人かのアーティストや一般市民と皆で1ヶ月かけて縫い上げて、6,000㎡の会場に敷き詰めました。本当に日本中のたくさんの人が協力してくれて、巨大な風呂敷を完成させたんです。その景色は壮観そのものでした。このおかげもあって、フェス

福島大風呂敷
Furoshiki for the festival
Photo: k-osamu 菊池修
(Osamu Kikuchi)

ティバルは大成功でした。13,000人もの人が会場にきて、25万人もの人がUstreamの生放送を見てくれたんです。でも、私は決して満足はしませんでした。なぜなら、フェスティバルをやったところで放射能の現状そのものは決して良くはならないからです。ただ僕らは、放射能のなかでどうやって生きていけばいいのか、素朴ではあるけど、指針のようなものは示せたと思っています。それは、現状を正しく把握し、隠蔽せず、専門家とともに様々な分野の人や一般の市民達と協力し、ネットワークをつくりながら、住むにしろ避難するにしろ、自分自身で判断し行動をしていくということです。最初の段階では、国も行政も何も助けてくれませんでしたから。

福島の問題は終わることがありません。終わることがないというのは、まだ今後10年、15年どころではなく、それ以上の長い年月がかかるということです。僕らはこの問題について考え続け、対策し続けなくてはいけない。だからといって、もうすでに起こってしまったことを嘆いても何も生まれません。この問題を解決していくなかで、次のより良い未来を考えていくしか僕らには道がない、そう思います。そんななかで福島の人同士、そして福島の人と世界の人をつなげることの手助けをしつつ、ひとつのメディアとしてプロジェクトが機能すればいいなと

考えています。オフィシャルメディアでは出来ないような、例えば現地の方々の経験を伝えたり、いろんな方の声、とりわけ顔の見える関係での声に耳を傾けたりするといった、よりインディペンデントなメディアとしてやることが出来ればと思っています。現在たくさんのアーティストが福島や東北地方で活動しています。たくさんの違った意見があって、それらは決してひとつになるようなものではありません。「プロジェクト FUKUSHIMA!」での活動では、こうしたいろんな意見、表現が共存していく形を実現出来ればと思っています。アーティストであれ、一般の市民であれ、それぞれのリアクションを自分たちで考え決定することが重要で、かつその行動を互いに尊重しなければならないと思います。アートを発信する側と受け取る側というふうに分けるのではなく、この状況に置かれた皆が、協働しながら何かをつくり発信し、互いにつなげていくような、そんな新たな発想で活動出来ればいいと考えています。

Yoshihide Otomo
Musician

When the earthquake happened, I was at a recording studio in Yoyogi, near Shinjuku, recording some songs. I felt the quake in Tokyo and immediately after I learned about Tohoku and Fukushima on the TV news. The quake was so big even in Tokyo that I assumed that damage had to have been very severe at the seismic center.

I instantly thought about Fukushima City where my family lives, and the Fukushima nuclear power plant. But there was no information. Since the destruction caused by the tsunami was so severe, information about Fukushima City, which is inland from the ocean, was hard to find. There was no immediate official announcement regarding the nuclear power plant. Later that night, I heard on the radio and TV about the mandatory evacuation order issued for those who lived within 5km of the plant. I had kind of expected this.

At that time, people in Fukushima could not do anything without a machine to measure radiation dosage. Ordinary citizens not only in Fukushima but in the whole of Japan could not judge properly what was happening. I wanted to rush to Fukushima but I could not go there because there was a shortage of gasoline and the roads to Fukushima were all wrecked. I canceled all my European tours scheduled for March and remained in Tokyo. I felt strongly that I could not leave Japan. I did not want to leave Japan.

To understand the situation better, I looked for any information available online. One of my two brothers, both of whom live in the south of France, came back to Japan and went to Fukushima one week after the disaster. He has all kinds of survival skills and he helped with aid work. It was April 11th, one month after, when I finally made it to Fukushima for the first time. To understand what had happened to them, I had a lot of conversations with my old friends as well as people I met online. They all seemed to be bleeding from the heart. I thought, no one was reporting on this inhumane situation. You can't see radioactivity. You don't feel it at all. The sky and the mountains, all of the beautiful environment looked as if nothing had changed but nothing was the same as it had been before 3.11. But we didn't get any information and the people in Fukushima were in despair, as they didn't know what to do. No one could speak out and spread the word. That was what was happening at that time.

I thought I had to do something but I didn't know what I could do. I met Ryoichi Wago, a poet who lives in Fukushima. Ever since 3.11 Ryoichi has been writing poems on Twitter every day about Fukushima's situation. I talked with him for two nights in a row, and one night after another I talked to my friends about what we could do. I also had a series of conversations with Michiro Endo, a Fukushima native and punk rocker, and then we finally decided to organize a festival in August. People in the disaster areas needed emergency supplies in the early days, but as the days went by, they needed something they could rely on emotionally. We were aware that we would get both approval as well as disapproval once we made a public announcement about organizing a festival. I thought this process would expose the issues of radioactivity, which would lead to the discussion of whether or not it was appropriate to have a festival in that environment. We needed to make every process transparent, especially given that our government was hiding everything. We needed to do the complete opposite to this. We decided to organize the festival on August 15th, the anniversary of when World War Two ended, as Michiro suggested. We had the sense that what we are facing right now is directly connected to postwar problems. We didn't have a definite plan at that time, though.

To organize the festival, Michiro, Ryoichi, and I came together as central members, with about fifty people both from and outside Fukushima, and we founded Project Fukushima on May 7th. We started off by producing a Ustream TV program, *Dommune Fukushima!*. We broadcast two shows every other Sunday while we were preparing for the outdoor festival in Fukushima.

We first started by looking for an expert on radioactivity. On May 15th, NHK aired a TV show about mapping radioactive contamination through a network of individual scientists. It was really a shocking program, the first TV program that told the reality about Fukushima, which had not been available before. A central person who appeared in the program was Dr. Shinzo Kimura. With his background in researching Chernobyl, he had retired from the public institution he had worked for before 3.11 so as to conduct fully independent, scientific research in Fukushima. NHK made a report about him and his research. Right after watching this program, I immediately contacted him and asked for his collaboration. We asked him to investigate the conditions in Fukushima, including the festival site, and then we made the findings public. While many differing opinions were expressed over our actions, we needed to understand the situation properly and engage in discussion.

The site selected for the festival had relatively low radiation and a lot of people live in the surrounding area. Nevertheless, we had to work out a careful strategy given that people outside Fukushima were expected to come. Based on Dr. Kimura's idea, we came up with the idea to place large "sheets" over the ground of the festival site to prevent cesium from rising up. For the sheets we used traditional *furoshiki*, a roughly 1m^2 piece of cloth for folding and carrying objects, and which every Japanese person has. Upon collecting massive quantities of *furoshiki* cloth, several artists and ordinary citizens sewed them together for a month and laid them out over the 6,000m^2 festival site. A lot of people from all over Japan cooperated together and made the massive *furoshiki*. It was a magnificent scene. Thanks partially to this idea, the festival turned out to be a huge success. 13,000 people came to the festival and 250,000 viewers watched the festival streamed live online. But I wasn't completely satisfied with the result because organizing the festival did not improve the environment contaminated by radiation. What we could show was a kind of simple guideline for how to live with radioactivity. That is, we need to understand the situation properly without hiding information and collaborate with experts as well as the general public to create a network of people. And each individual makes his or her own judgment and acts upon it as to whether to remain in Fukushima or evacuate. It was clear that both the national and local governments did not help us at all in the early days.

Fukushima's problems will never end. It will take much more than ten to fifteen years. We have to keep thinking about Fukushima and coming up with measures for it. Nothing comes about by just complaining about what has already happened, though. We have nothing left but to imagine a better future through solving the issues. I want Project Fukushima to function as a medium that connects people within Fukushima and Fukushima people with the outside world. As an independent media, it can deliver stories experienced by people in Fukushima, and conduct face-to-face, intimate interviews. A lot of artists are working actively in Fukushima and Tohoku area right now. There are a lot of different opinions and we can't merge them all as one voice. Project Fukushima wishes to realize a form for these diverse opinions as well as creative expressions to coexist together. Regardless of whether they are artists or regular citizens, what's important is that each individual thinks and comes to reach his or her own decision while respecting others. Instead of dividing between those who provide art and those who receive it, everyone under these circumstances is collaboratively working together to create something and showcase it, and connect with one another. That's how Project Fukushima wants to work in the future.

甲斐賢治

せんだいメディアテーク 企画・活動支援室室長

せんだいメディアテークは、2001年に仙台市の生涯学習施設としてオープンしました。世界的な建築家・伊東豊雄氏の設計による館内には、図書館をはじめとして1階の広場、ギャラリー、映画館、会議室やスタジオと呼ばれるメディアを用いた市民活動の拠点などがあり、オープン以来年間100万人が利用しています。私は、2010年4月に企画を担当する部署の任期付きディレクターとしてここに就任しました。

東日本大震災によって7階の天井が一部落下しました。幸い来館者やスタッフにけがなどもなく、また建物の構造にも問題がなく、大きな被害には至りませんでした。施設の被害状況がおおむね確認できた後は、東北エリアの文化拠点のひとつである施設としてこの混乱した状況下においてどのように活動すべきか、どのような取り組みが可能かなどスタッフや市の担当者などと議論を始めました。

メディアテークは美術館ではなく、アートまたはメディアを用いた市民活動、生涯学習活動を支援する施設ですので、その設置理由に基礎づけられた企画を進めるためにいくつかの条件がありました。まず、非常事態であっても基本的には政策に沿っていること。また、あの状況下、できる限り予算が少なくとも進められる事業であることや、スタッフも周囲の状況に混乱していたので、全く新しいことをするのではなく既存のスキームを生かす必要がありました。そして、取り組むものが市民からの共感をもって迎えられるものでなければならないとも思われ、検討を重ねました。

結果、2011年5月3日の一部開館に合わせて、大きく分けて2つの事業に取り組み始めました。まずメディア活動として、震災復興の過程を市民自らが記録し、保存していくためのプラットフォーム「3がつ11にちをわすれないためにセンター（通称:わすれン！）」を開設しました。震災以前より7階のスタジオにはメディアセンターとしての機能があり、さまざまなデジタルメディアを用いるプロジェクトを市民グループが申請し、受理されるとスタジオの設備、環境、

機材が無償提供されるという仕組みがありました。その際、最終的な活動の成果を寄贈いただくということが提供の条件となっていました。つまり、市民が活動することで得られた成果を、メディアテークにも保存、階下のライブラリーなどへの配架を通じ、さらに広く市民が再利用していくという仕組みがありました。天井が落下した7階を除く一部を開館している現在、このスタジオのスキームを2階に移設し、被災者自らが震災の記録を行う機会となるよう、この「わすれン！」を進めてきました。

「わすれン！」は、参加登録をした人々が、震災復興の記録・発信活動をすることによって得たデータを仙台市に保存していくプロジェクトです。現時点で90人ほどの参加者がいます[1]。あくまでも概算ですが、そのおよそ半分が仙台市に暮らす人々で、残りは首都圏など他の地方から来られた人々です。また全体の半分ほどがアーティストや映画監督あるいは人権団体など何らかの専門性をもっていて、そして残りの半分は一般に言う市民で、専門性、技術などのほぼなかった方々だろうと思われます。登録された参加者には取材用のキットをお渡しし、その活用をお願いしています。キットには取材の現場などで渡す「わすれン！」の趣旨が明記された名刺代わりとなるものとともに、取材対象者となる方々の肖像権を処理するためのサインをもらう書類が入っています。これによって参加者の取材を円滑なものとするとともに、肖像権処理された、将来的に2次利用可能なデータの保存ができることとなります。また「わすれン！」では、参加者の取材や記録作業への指示などは一切行いませんし、仙台市域での活動に限定することもなく、どこに行っても問題はありません。こうして寄せられた映像や画像は、肖像権処理の書類などの提出と併せて仙台市にも利用を許諾していただき、メディアテークに保管されます。基本的にデジタルデータとなりそのコピーを預かりますので、参加者ももちろんそのデータをどのように用いていただいても構いません。なかには映画を作られている方々なども含まれていますが、その映画そのものは配給され、その素材となる映像だけが保管されていくようなケースもあります。これらは、徐々にメディアテークの映像音響ライブラリーに配架、活用されていくと同時に、将来的になんらか開設されるであろうメモリアル施設などへも移管されていく予定です。また、これら「わすれン！」の活動がオランダ政府から支援を受けることとなり、これから一部の映像に字幕をつけた英語のサイトを作っていこうとしています[2]。

余談ですが、今回のようなアーカイブの取り組みは、これまでの学術や公文書

[1] 2013年3月31日時点 140名

[2] http://recorder311-e.smt.jp/

甲斐賢治

を取り扱うような、こつこつと時間をかけ構築されていく「静的」な性質のアーカイブとは異なります。今、進行している出来事が記録されるとともに一部発信され、またそれらが復興の現場に何らかの影響を与えていくような状況も少なからずあり、そういう意味において「動的」なアーカイブではないかという指摘が学識研究者からありました。

一方、アート分野での取り組みですが、震災がなければ展覧会開催を目的とした助成を受ける予定だったのですが、やはりあの事態のなか、一般的な展覧会を行なうのは適切ではないと考えました。スタッフとの議論を重ねるなか、今、人々が集いさまざまに意見を交換するような場が必要なのではないか、また、この事態を端的に捉えることに留まらない、考え続けていく取り組みがなんらか必要ではないか、とそのような機会を発生させる事業を構想し始めました。助成元に申請内容の変更を説明し、理解をいただくことができたので、1階の広場を拠点に6月ごろから人々が集まって話し合う、「考えるテーブル」というプロジェクトを始めました。まずその際、外から眺める人にとって、広場にたった15人でも20人でも集い話している景色がとても大切な時間で、なにか尊厳に満ちた様子に感じられるようなものができないかと、アーティストの豊嶋秀樹さんにその集う場となる家具の製作を依頼しました。同時に、震災以前から市民グループによって7階で取り組まれていた哲学カフェ「てつがくカフェ@せんだい」の皆さんに呼びかけ、人々がそれぞれの社会的属性を外した上で、震災にまつわるテーマについて語り合う取り組みを進めるとともに、

本来、ライブラリーである2階に開設された「3がつ11にちをわすれないためにセンター」のスタジオ
Studio of the "center for remembering 3.11" that originally opened on the second floor of the library
©2013 Sendai Mediatheque

102　甲斐賢治

名取市在住のアーティスト・志賀理江子さんのトークなども「考えるテーブル」の企画として進めました。また周辺プロジェクトとして、アーティストのタノタイガさんが取り組んでいたドロかきボランティア活動「タノンティア」によるバスツアーなども主催し、首都圏からの支援者をタノタイガさんの活動へと結びつけました。

これらの2つの事業には通底しているコンセプトがあります。時期は遡りますが、再開した5月3日の翌日、哲学者の鷲田清一さん[3]を招き、1階の広場で無料のトークを開催しました。当時私自身も含め、まだまだ多くの人々が混乱していたように思えました。どなたか社会的に広く信頼されている人物に語っていただき、その話を聴くことから各々の気持ちをそれぞれに整理していく。そこから始められないかと考え、伊東豊雄さんなど幾人かの人々に併せ、鷲田さんにも講演を依頼しました。その際、当時の私たちが漠然と考え、言語化できていなかった事柄について、彼の言葉が大変大きな示唆を与えてくれました。

彼は「隔たり」という言葉を使いました。厳密に彼の言葉をなぞるものではありませんが、いわばあのような事態のなか、いわゆる被災地と被災地以外、沿岸部と都市部、圏内と圏外というような、被災の度合いによるありようの違いが起こります。また、それ以前には見えにくかった差、資本力や文化の違いなどの社会的な差異も改めて顕在化します。つまり、地続きである沿岸部と都市部のその距離が、その物理的な距離以上にどんどん広がっていくような現象が起こります。「被災格差」などという言葉さえ頭に浮かびましたが、これらの差異、すなわち「隔たり」が起こりうることが予想され、それは震災後の大きな社会課題のひとつとなるであろうという認識が震災直後の私たちにもありました。それは、さまざまな孤立への原因にもなりえるのではないかとも考えていました。

そのような「隔たり」が、震災にまつわるあらゆるトピックに見え隠れし感じ取れるなかで、メディアテークとしては、そのこちら側とあちら側を「越えていく回路」をプログラムすることが人々の「学び」へと通じるのではないか。その回路を通じ他者を知り、慮ることがこの世界や事態を捉えなおし、考える機会となるのではないかと考えました。鷲田さんによる「隔たり」という言葉を得て、そのような認識が強化されていったように記憶しています。

具体的に言うと、例えば仙台の都市部に暮らす人が、沿岸部の仮設で暮ら

3. 2013年4月、鷲田氏はせんだいメディアテークの館長に就任した。

す知り合いのところへインタビューに行く。知り合い同士のおしゃべりではなく、ビデオカメラを挟んだ少し公的なこの「インタビュー」という形式をもってして話を聞くことで、相手の経験や想いを引き出すことができ、ほんの少しながらでも新たな理解の糸口が得られるように思います。その結果、自身が以前より深みのある配慮や考えへと進むことができるのではないか。さらには、その映像がネットにあげられ、その映像を鑑賞する方もまた、同様の糸口を得ることができるかもしれない。つまりは、ビデオカメラが「隔たり」を超える回路となりえるのではないかと考えました。また、哲学カフェの目指すところも似通ったものかも知れません。明らかに年齢も所属も異なる者が集い、この事態にまつわるさまざまな現象について共に語り、模索・検討を重ねるなかで、端的な物事の捉え方から少しずつ外れ、多様な考えが場に提出されていくプロセスを目の当たりにします。こうして戸惑いながらも他者を知り、自らの世界観を捉え直し、また更新していくこととなるのではないか。そしてまた新たに感じる違和感をもとに、さらに考え続けるという態度が学習されていくのではないかと思います。

最後に、今回のような大きな災害・事故を経てとても強く感じられるのは、多くの人々のその主体性の高まりです。メディアテークでもこれまで数多くの事業を行ってきましたが、どうもそれらのときと少し異なる、人々の意思ある参加が得られているように思えてなりません。これはこの歴史的な事態によってそれぞれの世界観がなんらかの影響を受け、例えば一度崩れ、個々にそれを再構築するための機会や場を必要としていることの証のようにも思えます。生涯学習施

「てつがくカフェ@せんだい」開催の様子
2011年6月18日
Philosophy café @ Sendai (June 18th, 2011)
©2013 Sendai Mediatheque

設であるメディアテークはこれに応えねばなりません。

しかしながら同時に、早くも、時が経つことによるその主体性の目減りも感じつつあります。今後も、この震災によって図らずも改めて見いだされた、人々の「力」を少しでも目減りさせることなく引き出すことのできるような活動に、引き続き取り組んでいきたいと考えています。

2011年5月4日。一部再開とともに開催した「歩きだすために」出演の鷲田清一氏
Lecture "in order to start walking" by Kiyokazu Washida (May 4th, 2011)
©2013 Sendai Mediatheque

Kenji Kai
Program Director, Sendai Mediatheque

Sendai Mediatheque opened in 2001 as a lifelong learning facility for the city of Sendai. The building was designed by renowned world architect Toyo Ito and has a library, a first floor open space, gallery, cinema, meeting rooms, and studio space that is a base for citizens' activities using media. 1 million people have been using Mediatheque annually since its opening. In April 2010 I became director of programming for a fixed term.

Due to the 2011 Tohoku earthquake and tsunami, some parts of the seventh floor ceiling collapsed but luckily no visitors or staff were injured. Mediatheque did not suffer major damage or structural problems. After checking the extent of the damage, we started discussing with the city officials and fellow members of staff about what the Mediateque, one of the cultural centers in Tohoku region, should do and what types of activities we could possibly engage in during this very confused time.

Sendai Mediateque is not a museum, but an institution supporting citizens in civic activities and continued education through art and media, which means that there are certain institutional conditions we have to follow when planning a program. Firstly, a program should be in accordance with the institutional principals even when there is an emergency. And a program needed to be able to move forward with a small budget. Given that staff were also confused by the circumstances, a program needed to use existing schema rather than do something completely new. Finally, what we did had to be accepted and welcomed by Sendai citizens. We had many discussions about all this.

As a result, in addition to partially reopening the building on May 3rd, 2011, we started working on two main projects. First as a media activity, we created a platform called "The center for remembering 3.11 (recorder311)" that aims for citizens to take an active role in documenting and archiving the reconstruction process. We had a media center on the seventh floor even before 3.11. It worked like this: A group of citizens would be offered the studio equipment with digital media facilities to use for free once their project application had been accepted. The only condition we asked of citizens was that they donate the project results. In other words, the Mediatheque preserves the outcomes of citizens' activities through placing their media work in the downstairs library so that more citizens can access it. With Mediatheque partially open except for the seventh floor, where the ceiling had collapsed, we moved the studio to the second floor and proceeded with offering opportunities for the victims to document the disaster by themselves.

"The center for remembering 3.11" is a project that archives and disseminates what registered participants document for the city of Sendai. We have around 90 registered participants.[1] We estimate that about half of the participants are Sendai citizens while the rest are from other regions like the Tokyo metropolitan area. Around half of the participants are people with some kind of expertise, such as being artists, film directors, or people working for human rights organizations. The rest are so-called ordinary citizens with no expertize or techniques. We hand over an interview kit to the registered users. The kit includes a card printed with the center's mission statement, which functions as a business card the users can give to interviewees, as well as a document that interviewees are asked to sign to give up their portrait rights. These tools enable the users to collect materials smoothly and allow us to preserve data free of image rights for secondary use in the future. The center does not give any direction as to what users should do when collecting materials and documenting. Users are also not restricted to working within Sendai but are free to carry out activities anywhere.

The videos and images, along with documents signing off on the portrait rights, are all kept in Sendai Mediateque. We keep copies of the digital data and, of course, users are free to use their data for whatever purposes they like. Some people make films and these have been distributed, but the original materials used for the film are still kept at the center. The data will gradually be placed and used in the Mediateque's media and sound library, though they are likely to be moved to a kind of memorial institution, which is planned to open in the future. We are going to create an English website with English subtitles on select videos through generous financial support from the Dutch government.[2]

On a side note, our archiving project is different to "static" archiving of academic and official documents that are accumulated over a long period

[1] 140 people as of March 31st, 2013.

[2] http://recorder311-e.smt.jp

of time. The center documents ongoing incidents, some of which are made public right away, which even somehow influences the ongoing reconstruction effort. Some academic researchers have pointed out that our archiving is actually "active."

As for our art department, we would have received a grant for holding an exhibition if the disaster had not happened. But we did not think it was appropriate to organize a regular exhibition as planned under the extraordinary circumstances. Through discussions with our staff, we came to think that we needed a place and project that enabled people to gather, exchange ideas, and continue to think about the situation, rather than limiting them to grasping the surface of what was happening. Upon explaining our intention to change the plan to the grant provider and getting its approval, we started a project called Kangaeru Table (Thinking Table) in the first floor open space. We felt that it was important for passers-by to see a group of people even as small as fifteen or twenty gathering together and talking, which would be a valuable time for them, something dignified. We asked artist Hideki Toyoshima to design furniture for the gatherings. Simultaneously, we invited the group philosophy café @ Sendai, who had been organizing a philosophy café on the seventh floor before the disaster, to continue the café aiming to encourage people to talk freely to each other about issues related to the disaster and without any social attributions. Kangaeru Table also includes lectures by Eriko Shiga, an artist based in Natori. As a fringe project, we organized a bus tour with tanonteer, the volunteer project to clear mud in the disaster zones run by artist Tanotaiga, connecting people from the Kanto region to Tanotaiga's project.

These two projects share a concept. Going back further, we organized a free lecture by Kiyokazu Washida[3] in the first floor open space on May 4th, the day after we reopened. As many of us at that time, including myself, were confused, we wanted to order our personal thoughts by listening to people regarded highly in society. We invited people such as Toyo Ito and Washida to give lectures. Their words gave us hints about ideas we had not been able to verbalize.

Washida used the word "gap" during his lecture. While I am not going to describe his lecture word by word, he talked about how, depending on the level of damage from the disaster, what had surfaced in this situation was disparity—between the places that were hit by the disaster and those that weren't, between coastal and urban areas, and between Sendai and the outer

3. Kiyokazu Washida became the Director of Sendai Mediateque in April 2013.

Sendai area—as well as how the gap in capital strength and cultural capital, invisible before the disaster had surfaced once again. In another words, a phenomenon emerges how the distance between coastal and urban areas is wider than the actual physical distance. The word "disaster inequality" came to mind and we expected that this difference, this "gap," would be one of the big social issues right after the disaster, and would be a cause for different kinds of isolation.

These "gaps" could be glimpsed in every topic related to the disaster and we thought that Mediateque could make a program that crosses over from one side to the other, which would then lead people to "learnings." This path enabling people to understand and care for others provides an opportunity for them to recapture the world and the disaster. I remember Washida's word "gap" as reinforcing the initial concept we had.

For example, a person who lives in the center of Sendai visits an acquaintance in temporary housing to conduct an interview. Listening to his or her stories through this slightly official video "interview" instead of mere chatting among friends enables the interviewer to collect experiences and thoughts, and to gain a clue as how to care for and understand others more deeply than before. Moreover, once the video is uploaded online, viewers may be able to acquire the same clues. A video camera could be a path to traverse these gaps, which might be similar to what the philosophy café aims to do. Through a process of gathering, talking together, exploring, and investigating various issues connected to the disaster, people from different ages and social groups encounter a range of ideas and gradually move away from a simple way of looking at things. In this way, people learn about others and re-understand their own worldviews all while still being confused, and they continue to learn based on a feeling that something is not quite right.

Finally, as a result of the massive natural disaster and Fukushima catastrophe, we saw an increase in people's independence. Much more than in the many past programs we have organized, participation felt active. This implies that people are eager to have opportunities and places to reconstruct their worldview that was influenced or somehow destroyed by the historic disaster. The Mediateque, a place for life-long education, should respond to this.

At the same time, we have witnessed how active participation is in decline as time goes by. Our mission is to continuously engage in activities that nurture the power people have gained through this disaster so that it is not lost.

加藤種男

公益財団法人　アサヒグループ芸術文化財団　顧問
公益社団法人　企業メセナ協議会　代表理事専務理事

　3月11日後、多くの活動に携わりました。私はアサヒビール芸術文化財団と公益社団法人企業メセナ協議会で仕事をしているんですけど、双方の団体とも3月11日を境にいくつかの経験をしました。
　アサヒの方のことをまず一つお話すると、アサヒビールではもともとアサヒ・アート・フェスティバル（AAF）を行っていて、今年で10年目になるんですね。で、全国のコミュニティにおけるアート活動とネットワークを形成していったんです。今年の参加チームの中に今回被災を受けた地域がいくつも含まれているんです。一番象徴的な町は宮城県の南三陸町。去年（2010年）、そこに行ってプロジェクトに一緒に参加したんですね。このチームは、一種のツールを開発したんです。それは「きりこ」と呼ばれていて、切り絵なのですが、それを一軒一軒の家の前に飾ったんですね。[1]
　きりこはそれぞれの家の特徴を表していて、例えば、あるお店ではえびの天丼のえびが大きいのでそのえびを切って飾ってみたり、またあるお店では大きな招き猫があるのでそれを絵にして飾ってみたりという具合にね。
　それで、この活動をするには、それぞれの家の特色を聞き出す必要があったんで、それを聞くのに15人位の地元の人が協力したんですよ。それでこの経験を通して、こういうある種の過疎地でも実はお互いにコミュニケーションをあまり取れていないっていうことが分かってきたんです。それで、これをきっかけにお互いがコミュニケーションを取るようになったともいえる。で、この活動中大変面白いことが起きたんですが、参加者の中に、中国から日本に嫁いで来た人がいたんですよね。彼女はまだ南三陸町のコミュニティに溶け込んでいなかったわけね。ところが、そのきりこの作業を見て「これは中国にもある」と言い出したんですよ。彼女の町では全員女の人はこれをしょっちゅう作ってると言うんです。日本では神様に供えるために白い紙を使っていたんですけど、中国では赤い紙をお祭りの時の飾りとして使ったわけですね。それで、彼女が色々みんなに教えて、今度は赤いきりこを初めて南三陸の人が作っていったんです。それ

1. 参加者の思い出や宝物を「きりこ」と呼ばれる切り紙で表すもの。

でお互いに初めて、コミュニケーションが円滑に進むようになったんです。

それで、この活動を最初は志津川エリアだけでしていたのを、今年は南三陸町全域に展開しようねって言ってたのね。で、ところが3.11で町が何もなくなってしまった。それでともかく、AAFには全国のネットワークがあるから、全国のAAFの人たちが南三陸町の人たちを応援するために、全国でそのきりこを作って、私たちは南三陸町のことをちゃんと覚えているよっていうようなメッセージを発信しようと、全国でその活動を展開したんですよ。最終的には南三陸町できりこをやったんだけれども、それは大分時間が経ってから。当然のことなんだけど、南三陸町自体がこの活動をする余裕がなかったから、それができたのは何ヶ月か経ってからなんだけれどもね。いずれにしても8月に南三陸町で南三陸町のきりこと全国から集まったきりこを一緒に並べ展示しました。私が南三陸の現地へ震災後最初に行ったのは5月4日、で、その展示を現地で見たのは8月16日でした。それで、こういうAAFの活動のおかげで、南三陸町と全国とはわりあい早くコミュニケーションが取れたんですね。

もう一つの方、企業メセナ協議会では3.11の後、GBFundっていうのを作ったんですよ。Gは芸術のG、Bは文化のB、そしてFは復興のFなんです。つまり、文化と芸術によって復興の支援をするためのファンドです。ご存知のように復興のためにいろんな人、会社がそれぞれの形で復興を支援してきたわけですよね。

我々はもちろん生命の救助も重要と考えたけれども、3日後からは絶対に文化が必要になると思った。だからと言って3日後には何も出来ませんでしたが、震災後の1ヶ月が勝負だと思ったのね。1ヶ月以内に何か文化の応援が出来ないと、心の問題は手遅れになると思っていたわけです。それで、このGBFundを作ってですね、何とか被災地における文化活動、芸術活動を使ってどうやったら応援できるだろうかって考えていました。最初、我々が予想していた事柄は、多くのアーティストが現地に赴き、例えばコンサートを開いたり、絵を一緒に描いたりというような、様々な活動を現地の人と行っていくことが起きるんだろうなって思ってたんです。他に、セラピーを使った、そういう人たちと一緒に例えばダンスを通してのワークショップみたいな、そういうことがいっぱいあるんだろうなと思っていて、そういう人たちを応援するのが重要だねって思っていたんです。事実、最初の頃、震災から1、2ヶ月後とか、3ヶ月ごろというのは、外から来たアーティストが様々な支援をするという案件が多かったんですよね。例えば、映像のアーティストがすべてのことを記録していったり、他にも写

加藤種男 | 111

真家が見つかった写真を集め、洗浄し、持ち主に返すためにその集めた写真でアルバムを作り、ポスターなどで色々な避難所(当時はまだ仮設住宅が建てられていなかったため)にお知らせするという活動っていうのがありましたね。

そういう外から来るアーティストたちの色々な創造的活動もこれはこれでとても価値があるんだけど、そのうち夏前になって、一つの大きな変化があったんです。それは、地元の人たちから地元の郷土芸能、いわゆる神楽とか祭りを今年2011年の夏に絶対に復活させたいという声がたくさん上がってきたんですよね。つまり、それぞれの小さな町や村でずっと伝承されてきた郷土芸能を7月、8月にしたいということですよ。8月は日本の仏教において非常に重要な月で、亡くなったご先祖をお祭りする「お盆」という行事があるんですよね。そして、今年亡くなった方をお祭りするのを「新盆」といって特に重視するわけです。だから、今回のこの震災で肉親を失った多くの方々が、亡くなった肉親のためにこの新盆をなんとかやりたい。で、お盆には盆踊りをはじめとする様々な行事があるわけですよね。しかしながら残念なことに人手が失われ、それに使われる衣装、楽器、神楽殿と呼ばれる場所も失い、やりたくても出来ないという状況が生まれたんですね。それでまあ、すべてを元通りにとはいかないまでも、例えばそのうちの何か一つ、例えば太鼓とか鹿踊に使う鹿の角を使った仮面を復活できれば、人々のやろうとする気にはずみがつくわけね。

それで、そういうのっていくらするのかよくわからないんですけどね、50万、100万円位あったら何か始まるか聞くと、もちろん始まりますと言うんです。例えば太鼓が一つ買えますとか、鹿がたくさんいる所の人が角を送ってあげるって言ってくれるわけですね。で、そういう案件を我々がGBFundで応援して、8月にお祭りができたケースは15件位はあるんですけど、来年は100件応援しようと思っているんですよ。それで、専門家によるとおそらく1000位のこうした郷土芸能が被災していると言われているので、せめてその1割を我々のファンドで応援する形を作りたい。

いずれにしても、この震災で、我々は東北地方にこれほど多くの郷土芸能が残っていて、いくつか有名なのがあることは知っていたんだけど、こんなに数が多いとは知らなかったですね。しかも重要なのは、その郷土芸能が人々の生きる力にとっていかに重要か、あるいはコミュニティの人々の間を取り持つ絆としていかに重要かということがやっと分かったんです。

一方で、アサヒ・アート・フェスティバルのような新しいコミュニティ創造型の活動や一度なくなったコミュニティが新しいコミュニティを作り出すコミュニティ再生型アート活動をやってきたおかげで、今年の6月のアサヒ・アート・フェスティバルの「グランドオープン・パーティー」に南三陸、あるいは福島のいわき市の皆さんに東京に来て頂いて交流が出来たんです。

で、現地に行くことも大事だったんだけど、現地の人が、現地を離れてみることも気が楽になったみたいですよ。それで、申し上げたように、コミュニティの再生をしようとするイニシアチブも大切なんですけど、一方で我々が気づかなかった地域に根ざした伝統的文化活動がたくさんあった。で、被災地を見てわかったことは、これらの活動は部分的ではあるけれどもコミュニティを維持させるために役立っていた。だから、我々のこれからの課題は、伝統的なコミュニティに根ざしたものと、新しく我々が作ろうとしているコミュニティ再生のためのアート活動との間に、どういう接点が作れるかなっていうこと。

どのようにしてこの2つを結びつけることができるのか？なぜこのようなことを考えるかというと、例えば、あるお祭りを行うためもともと2つの組があって、ひとつは上組、もうひとつは下組っていうのがあった。でも、今回の津波で下組の人たちの家はすべて流された、ところが上組の人たちの家は高台にあったから津波から逃れることができた。このお祭りをするために組があったおかげで、上組の人たちは下組の人たちに泊まってもらってという形で支援しました。それはお祭

きりこ展示@南三陸
全国でつくられたきりこは、2011年8月に南三陸で展示された。
Kiriko (traditional paper cutouts) exhibition at Minamisanriku
Kiriko made throughout Japan was exhibited at Minamisanriku in August 2011.
©AAF Network Executive Committee

加藤種男

りを一緒にやるコミュニティが仲間を助け合う仕組みの根拠になっているわけですよね。
でも、こういったコミュニティにも欠点があるんですよね。それはその仲間に属してない人たちについては結構排他的なのね。これを何とかするため、我々は新しい形のコミュニティ作りを模索しているんです。で、そこにアートが機能するのではないかと思っているのね。

きりこワークショップ@東京
南三陸へ応援のメッセージを込めて、全国できりこをつくるワークショップが行われた。
Kiriko workshop in Tokyo
Workshops making *kiriko* with messages of support for Minamisanriku were held throughout Japan.
©AAF Network Executive Committee

アサヒ・アート・フェスティバルはそういう閉鎖的な問題を克服し、内容は伝統的なものでだけでなく、新しいものを中心に、全国のそれぞれの独立しているコミュニティのアート活動のネットワークを作りたいと思っているんです。だから、それぞれの自立と、でも広く開かれたという状況を作っていきたいわけね。この課題は私がずっと考えていることのうちの一つで、これには前提として東京や大都市と過疎化の進んだ地方都市の課題もあるんだけれども、やっぱり大都市には人々の孤立という問題があるんですよね。日本は今のところ世界的に見ると治安がいいほうだけども、やっぱり問題はあるよね。こういった意味での孤立と不信は大きな問題だと思うんですよ。一方、地方のコミュニティは崩壊しつつあるので、我々はどのように新しいコミュニティを作ることが出来るか考えているんです。で、それがアートの力を媒介すると新しい手段として役に立つのではないかと思ってるわけですよね。
最後に、日本はアジアの中でも孤立しているという問題があるんです。例えば、韓国は文化と産業を結びつけ、新しいクリエイティブな産業を生み出して

く。反対に日本はそういった戦略もなく、困難に直面しているんです。国レベルだと時間がかかるので、民間や都市間で動くより早く機能するかもしれない、新しい戦略ビジョンを持ってヨーロッパとの交流とアジア諸国との交流が重要なんです。ひとつのアイデアとして、年に2都市ずつ東アジアにおける文化首都を選んで、それぞれの自治体で文化都市活動をするというような、東アジアでの、EUの発明した「文化都市構想」の考えは役に立つと思っているわけです。横浜で「クリエイティブシティ・ヨコハマ」に携わっていた経験を活かして、アジア版クリエイティブ・シティのネットワークを作っていきたいですね。

南三陸きりこ
AAF2010参加プロジェクト「"生きる"博覧会2010」（主催ENVISI）で南三陸志津川地区を飾ったきりこ。
Minamisanriku *Kiriko*
AAF2010 project decorating the Minamisanriku Shizugawa district with *kiriko* as part of "Live Exhibition 2010" (ENVISI)
©AAF Network Executive Committee

じゃんがら踊り
いわき市の郷土芸能「じゃんがら念仏踊り」。AAF2011グランドオープン・パーティにて披露していただいた。
Jangara Nembutsu Odori (ritual dance) from Iwaki City, performed at the Asahi Art Festival (AAF) 2011 Grand Opening Party
©AAF Network Executive Committee

加藤種男 | 115

Taneo Kato

Secretary General, Asahi Beer Art Foundation
Executive Director, Association for Corporate Support of the Arts

I have been involved in lots of activities since March 11th. I work for the Asahi Beer Art Foundation and Association for Corporate Support of the Arts, and I have experienced several things with both organizations since March 11th.

To start with Asahi, Asahi Beer runs the Asahi Art Festival (AAF), which reached its tenth year in 2012. It forms a network with art activities from communities all over Japan. 2012's event includes participating teams from some regions that suffered in the disaster. The most symbolic town is Minamisanriku in Miyagi Prefecture. We took part in a project together that happened there in 2010. The team is developing a type of tool. It's called *kiriko*, paper cutouts (*kirie*) which are hung out in front of each house.[1]

The *kiriko* express the characteristics of each house, displaying, for example, an image of a shrimp because it's a restaurant that serves large shrimp rice bowl dishes, or a picture of a certain restaurant's large Maneki-neko.[2]

To do this kind of activity it was necessary to elicit each building's characteristics and so to investigate this we worked with around fifteen local people. Through this experience I came to see that in this kind of depopulated area, which is supposedly very tight-knit, there isn't much communication between people. So we could say that this became a catalyst for better communication. During the activities, something very interesting happened. Among the participants there was someone who had come from China to marry a Japanese man. She didn't seem integrated into the Minamisanriku community yet. But when she saw what was being done with the *kiriko*, she said, "We have this in China too." She told us that in her hometown, all the women are always making them. In Japan, we use white paper in order to make an offering to the gods, but in China they use red paper as decoration during festivals. She taught the others all kinds of things and so then the

1. It represents the memories and treasured things of participants on paper cutouts (*kirie*) called *kiriko*.

2. The Beckoning Cat figure commonly found in restaurants or businesses.

people in Minamisanriku made red *kiriko* for the first time. In this way, communication with each other was able to move forward smoothly for the first time.

This activity was done at first only in the Shizugawa area and in 2011 it was set to expand to the whole of the Minamisanriku district. But then in 3.11, the town was destroyed. AAF has a national network so AAF people from all over Japan made *kiriko* in order to support Minamisanriku, mounting activities nationwide that broadcast the message that we are properly remembering Minamisanriku. In the end, *kiriko* were also made in Minamisanriku but not until a long time had passed. It goes without saying that Minamisanriku itself didn't have the capacity to do this kind of activity, so it could only be done after several months had gone by. At any rate, in August the *kiriko* from Minamisanriku and the ones collected from around the country were exhibited together in Minamisanriku. I first went to Minamisanriku after the disaster on May 4th, and I saw the exhibition at the site on August 16th. And so it is thanks to this kind of AAF activity that Minamisanriku and the whole country were able to communicate with each other relatively quickly.

The Association for Corporate Support of the Arts, on other hand, created the GBFund after 3.11. The "G" is the "g" from *geijutsu* (arts); "B" is the "b" from *bunka* (culture); and "F" is the "f" from *fukko* (reconstruction, rebirth). In other words, it is a fund for supporting reconstruction via culture and the arts. As you know, all sorts of people and companies have been supporting the reconstruction in their own ways.

Of course, we knew how important it is to rescue human life, but after three days we also thought that culture would definitely be needed. Saying that, three days after the disaster we couldn't do anything. One month after felt like make-or-break. I thought that if we didn't do something cultural within one month, it would be too late for people mentally. And so we made the GBFund to see if we could support the victims somehow by using cultural and artistic activities in the areas hit by the disaster. What we were anticipating at first was that many artists would take themselves to the sites, and then all kinds of activities could take place with local people, for example, holding concerts or painting pictures together. There were also things that used therapy, such as dance workshops, as we thought supporting people like that was important.

The reality was at the start, one or two or three months after the disaster, external artists were coming and giving all kinds of support. There were activities such as a video artist coming and recording everything, while a photographer collected photographs, washed them and then made a photo album for returning them to their owner, and the photographer also made posters and so on to inform the various evacuation centers (at the time, temporary housing had not yet been erected).

These kinds of various creative activities where artists come in from outside have great value in their own right, but there was a big change just before the start of the summer. This was when the local people began to say they wanted to revive the local performing arts in summer 2011, *kagura* (Shinto music) and *matsuri* (festivals). They wanted to put on these local July and August entertainments that had been handed down over the ages in each small town and village. August is an extremely important month in Japanese Buddhism, where there is a festival called Obon that celebrates your ancestors. And it attaches important in particular to celebrating those who have died that year, which is called Ninbon. So in 2011, there were lots of people who had lost relatives in the disaster who wanted to hold Ninbon for their dead family. In Obon, there are all kinds of festive events, such as the Bondori (Bon Dance). Sadly, now there weren't enough people to do it and the costumes, musical instruments and places like the performing stage had been lost, so the situation was that though they wanted to do it, they just couldn't. But regardless, even if not everything could be done the way it used to be, people's motivation would be boosted if, for example, we could restore the drum or horned mask used in the deer dance.

But then comes the question of how much that kind of thing costs. We asked locals if they had about ¥500,000 or ¥1 million, would they be able to start doing something? "Of course," they answered. For example, we could buy a drum or people would send in horns from places where there are lots of deer. We supported these kinds of cases through the GBFund and so in August 2011 there were around fifteen festivals, and I want to support around 100 in 2012. According to experts, there are around 1,000 cases of local performing arts affected by the disaster, so at the least I want to create a platform for supporting 10% of these through our funding.

At any rate, we knew a few were famous, but we had no idea there were so many local performing arts remaining in the Tohoku region. Moreover, what is important is that we finally understood that these performing arts are vital for people's ability to live, that they are important for the bonds that create communication between people.

And on the other hand, thanks to doing activities such as the Asahi Art Festival that create communities, or community regeneration-style art activities where temporarily lost communities create new ones, people from Minamisanriku and Fukushima's Iwaki City came to the Asahi Art Festival opening reception party in Tokyo in June 2012 and interacted with everyone.

So going up to the site was important, but it seems that local people also feel better if they can leave the area. The initiatives I mentioned that tried to regenerate communities were also important, but there were also many traditional cultural activities rooted in the region of which we were not aware. What we saw and understood in the areas afflicted by the disaster was that these activities played a role, albeit partially, in sustaining the community. And so our challenge from here on is what kind of interface we can build between these traditional things rooted in the communities and the art activities for regenerating communities that we are trying to create anew.

How can we connect these two? And why are we thinking in this way? For example, in order to conduct a certain festival, there were two organizations. One was called the "top," located at the top of a hill and the other was the "bottom," located at the bottom of a hill. In the tsunami, the houses of the people in the "bottom" group were all swept away, but the houses of the people in the "top" group were on higher ground and so they could escape the tsunami wave. Thanks to there being these two groups for doing the festival, the people from the "top" group supported their "bottom" peers by letting them stay in their homes. Here we have a foundation in this structure for helping each other out in communities that make festivals.

But there are shortcomings in these kinds of communities, and one is that they can be excluding to people who are not members. We are seeking out new forms of community-building to do something about this, and we think art can function here.

Asahi Art Festival wants to overcome these problems of exclusiveness, and build a network of art activities for independent communities around the country, focusing not only on traditional content but also on new things. And so we want to create a situation where each stands by itself but has also been opened up. This challenge is one of the things I have been thinking about for a long time, and in it there is the assumption of the challenge of Tokyo and the large cities versus the regional cities which have become depopulated, though in a large city there is also the issue of isolation. If we look globally at Japan today, while law and order are fine, there are problems. I think that isolation and distrust in this sense are large issues. On the other hand, regional communities are being eroded, and so we are thinking how we can build new communities. And this is where we feel that mediating through the power of art will be useful as a new method.

Lastly, there is the problem of Japan becoming isolated within Asia. For example, Korea is producing new creative industries that link culture and industry. In contrast, Japan does not have these strategies and is facing difficulties. It takes time at the state level, so getting things going in the private sector or between cities would likely function more quickly. It is important to have new strategy visions and engage in interchange with Europe and Asian nations. One idea which I think would be helpful here is to have a scheme like the EU Cultural Capital in East Asia, choosing two cultural capitals per year in East Asia, and where cultural capital activities would be carried out by the local government in each. Taking advantage of my experience of being involved with Creative City Yokohama, I want to build a creative city network in Asia like this.

假屋崎 省吾
華道家

3月11日の地震が起きたとき日本に居ました。実は東京にはおらず、京都で個展を開催していましたので、私自身直接被災はしておりません。

京都では「歴史的建造物に挑む」シリーズの個展のため、京都の長楽館にお客様と会場にいて、作品の説明等をしておりました。関西地区でしたので揺れを全く感じず、15時過ぎまで状況を把握できませんでした。事務所に電話をしても全く通じなかっため心配をしていたところ、長楽館の事務所の方からテレビのニュースで関東以北が大変なことになっているとの報告を受けました。その時には既に通信手段が一切通じなくなっていたため、花教室スタッフの安否の確認をするのに何時間もかかり、気が気ではありませんでした。

震災前から予定されていた新しい企画や活動の予定が山のようにたくさんありましたが、イベントなど中止になったもの、延期になったもの、実行されたもの、様々でした。

様々な活動をしているなか、私は華道家であるので、花を通して被災された方々のお役に立たせていただきたいと考えました。震災直後に鹿児島県のスプレー菊生産者の友人に相談をし、特に被害の大きかった被災地の1つである岩手県陸前高田市やその近隣の町に、スプレー菊を何度かに分けて1万本程送らせて頂きました。現地の方に伺ったところ、何千何万の方々が亡くなっているのに弔い花が全くない状況だとのことでしたので、皆さんにとても喜んでいただけました。

また、教室の生徒や、各地で行った講演会などのイベントの折に、義援金を募ってボランティア団体に寄付もさせて頂きました。その他にも、テレビやラジオを通して様々なチャリティーの呼びかけをしたりもしました。2011年11月の目黒雅叙園の展覧会でも、被災地で栽培されたリンドウ、ガーベラ、カーネーションを使用し、被災地への応援を込め、心を込めていけさせていただきました。

そして、震災から一年経つ2012年3月11日にJALさんの企画で行われた仙台空港で行った鎮魂式に、私は華道家として会場に鎮魂の意を込めるとと

もに、復興と再生への夢と希望を託して花をいけさせていただきました。津波の押し寄せた被災地は、震災後も塩害で田畑が使い物にならなくなってしまい、しばらくは何も育たない不毛地帯になってしまうだろうと言われていましたが、その後JALさんの復興プロジェクトで比較的塩害に強いと言われる綿花をその地で栽培し、復興支援を行っています。3月11日の鎮魂式では、その綿花も使用していけ花を作成いたしました。

先日NHKのあさイチの番組で、茨城県のひたちなか市や福島県のいわき市まで行って収録を行い、今現在の被災地の現状等々のレポートをしたり、2012年8月4日＆5日に東京国際フォーラムで行われた「福島まごころフェスタ」ではパネリストとして招待されて様々なゲストの方々とディスカッションを行った他、そのイベントの一環として福島県内の花農家に伺い、風評被害や現在の震災後の生産状況を伺ったり、福島県立明成高校に伺い、いけ花を通じて応援メッセージを贈らせていただいたりしました。

毎年の恒例行事となっている目黒雅叙園で行う展覧会を、今年は11月1日–18日まで行いますが、そこでもまた被災地で栽培された花を使用したりと、何かしらの形で私にできる限りの被災地支援をしていきたいと考えています。

鎮魂花
Flower requiem
©Shogo Kariyazaki

福島
Fukushima
©Shogo Kariyazaki

目黒雅叙園
Meguro Gajoen
exhibition
©Shogo Kariyazaki

Shogo Kariyazaki
Floral arrangement artist (Ikebana artist)

I was in Japan when the March 11th earthquake occurred. Actually, though, I was not in Tokyo but in Kyoto for a solo exhibition, so I did not have any direct personal experience with the disaster.

At the time, I was at the Chourakukan hotel in Kyoto giving a talk about my work displayed there as part of a series of art exhibitions in historic buildings. I did not feel any shaking since I was in the Kansai region, and more than fifteen minutes passed before I fully realized what had happened. I tried calling my office but could not get through. Just as I started to worry, the news on the hotel office's TV reported that the situation in the Kanto area and north of it was serious. At that point all means of communication were already cut off, so it took a while to confirm the safety of the staff at my flower arranging school. I was very uneasy.

Before the disaster I had been planning many, many new projects and activities. Some of these were canceled, some were delayed, and some went ahead as scheduled.

Since I am a floral arrangement artist, I thought I could use flowers to help people hurt by the disaster. I immediately got in touch with a friend who grows spray chrysanthemums in Kagoshima Prefecture, and together we were able to send around 10,000 flowers in several batches to Iwate Prefecture's Rikuzentakata City and its surrounding area, which was one of the worst-affected places. When I spoke with local people, I learned that although several thousand people had died, there were no flowers for funerals, so the chrysanthemums we sent were eagerly welcomed.

I also had the honor of donating funds contributed by flower arrangement students and raised at lectures and other events around the country. I also put out calls for various charities during TV and radio appearances. At a flower arrangement exhibition at the Meguro Gajoen hotel in November 2011, I used bellflowers, gerbera daisies, and carnations grown in areas affected by the disaster. I arranged these flowers with a heartfelt desire to give encouragement to these places.

At a requiem ceremony hosted by JAL at Sendai Airport on March 11th, 2012, my job as floral arrangement artist for the occasion was to create an arrangement that honored the souls of those lost, while also expressing dreams and hopes for restoration and rebirth. The soil of areas hit by the tsunami was said to be unusable for crops due to salt damage, and it seemed that it would be unable to grow anything on the land for a while. However, as part of a JAL restoration project, I have been involved in cultivating cotton, which is said to be relatively hardy in salty soil and has contributed to the area's revival. I used this cotton in my flower arrangement for the requiem ceremony.

I traveled to places including Ibaraki Prefecture's Hitachinaka City and Fukushima Prefecture's Iwaki City to record the NHK morning show *Asaichi* and reported on current conditions in areas affected by the disaster. At Fukushima Magokoro Fest, a benefit held at the Tokyo International Forum on August 4th and 5th, 2012, I held discussions with a variety of guests as a panelist. In connection with the same event, I had the privilege of interviewing Fukushima flower growers, investigating harmful rumors and post-disaster production levels, visiting Fukushima Meisei High School, and offering messages of support through flower arrangements.

My arrangements for the November 1st-18th, 2012 Meguro Gajoen exhibition—now an annual event—featured plants grown in disaster-stricken areas. Through actions such as these, I hope to help places impacted by the disaster as much as I can, in any way I can.

黒瀬陽平
CHAOS*LOUNGE 代表
美術評論家

日本のアートプロダクションの現状はとても特殊だと思います。「日本にはアートマーケットがない」とよく言われますが、正確にいえば、国内の小さなマーケットがグローバルなマーケットときちんと接続することなく、閉じた状態である、ということだと思います。唯一、世界のマーケットに対して大きな影響力を持っているのが「カイカイキキギャラリー」、つまり、アーティストである村上隆が自ら経営するギャラリーだという事実は象徴的です。その状況は、3.11以前も以後も変わっていません。

ではアーティストたちのリアクションはどうだったか。一言でいえば、まだバラバラの状態にあると思います。3.11に対する日本のアーティストたちの反応は、ひとつのムーブメントやシーンを形成するに至っていません。だから日本のアーティストが今何を考えているのか、ということについては、外からでは非常にわかりにくいでしょう。

デモなどを通して社会にコミットメントしようとしているアーティストたちもいます。戦後日本において定期的に繰り返されてきた、権力への抵抗を旗印とした「政治的なアート」が3.11後に再び復活しつつあるようにも見えます。あるいは、アーティストが被災地へ行ってワークショップを行うような、いわゆる「コミュニティ・アート」のようなものも盛んになってきています。

しかし、僕たちはそれらのいずれとも違う回路で、社会と関わるアートを模索しています。CHAOS*LOUNGEは3.11以前から、日本の平均的なファインアートに比べてかなり極端にサブカルチャー、ネットカルチャーに寄り添って活動してきました。なぜなら、日本では、ファインアートよりサブカルチャーの方がリプレゼンテーションとしての文化の役割を果たすと同時に、「日本の無意識」に触れることができているからです。

例えば、3.11以後、いち早く「日本の無意識」の層に触れることができた作品のひとつは、「週刊少年ジャンプ」で連載している冨樫義博さんの「HUNTER×HUNTER」という漫画だったと思います。「HUNTER×

HUNTER」は、今日本で起こっていることをすべて漫画という表現のなかに織り込むように創作をしています。ほとんどシャーマンのような存在です。偉大なアーティストだと思います。

ただ、現状をリプレゼンテーションした上で、それへの応答や新しいヴィジョンが描けていなければ、単なる社会反映論に留まることになると思います。ですが、仮に現在の社会反映に留まったとしても、冨樫のように「日本の無意識」に触れるような作家は、本来であればファインアートの世界から輩出されるべきでしょう。日本では、冨樫のように現実を自分の中に取り込み、それを消化して作品に出来るタイプの人がサブカルチャーからばかり出る。

ですが、さらに深刻なのは、3.11以後のサブカルチャーは徐々に国内の現実を捉えられなくなってきているのではないか、という兆候も見られることです。冨樫のような例外はあるとしても、日本のサブカルチャーは、経済的にも精神的にも震災の影響から無縁ではいられないにもかかわらず、その現実と向き合うことを避けているように見えます。その意味において、僕たちは少しサブカルチャーと距離を感じ始めています。今までのように、サブカルチャーの中に自分たちの身を埋めてアート活動をすることが正しいのかどうか、ためらいを感じるのです。これが僕らにとって一番大きな変化です。

3.11がサブカルチャーに与えた影響のほとんどは、3.11以前から存在していた問題の連続であると言うこともできます。3.11以後の経済的困窮は、当然ながら産業としてのサブカルチャーへ打撃を与えています。しかし、もしも日本のオタク産業が、国内でアニメのDVDやフィギュアを売るだけではなく、デジタル時代のグローバルなコンテンツとしてのマネタイズを構築していたなら現状は違っていたでしょう。

例えば、任天堂の『ポケモン』は日本発で世界的にヒットし続けているコンテンツですが、それは『ポケモン』がゲームという産業をベースにして、極めて例外的なマーケティングを行なっているからです。ですが、多くの日本発のオタクコンテンツは『ポケモン』のような戦略を持っていません。作品やキャラクターは世界中で愛されていても、そのユーザーたちの支持をマネタイズすることについて大きく出遅れてしまったのです。自分たちが生み出し、育てたクリエイティビティを守りつつ世界に浸透させるためのブランディングと、その基盤となるマーケティングをまだうまくできないのです。

加えて、日本では文化に対する国からの援助がうまく機能していません。アート

の助成金ももちろんですが、「クールジャパン政策」にも多くの批判が集まっています。オタクコンテンツのような日本独自のサブカルチャーを他文化の人たちに紹介するためには、もっと高度な翻訳能力（言語的な翻訳だけでなく）が必要です。そして、物珍しげなオリエンタルな視線で消費されるだけでなく、和製サブカルチャーが体現する思想とは何なのかを伝え、日本人がイニシアチブを取るためにはどうすればよいのか、ということを考えるべきです。そのためにはもっと批評的な視座が必要となるでしょう。

例えば、ぼくたちが考えるのは、3.11以後の「新しい日本像」についてです。オタクとはまさに、3.11以前の日本像、日本人像として機能していました。オタクという未成熟で、イノセントで、無垢な少年少女というイメージは、戦後日米の関係のもとで屈折しながら育ってきた日本文化をリプレゼンテーションするものだったのです。

しかし、震災以後その自己像は更新を迫られていると思います。なぜなら、3.11が世界に印象付けた日本の姿とは、世界有数の災害の国であり、世界の海に放射性物質を垂れ流す国だったからです。そのことは、これまでのオタクという自己像が持っていた「アメリカに去勢された被害者」としてのイメージを吹き飛ばすに足る事実です。3.11以後の放射能汚染に関していえば、日本は「加害者」としてのイメージも背負うことになるでしょう。

3.11を経て、日本は明らかにひとつの区切りを迎えました。CHAOS*LOUNGEは、この区切りが何だったのか、そしてこれからぼくたちはどのように生きていくべきか、ということを考え続けています。

これはCHAOS*LOUNGEが3.11後に世に出した最初のイメージです。CHAOS*LOUNGEのアーティスト梅沢和木の作品ですが、この画面には二つの「大地」があります。津波で流された大地から隆起するようにもう一つの大地があります。しかし、新しい大地を持ち上げているのはまるで津波そのもののように描かれているので、破壊と再生が同居した風景になっています。そして、この風景は、インターネット上で流通している雑多な画像の集積でできているのです。

ぼくたちは常に、インターネットとサブカルチャーを介して現実にアプローチしようとしています。インターネット上という巨大なネットワークを経由して立ち現れてくる「現実」を捉えることの重要さを、梅沢の作品はよく表していると思います。ぼくらの思想は、ジャン・ボードリヤールのポジティブ版と言えるかもしれませ

梅沢和木《とある人類の超風景》2011年
Kazuki UMEZAWA, *A Certain Mankind's Super Landscape* (2011)

Courtesy of CASHI, in cooperation with Kenshu SHINTSUBO This collage contains some elements of photography taken and owned by Kenshu Shintsubo.

ん。彼が20世紀に記述した情報社会のヴィジョンでは、そこではもはやアートは消滅していると予言されていますが、ぼくたちは新しいアートをつくろうとしているのです。

一方で、梅沢をはじめとしたCHAOS*LOUNGEの作家は、インターネット上の画像を収集して作品を作っているので、現在オタクたちとの間で深刻な問題になっています。つまり、ぼくたちの作品はコピーライトの侵害であり、犯罪である、というバッシングを受けているのです。この問題は海外の人にはわかりにくいと思います。アートがコラージュやサンプリングという手法で著作物の一部を使用することは一般的だからです。しかし日本では「これはアートであり、オリジナルな創作物である」という主張は通用しません。なぜなら、多くの人が現代アートに価値を見出していないからです。それによってぼくたちは、ネット上の匿名の存在たちから、国内での活動を極端に制限されるほどの弾圧を受けることになりました。しかし、この現象自体がこの国の姿を映しているとも言えます。ある程度時間が経てば、ぼくたちが受けた激しい弾圧は、日本の現代アート史の事件として記録されるでしょう。

今、次の展覧会の構想を練っているのですが、これははっきりと、3.11以後の日本と世界の関係について考えるものになるはずです。タイトルは「Little Akihabara」です。この展覧会は、3.11以後のオタクの運命をシミュレーションしたものです。

ストーリーはこうです。3.11以後、日本が経済的な復興を遂げることがで

黒瀬陽平 | 129

きず、現在のような規模のオタク産業を支えられなくなる。それにともなって、オタクカルチャーの中心も日本からアジア諸国へと移ってしまう。「Little Akihabara」の主人公は、そんな状態の日本を脱出し、外国で生きることを選択したオタクたちです。彼らはより良い生活を求めて外国へ移住したものの、3.11以前の日本を忘れられず、異国の地に「Little Akihabara」を作ってしまう、という話です。展覧会は、架空の「Little Akihabara」をインスタレーションとして作るつもりです。この「Little Akihabara」の姿を描くことが、オタクカルチャーにコミットしながらアートについて考えてきたCHAOS*LOUNGEの表現なのです。

Yohei Kurose
Director, CHAOS*LOUNGE
Art critic

I think Japanese art production is very peculiar. It is often stated that "there is no art market in Japan," though it's more precise to say that the small domestic market is closed and not connected to the global market. The fact that Kaikai Kiki Gallery, the gallery run by Takashi Murakami, is the only gallery with a major influence on the world market, says something about this reality. This hasn't changed before or since 3.11.

What were the reactions of artists to 3.11? To summarize in one phrase, all I can say is that reactions varied. The responses of Japanese artists to 3.11 haven't formed a movement or scene. From the outside, it seems difficult to see what Japanese artists are thinking about right now.

There are artists who try to engage with society through anti-nuclear power protests. This seems to represent a comeback of the "political art" with an anti-authority agenda that repeatedly surfaced in the postwar era. Or the kind of art genre called "community art" in which artists are going to the devastated areas and doing workshops has also been popular.

But we were trying to find a path to engage the society differently to both these discourses. Before 3.11, CHAOS*LOUNGE had been working extremely closely with Japanese subcultures and Internet culture compared to average Japanese fine art, because in Japan subculture functions as representational culture and you can touch on "Japanese unconsciousness" better.

For example, one of the works that touched on this "Japanese unconsciousness" is the manga *HUNTER × HUNTER* by Yoshihiro Togashi, featured in Weekly Shonen Jump. *HUNTER × HUNTER* illustrated everything happening in Japan right now expressed through manga. This great artist is almost like a shaman.

Even if work represents reality, it ends up as a mere reaction if it does not offer a response and new vision. And even if it is limiting itself to simply reacting to current society, an artist like Togashi who touches on "Japanese unconsciousness" should originally come from fine art. In Japan, though, someone like Togashi who takes on reality and digests it into an artwork will always come from subcultures.

However, I see indications that subcultures after 3.11 have not been able to grasp the domestic reality. Japanese subculture is in no way disconnected from the financial and mental effects of the disaster, but it seems to be avoiding confronting reality, with the exception of Togashi. In this sense, we have gradually started to feel a distance from the subculture. I have begun to doubt whether placing ourselves within this subculture and creating art is the right thing to do. This is the biggest change that has happened to me.

The impact of 3.11 on Japanese subculture is a consequence of the problems that existed before 3.11. The economic depression after 3.11 obviously hit the subculture hard, but if the *otaku*[1] industry had explored ways to monetize content for the global digital era instead of just selling anime DVDs and figures domestically, the situation would have been different.

For example, the globally successful *Pokemon*, created in Japan by Nintendo, employed an exceptional marketing strategy based on the video game industry. But most of the *otaku* content made in Japan does not have the same strategy as *Pokemon*. While the works themselves and their characters are popular among fans around the world, the industry lags behind in monetizing users' support. People have difficulty marketing and branding their work to spread it overseas while protecting their creativity.

In addition, governmental financial support to the culture industry does not function properly. There is a lot of criticism directed towards art grants as well as at the "Cool Japan" policy that promotes Japanese cultural capital.[2] In order to introduce *otaku* content, which is a very unique culture, you have to have a high level of translation proficiency, and not just in the literal sense of the word. While avoiding orientalist consumption, we need to deliver the ideas represented by made-in-Japan subcultures and consider what we have to do to take the initiative. To do this, we need a more critical perspective.

Let me talk about a post-3.11 "new image of Japan." *Otaku* used to function in illustrating the image of Japan and Japanese in the pre-3.11 era. *Otaku* have an image of being immature, innocent, and naive boys

1. Japanese "geeks" famous for their consumption of various kinds of manga, anime, videpo games or "idol" subcultures.

2. A Japanese government policy for promoting Japan with an emphasis on manga and anime popular culture and subcultures.

and girls, which represents how Japanese culture developed in a warped way under the postwar relationship with the US.

However, since the disaster, this self-image needs to be updated. This is because 3.11 has given the world an impression of a country of disasters, a nation that released radioactive substances into the world's oceans. The *otaku* self-image until now was that of a "victim emasculated by America" but the fact is that this has been blown away. In terms of radioactive contamination post-3.11, Japan also has to shoulder the image now of being a "perpetrator."

Japan saw a turning point after 3.11. CHAOS*LOUNGE has been thinking about what this turning point really means and how we should live in the future.

This is the first image that CHAOS*LOUNGE released after 3.11. It is artwork by CHAOS*LOUNGE artist Kazuki Umezawa. It depicts two "grounds" in the canvas. A second ground is rising from the ground washed away by the tsunami. As the artist draws a force lifting up the ground in a way that resembles a tsunami, the scene looks as though destruction and rebirth are coexisting in one canvas. This image is actually an accumulation of unsorted images circulating online.

We always approach reality through the Internet and subcultures. I think Umezawa's work illustrates the importance of capturing the "reality" that is surfacing via a massive online network. Our ideas could be a positive version of Jean Baudrillard's. While the vision of the information society he described in the twentieth century predicts that art would disappear, we are trying to create new art.

Artists represented by CHAOS*LOUNGE including Umezawa create their work by collecting online images, which causes serious issues, especially in relationship with the *otaku* population. We have been accused of violating copyright and committing crimes. Foreigners might have difficulty understanding this issue because it is acceptable overseas for artists to use some copyrighted materials in the methods of collage or sampling. But insisting that "this is art and an original creation" is not accepted in Japan because many people do not see any value in contemporary art. Due to this situation, we have been oppressed by anonymous people to the extent that we have had to limit our domestic activities. This phenomenon reflects the conditions in Japan. After a certain time has passed the extreme oppression we have experienced will be recorded as an incident in the history of contemporary art.

We are currently planning ideas for an upcoming exhibition that will enable us to think about the relationship between post-3.11 Japan and the world. Entitled *Little Akihabara*, the exhibition is a simulation of the fate of *otaku* after 3.11.

The story goes like this: With the Japanese economy unable to fully recover after 3.11, it cannot sustain the current scale of the *otaku* industry, so the center of *otaku* culture moves from Japan to other Asian countries. The protagonists of *Little Akihabara* are *otaku* who decide to escape from Japan. While migrating to foreign countries for better lives, they are unable to forget the pre-3.11 Japan and create a "Little Akihabara" overseas. We are going to create a virtual "Little Akihabara" as an installation. Portraying this "Little Akihabara" represents CHAOS*LOUNGE's creative endeavors that always consider art through engaging with *otaku culture*.

後藤和子
前文化経済学会〈日本〉会長
国際文化経済学会理事(2006–2012)
埼玉大学経済学部教授

文化やアートが、震災復興の役に立っているかどうかは、いまだに、はっきりした答えがないというのが正直なところであろう。理念としては、文化は人間や社会にとって根源的なものであり、地域文化の復興こそ、人々を勇気づけ復興に向かう力になるなど色々なことがいえるが、果たして、それが、今回の被災地で本当に起こっていることなのかどうかは、長い時間をかけて検証される必要があるだろう。

被災地でアーティストが活動するというスタイルは、すでに、1995年の阪神淡路大震災の時に始まったもので今回が初めてではない。また、新潟県十日町を中心とするエリアで3年に1度開催される「大地の芸術祭」の関係者は、2004年の新潟県中越地震の際に、被害を受けた芸術祭開催地域の支援を行っている。2011年の東日本大震災の翌日には、新潟県に隣接する長野県北部でも大きな地震があり、芸術祭作品の1つであるオーストラリア・ハウスが倒壊したが、2012年にはオーストラリア政府などの支援で見事に再建された。私としては、むしろ、こうした日ごろからアートや文化を通した繋がりがあり、その繋がりが被災地支援に向かうという自然な流れに着目したいと思う。なぜなら、新潟県越後妻有エリアを開催地とする「大地の芸術祭」は2000年以降、継続的に開催され、過疎で高齢化が進む地域を少しずつ変えてきたという、長い時間の流れの中での被災地支援という確かなものだからである。

さて、今回の震災は、地震と津波に加えて、原子力発電所の事故を伴ったこともあり、科学の一端を担う私たち研究者にとっても、国際的責任の重さを痛感させられる出来事であった。私自身は、2006年以降、国際文化経済学会の理事を、また、2010年から2012年にかけて文化経済学会〈日本〉の会長を務めた。2008年のボストン大会時に、国際文化経済学会の理事会を通して2012年の日本での開催を、初めて提案させていただいた。国際文化経済学会は1970年代からの歴史のある学会であるが、アメリカとヨーロッ

パ以外で大会を開催したことはなく、日本での開催など考えられないという雰囲気もあった。

しかし、日本側の熱心な準備状況を伝え、2009年のパリで開催された理事会で、他の候補をおさえて日本開催が決定され、2010年のコペンハーゲン大会で歓迎のスピーチを行うことができた。そうした中で起きたのが、東日本大震災であった。被災地の皆様のご苦労に比べれば、はるかに小さな影響ではあるけれど、震災直後からの原発事故をめぐる国際的反響は非常に大きかった。毎日届くメールによって、海外でどのように報じられ、どのような反響をよんでいるのかヒシヒシと伝わってきた。経済学とはいえ、科学の一端を担うものとして国際社会での責任を痛感せずにはいられない日々であった。そのため、当時の日本の状況を、「可能な限り正確に正直に」メーリングリスト等で国際文化経済学会会員全員に伝える努力をした。

しかし、2011年春にイタリア・シチリア島で開催された理事会では、日本での国際学会大会開催を懸念する声が出され、大きな議論になった。日本の理事は私一人である。日本の会員は、学会創立20周年記念としての国際学会開催をとても楽しみにしている。日本の正直な現状を話すとともに、開催予定の京都と福島との距離や、日本の会員が国際学会開催のために大きな努力を積み重ねていることを伝え、「開催しないという選択は一度も考えたことがない」と述べた。放射能を心配する意見ももっともであるし、もとより日本で開催すると「遠い」「滞在コストが高い」という理由で参加者が減るのではないかという心配もあった。しかし、議論を尽くした末に、理事会は日本開催を支持してくれた。

2012年6月に開催された国際大会には、250名近いヨーロッパ他の海外からの参加と100名を大きく超える国内からの参加があり、国際文化経済学会大会史上最高の参加者となった。インターネットによる著作権侵害が、音楽産業にどのような影響を与えているか分析したテキサス大学教授のS.リーボウィッツ教授の講演に続き、「バベルの塔」を引用し、人間の言語が多様なのは、神の罰か祝福かと問いかける経済産業研究所の藤田昌久教授の講演は、文化多様性と都市発展の関係を経済学の視点から解明し大好評であった。

東日本大震災に触れた近藤誠一長官の挨拶、京都の都市形成について宗教学の視点から分かりやすく説いた山折哲雄先生、ユネスコにおける無

「六斎念仏」は10世紀に伝染病を終わらせる為に僧空也によって始められたと伝えられる踊念仏
The Buddhist religious dance Rokusai-Nenbutsu, originating from the Priest Kuya's dance praying for the end of a plague in the tenth century

形文化遺産保護の経緯と意義を語った松浦晃一郎氏の講演など、いずれも意義深いものであった。大会プログラム作成のイニシアチブをとり、魅力的な大会へと作り上げてくださった次期国際文化経済学会会長(現会長)のF. Benhamou教授とは毎日メールで連絡を取り合う日々であった。

2011年には、日本で開催される予定であった美術館展示や学会等が、数多くキャンセルになった。被災地からは遠く、原子力発電所からも遠い地域でも、様々な理由で開催が困難になったのである。そうしたなかで、アジアで初めてとなる国際文化経済学会大会を開催できたことは、国際文化経済学会理事をはじめとする国際的な支援の賜物である。心から感謝したいと思う。

復興への道のりはまだ続いている。今でも被災地に寄り添い活動を続けているアーティストがいる。アートや文化が人々の心の奥底に届き、復興への歩みを支えることができるかどうか、これからが正念場である。

Kazuko Goto

Former president, Japan Association of Cultural Economics (JACE)
Board Member, Association for Cultural Economics International (2006–2012)
Professor of Economics, Saitama University

I think it is not yet clear whether or not culture and art can be of help in Japan's post-disaster reconstruction. In principal, given that culture is a fundamental aspect of human life and society, rebuilding local culture encourages people to gain power for reconstructing their life. Whether or not this principal is working in the affected areas needs to be investigated over the course of a long time.

The phenomenon of artists working in the disaster areas is nothing new and it started in 1995 when the Great Hanshin-Awaji Earthquake happened. Also people working for the Echigo-Tsumari Art Triennale held in Tokamachi, Niigata Prefecture, supported the areas used for the Triennale's venues when the 2004 Chuetsu earthquake occurred. The day after 3.11, a big aftershock hit the northern part of Nagano, a prefecture next to Niigata. One of the Triennale's artworks, *Australia House*, was destroyed but it was rebuilt beautifully with help from the Australian government. I want to focus on how the pre-existing, everyday relationships made through art and culture naturally progress to support the related areas. For example, the Echigo-Tsumari Art Triennale is based in the Echigo-tsumari area, which has been periodically hosting the festival, little by little changing the aging and marginalized region. Aiding the damaged area in this case is a result of many years of collaborations.

In addition to the earthquake and tsunami, the accident at the Fukushima nuclear power plant was a part of the disaster. Researchers who are responsible for advancing science felt the weight of international responsibility. I have been a board member of the Association for Cultural Economics International since 2006 and a president of the Japan Association of Cultural Economics (JACE) between 2010 and 2012. At a conference held in Boston in 2008, I proposed through the board of directors that the 2012 conference be held in Japan. The Association for Cultural Economics International, with its long history since 1970, had never held a conference outside the US or Europe, and there was a feeling that organizing it in Japan wasn't realistic.

Japan was selected as host country at the 2009 board meeting in Paris after we conveyed that it was well prepared for hosting the conference. We were able to deliver a welcoming speech at the 2010 conference in Copenaghen. And then the 2011 Tohoku earthquake and tsunami happened. Its effect on us was rather small compared to the suffering of the victims, but we had a lot of international responses regarding the nuclear accident. The emails I received every day made me realize how the disaster had been reported and how it had drawn attention. Although my field of expertize is economy, I could not help but still feel a responsibility as someone who serves the advancement of science. I tried my best to tell others what was happening in Japan as accurately as possible through a newsletter distributed to ACEI members.

There were concerns over the possibility of holding the conference in Japan, voiced and discussed during the 2011 board meeting in Sicily. As the only Japanese board member, I told the board that Japanese members were looking forward to hosting the international conference, which would commemorate the twentieth anniversary of the association. While conveying the reality in Japan truthfully, I also talked about the physical distance between Fukushima and Kyoto, where the conference was to be held, and how Japanese members had been making a lot of effort in organizing the conference. I told them that "not hosting the conference was never on the table." I completely agreed with their concerns over radioactivity and there were also some who worried that the expense of staying in Japan would decrease the number of participants. After a series of discussions, however, the board supported the idea of hosting the conference in Japan.

The international conference held in June 2012 attracted nearly 250 international participants and more than 100 Japanese participants. The number of participants was a record high in the history of the conference. Popular contributions came from Stan Liebowitz, a professor from Texas University, who discussed how copyright violation affected the music industry, as well as from Masahisa Fujita, a professor at the Research Institute of Economy, Trade and Industry, who explained about the relationship between cultural diversity and urban development from an economical perspective, and drew on the biblical tale of the Tower of Babel to question whether diversity in human languages is God's punishment or a blessing.

Seiichi Kondo, the Commissioner for the Agency for Cultural Affairs in Japan, made a welcome speech touching on the 2011 Tohoku earthquake and tsunami, and Tetsuo Yamaori discussed Kyoto's urban development from a religious point of view, while Koichiro Matsuura's lecture was on the process and importance of UNESCO's attempt at conserving intangible cultural heritage. These lectures were all very meaningful. The days prior to the conference were occupied by email correspondence with Professor Françoise Benhamou, the president elect at that time (and the current president), who took the initiative in programming and creating this remarkable conference.

Many museum exhibitions as well as conferences were canceled in 2011 for various reasons, despite their venues being far from both the disaster zones and the Fukushima nuclear power plant. Being able to successfully organize the conference in this climate—and for the first time in Asia—was largely due to international support, including that of the board members.

The road to rebuilding still stretches far ahead, while there are artists who still continue to work close to the affected areas. From now comes the crucial time of deciding whether art and culture can resonate in our hearts and support the steps toward reconstruction.

小山薫堂
脚本家・放送作家
「kizuna 311」呼びかけ人

3.11の地震によって今まで僕がしたかったことはかわってないんです。僕がしなければいけないことはかえって伝えやすくなったと思います。例えばいくつかあるのですが、一つはNHKのドラマで「坂の上の雲」というのがあるんですけど、その中の主題歌の作詞をしたんです。主題歌は3.11後のほうがヒットしている、歌詞が人々に共感されるようになったことが一つ。同じようにもう一つ、毎年年末に国内外に放送されるNHK紅白歌合戦で白組司会を務めた嵐が「ふるさと」を歌いました。この歌は3.11以降また歌われるようになって、今年の紅白歌合戦でも拡大バージョンで歌われることになった。

あとは僕は熊本県の出身なので熊本県の観光をPRするためのショートフィルムを撮っていたんですけど、それを撮り終えた後、編集をしている時に地震が起こったんですね。それを見た人達の心にすごく刺さるようになったといえるところはあります。これは世の中がやさしさを求めたり、絆を求めたり、心のぬくもりを求める時代になったので、僕が作りたいテイストにすごく合うように震災以降の変化があったということ。つまり、僕は変わってないんですけど、すごく物が作りやすくなったという印象はあります。

僕がずっと言っていたのは、僕の好きな言葉で「幸せは探し出すもんじゃなく

熊本県観光フィルム「くまもとで、まってる。」より抜粋
Excerpt from Kumamoto Prefecture tourism film *I'm waiting for you in Kumamoto*

て気づくものだよ」。つまり、それまで人は、何が幸せかというものを常に自分より上にあるものばっかり探そうとしていたけども、いまはもうそうじゃない。僕は自分の置かれている環境の中でこれが幸せだと感じることが一番の幸せだと思います。人々は何もない普通であることそして生きているだけで幸せを実感し始めてた。

例えば、僕の故郷で撮影したドキュメンタリーの中で、おじいさんを撮影したんです。僕、おじいさんに何で片道たった150円にしかならない、たった一人の高校生のお客さんしかいないのに渡し舟を漕ぎ続けているんですかって聞いたんです。彼は私に「何でって言われても、これが私のつとめですから」って言ったんですよ。自分の仕事を幸せに感じながら自分がやらなければいけないことをやっていく人達を撮影しました。最初はみんな、これ退屈じゃない？って言ってたんですけど、震災があって世の中が変わり、日常の中にある幸せをすくい上げるようになった。僕はこういうことをメッセージとして送り続けたい。

僕ら、「kizuna 311」という活動を始めまして、それは、最初はメディアの中に光を作るということを目的にしました。どういうことかと言いますと、最初に渡辺謙さんが何かやらなきゃという気になって、それで何をしようかって一緒に考えたんですよ。

kizuna311.com
渡辺 謙
「雨ニモマケズ」朗読
Ken Watanabe reading the poem "Strong in the Rain" by Kenji Miyazawa
©kizuna311

雨ニモマケズ
風ニモマケズ
雪ニモ夏ノ暑サニモ負ケヌ
丈夫ナカラダヲモチ
慾ハナク
決シテ瞋ラズ
イツモシヅカニワラッテヰル
一日ニ玄米四合ト
味噌ト少シノ野菜ヲタベ
アラユルコトヲ

当初、言葉を何にしようか考えたんですね。「津波」という言葉が世界の言葉になっているじゃないですか。で、その津波よりももっと覚えて欲しい言葉は何だろうと考えた時に色々挙がったんですけど「絆」っていう言葉が一番覚えてもらえ易いかなって思ったんです。三文字で「つなみ」よりも「きずな」っていうふうになったらいいなって。だから「絆」に決めたんですね。

で、その中で思ったことが、震災直後って、テレビの中の映像は繰り返し津波の映像ばかり流れて、世の中がすごく暗くなる、真っ暗になってどうしようもないという時に、僕、ラジオ番組をやっているんですけど、ラジオはすごくテレビとは違って、ラジオというメディアを介して人々が手をつなぎ一生懸命前を向こうということをしているように感じたんですね。音楽が流れることによって人々は勇気をもらえるし、すごく役に立つ。実質的な情報を聞くことが出来るし、テレビはどちらかというと広い所に流すので強烈な映像をリピートするだけで救いがなかなか見つけられない。

だから全国のラジオ局にコンテンツを提供したいと思ったんですね。多分作るのも大変でしょうから。それで詩を朗読するということを考えたんですね。色んな俳優さんが元気になる詩を朗読して、それをCDで各ラジオ局にお届けしようと。で、各ラジオ局はそれを自由に著作権フリーでオンエアに使ってもらう。ウェブにものせました。一つは、ウェブ上ではカタログのようにラジオ局の人が使いたい詩を選んでオンエアに使う。そして、もう一つはラジオを聴かない人は、若者がアクセスしてこれを見ることによって被災地以外の人も元気になるという思いで作ってみました。協力をしてくれた人達はやりたいと言ってきた人、お願いした人両方います。

今、一番の活動はカレンダーで、僕らカレンダーにのせる言葉を募集しまして、これは「あなたが前向きになった言葉を教えてください」と。被災地の人に呼びかけまして、被災地の人達から主に頂いたんですね。でも全国から来ました。けど、なるべく被災地からの言葉を中心に選びました。それで、今その言葉を3日めくりカレンダーにしています。3月12日から始まるカレンダーを発売しました。それで、1冊2,000円で販売するんです。原価が1冊約1,000円かかっているんで、倍の値段で販売して、東京の人が1冊買ったらもう1冊が被災地の学校や病院、公共施設に寄付される。東京で買った人は3日に1回めくるたびに「あっ、自分のもう1冊のものを被災地の人がめくってるんだ」と思う。反対に、被災地の人はめくるたび「あっ、これをくれた人とつながってるんだ」と思う。それを意識することでつながっているという気分を味わう。そして被災地の人は今までずっと励まされているばっかりだと思うんですが、自分が前を向くきっかけになった言葉を発表することで自分の言葉で他の人も励まされるのではないか。つまり自分の生きているというか、存在価値を感じることが出来る。そこに元気の種が生まれるんじゃないかと思ってこういう企画にしました。

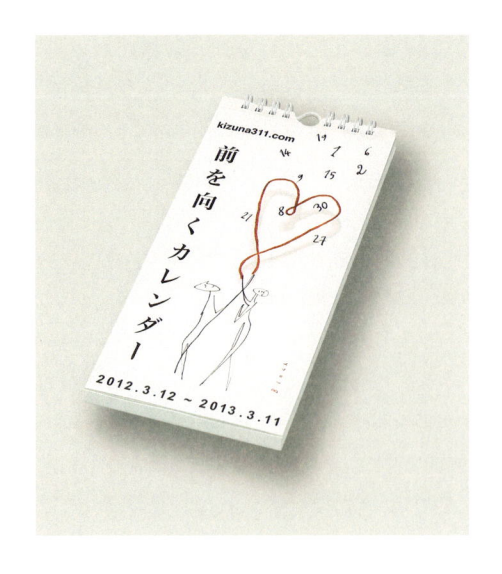

kizuna311.com
「前を向くカレンダー」
(kizuna311+PARCO)
kizuna311.com,
"Forward-looking Calendar" (kizuna311 +PARCO)
©kizuna311

最初に渡辺謙さんと一緒に背伸びはしない、出来る事をやる、長くやる。これを大切にしようと思っています。

実は今日、謙さんからメールが届いていて、彼は今、気仙沼に行ってるんですね。メッセージは「暗いうちから船の音がして町の息吹が少し感じられてうれしいです」という内容でしたね。前に行った時は本当に船の音さえしていなかったらしいので。

僕、大きいことをすることは考えたことがないんですね。それは、一人ひとりの事情が違うと思うから。僕は、例えば「誰かのためにこの人をどうしたらいいのか」というアイデアは出せる気はするんですけど、町をどうするかという大きなアイデアは考えても難しい。空虚なものになるのかなと思います。それを考えるより、どこどこに住んでいるだれだれさんをどうするかっていうのを一人が考える。その隣の家の人もまた誰か一人を考える。という意味では、皆で大きなことをすることを考えるより、一人が一人を支援する。つまり、マンツーマンの支援をどうしていくかということを考えるほうがいいかなと。あるいは十万人被災をしているとしたら一人について十人がついてあげたら、百万人の支援者がいたらそこは救われるわけですよね。そういう仕組みを作れないかなっと、もしそのアイデアがあるとしたら、そういう仕組みが何とか出来ないかなって思います。

[2011年11月]

Kundo Koyama
Scriptwriter, TV writer
kizuna 311 organizer

1. A 2009 NHK drama series adapted from a 1968–1972 novel by Ryotaro Shiba (1923–1996) set in Matsuyama during the Meiji Period.

2. A 2010 song with lyrics by Kundo Koyama first sung on the 2010 *Kohaku uta gassen* (Red & White Year-End Song Festival) and later performed at post-disaster NHK benefit concerts and following New Year's song festivals.

3. An annual New Year's Eve singing contest hosted by NHK with Japan's most popular musicians split into female- and male-led red and white teams.

The March 11th earthquake didn't change what I've been wanting to do until now. It rather made it easier to get across the idea of what I feel driven to do. For example, the theme song I wrote for the NHK drama *Saka no ue no kumo* (Clouds Above The Hill)[1] became more popular after the disaster, when it resonated with a lot of people. Likewise, popular Japanese boyband Arashi sang my song *Furusato* (Hometown)[2] as "white team" leaders during NHK's internationally broadcast *Kohaku uta gassen* (Red & White Year-End Song Festival).[3] This song was also performed again after March 11th, and an expanded version will be sung at the 2012 *Kohaku uta gassen*.

Another example is how I was editing a short film I'd shot to promote tourism in my native Kumamoto Prefecture when the earthquake struck. This film really moved audiences, and I think that's because the age we live in now has become one in which people are searching in the world for kindness, connections, and emotional warmth. There was a change after the disaster that fits very well with my own artistic tastes. It's not that I've changed, it's just that it's become easier for me to create what I want.

One of my favorite sayings, one that I've been repeating for a long time, is "Happiness isn't something you seek out. It's something you notice around you." Until the disaster people had been searching for happiness as something always above and beyond them, but not anymore. Now the best happiness is the kind you feel in whatever environment you find yourself in. People have started to feel happiness just in living their normal lives.

For example, in a documentary made in my hometown, I filmed an older man. I asked him why he continues to ferry a single high school student around when the trip only earns him ¥150 each way. He responded, "Because it's my job." I filmed people who find joy in their jobs just by doing what they have to do. At first everyone said, "Isn't this boring?" After the earthquake, however, the world changed and people started finding happiness in their everyday lives. This is the kind of message I want to keep sending.

When we began the kizuna 311[4] project, our initial goal was to create a source of light in the media. It started with Ken Watanabe's[5] feeling that something had to be done, so together we thought about what to do.

We wondered what to do for the name. "Tsunami" has become a global term, but we wondered if maybe there wasn't another word we'd rather people remember. We came up with several ideas, but "*kizuna*" (bond) seemed the easiest for people to remember. Like "tsunami," it can be written with three *kana* characters in Japanese, and we thought it had a nice ring to it. So that's how we decided on "*kizuna*."

Then I started thinking about how immediately after the disaster all that was being shown on TV was repeated footage of the tsunami, and the world seemed very dark. In this hopeless time of pitch darkness, I was doing a radio program. Radio is very different from TV, and I got the impression that through this medium people were coming together and putting all of their effort into moving forward. Radio is incredibly useful because you can find courage in the music played on it and get practical information. TV, on the other hand, just replays shocking images to reach wide audiences, which doesn't provide any relief.

So we decided we wanted to provide content for radio stations around the country, which we imagined were struggling to create programs. Poetry readings came to mind. We decided to have various actors read the poems that gave them strength and send CDs of these recordings to radio stations, allowing them to use the recordings on air free of copyright.

We also posted content on the Internet. One reason we did this was to make a sort of online catalog so radio stations could select and broadcast the poems they wanted to use. Another reason was so that young people and others who don't listen to the radio much, and people outside of the areas affected by the disaster, could also hear and take heart in the poems' messages. Both volunteers and invited guests participated in the program. Our top project right now is the calendar. For this, we asked people to send in motivational sayings which inspire them. We put out requests and accepted submissions mainly from people in the disaster-stricken areas, although we got responses from all over Japan. We mostly chose

4. A website that raises funds and features videos with support messages from celebrities and regular citizens for people affected by the 2011 Tohoku earthquake and tsunami. http://kizuna311.com

5. One of the most famous actors of his generation in Japan, he has also appeared in many major Hollywood films.

the words of people in places affected by the disaster, though. These sayings appear on the three-day flip calendar, which start from March 12th, 2012, went on sale for ¥2,000. The cost to produce each calendar is ¥1,000, and every time one is purchased, another is donated to a school, hospital, or public facility in an area affected by the disaster. So, every three days when one of the purchasers of the calendar, say someone in Tokyo, flips over a new page, he or she thinks, "Oh, the person I donated the other calendar to is also turning over a new page." At the same time, the recipient thinks, "I have a connection with the person who gave me this calendar." This awareness gives people a feeling of being united with others. Until now people in the areas affected by the disaster have mostly been on the receiving end of all the encouragement, but by expressing the words they find inspirational, they can see they are also cheering on others, which provides a sense of self-worth and plants seeds of hope. That's the project we're working on.

From the beginning, Ken Watanabe and I have been trying to do what we can, together, within our own limitations and over a long period of time. These are our priorities.

Just today I got an email from Ken, who's in Kesennuma. He wrote, "I can hear the sounds of boats in the dark and can feel a bit of the energy of the town, and it makes me happy." Apparently during his last trip there were not even any noises from the boats.

I have never thought of doing anything big. After all, everyone's personal circumstances are different, right? I feel like I can come up with ideas for how specific people can help others, but I find it hard to think of big ideas like what an entire town should do. That seems misguided to me. Instead I think of individuals, of how each individual can help so-and-so living in such-and-such place. Then, the person in the next house over can think of what he or she can do for one other individual, so that rather than everyone thinking of something big, people support each other on a one-on-one basis. Isn't it better to think of how we can help each other as individuals? Or, if 100,000 people are affected by a disaster and ten supporters reach out to each person, there will be 1 million supporters, which is surely enough to save everyone. That's the kind of system I think we have to build. If we have this idea in mind, I believe we can somehow make it a reality.

[November 2011]

近藤誠一
文化庁長官

1.これまでの文化庁の活動

震災が起きた直後から文化庁が行った活動は、次の7つの類型に分けられます。

（1）文化財・文化会館などの被災状況や、公演などへの影響の把握・調査
（2）被災した文化財・文化施設の救済・応急措置、本格的修復・復元
（3）埋蔵文化財や指定された史跡などへの規制の弾力的運用
（4）修理・復旧に必要な予算の確保、内外からの寄付の呼びかけ
（5）被災地を勇気づけるための種々の文化行事、公演、体験機会の提供や、右を行う意志のある芸術家・団体などと被災地のニーズをつなぐ仕組みの構築
（6）いわゆる風評被害を軽減するための措置
（7）過剰な自粛ムードを差し控えることの呼びかけ

まず最初に行ったのは、寺社や美術工芸品等の文化財、それらを収蔵・展示する美術館・博物館、音楽ホール等の文化施設の被災状況の調査です。これは、基本的に現地の都道府県に依頼し、実際に現場に行って調査をしてもらった結果を報告してもらう形をとりました。被害が大きい地域は、地元自治体が、人命救助や捜索、遺体の回収、被災者の当面の世話、ライフラインの確保など、最優先の人道案件を抱えているため、その活動に支障をきたさないためという配慮です。また中央政府から専門家を派遣するにあたっても、地元の受け入れ・支援体制がなければ、効果的な調査を安全に実施することができないからです。

これらの点で、阪神・淡路大震災の教訓が随所に活かされました。まず地元自治体からの報告が、早い段階から始まったことです。ある自治体からは、早くも震災の翌日に一部の文化財被災状況の報告が到達し、日増しにその数が増えました。原発事故によって一定地域への立ち入りができない福島から

の報告が遅れたのは当然でしょう。それでも原発がある程度コントロール下におかれた2012年初めに、直ちに重要な洞窟遺跡に調査隊が入って、一部の損傷を確認することができました。

こうして調査の結果、国宝や、重要文化財、特別史跡など国指定の文化財は、大被害のあった3県(岩手、宮城、福島)を含む1都18県で、744件に上りました。これは阪神・淡路大震災のときの173件を大きく上回ります。しかし幸い国宝の被害は5件で、かつ比較的軽微なものに止まりました。

また被災した文化施設の数は1都15県で290施設で、主な被害はホール天井の落下、舞台設備の損傷、壁や窓の破損、配管・電気系統の故障です。この結果安全をとって多くの公演が中止・延期になりました。

2. 国民の日常生活・社会の反応、アーティストの反応

この大惨事は、国民の生活、ライフスタイルに大きな影響を与えました。第一は、誰もが地震・津波・原発事故という三重の苦難の「意味」を考えたことです。「何が起こったのか?」、「何がいけなかったのか?」という問いが発せられました。ある哲学者によると、通常は問題が起こると、「どうすれば解決するのか?」という問いにあふれるのに対して、今回はこのように根源的な問いが多かったそうです。

それに対して、一方で科学技術への過信、危機管理体制の不備を指摘する声があがると共に、日本人が古くからもっていた自然への畏敬の念の喪失(自然は科学技術で制御できると考える人間の思い上がり)、近代西欧文明の負の側面(物質主義、効率主義、個人の欲望達成努力を奨励する)の表面化などの文明論的な議論も多くなされました。

またこのような惨事を前に、自分に何ができるかという問い、何も出来ないことへの苛立ちと無力感を感じた人は多く、それはアーティストや団体にも多くみられました。「こんな時にアートに何ができるのか?」「アートは社会に貢献していないことが明らかになったのではないか?」という苦渋に満ちた問いかけが多くなされました。

このことは2つの相反する動きにつながりました。ひとつは国民的な自粛ムードです。多くの尊い命が奪われ、多くの人たちが悲しみ、苦しんでいるのに、生き残ったものの何もしてあげられない自分たちだけが楽しい生活を続けて良いのかという発想が広がったことから、音楽会、演劇、落語、美術品展示会な

どのキャンセルを余儀なくされ、その状態が数ヶ月も続きました。日常生活に戻るきっかけが見いだせないままに毎日が過ぎ、アーティストや芸術団体の苦悩の日が続きました。誰が命令した訳でもないのに、日本人の間に歌舞音曲は慎まねばというムードが広がったのです（この社会的風潮は消費活動を冷えさせ、経済に悪影響を与える結果をもたらしましたが、同時に夏の電力消費の節約に大きく貢献し、懸念された需要ピーク時の停電などは回避できました）。

これに加えて、福島原発の事故の影響を懸念した外国のアーティストたちや、美術品所有者が、日本での公演や展示を直前にキャンセルする事態が相次ぎ、音楽会ホールや美術館に大きな経済的打撃を与えることになりました。こうした動きを懸念して、私は4月12日に、行き過ぎた文化芸術活動の自粛は、かえって社会を必要以上に沈滞させ、復興に必要な社会の力をそぐので止めようという趣旨のメッセージを発しました。文化芸術団体にファックスで送ると共に、文化庁のHPに掲載しました（文化庁HP参照）。これは多くの好意的な反響を呼びました。また在京の外交団をチャリティーコンサートや歌舞伎公演などに招き、日本が元気に芸術活動も行っているというメッセージを本国に送ってもらうようにしました。さらにこうした中でもあえて日本に来て公演してくれたアーティストたちに感謝の念を伝えるために、彼らを楽屋に訪ねたり、5月のラ・フォル・ジュルネ・イン東京では、海外からの出演者を歓迎するレセプションを開催したりしました。あるソプラノ歌手が、周りが止めるのも聞かず生後8か月の赤ちゃんを連れて来日し、予定通りオペラの主役を演じたことに感動し、楽屋にお礼を言いに行ったとき、彼女は赤ちゃんと、乳母、自分のお母さんを連れて現れ、「こういう時に日本に来て歌うことが、私が日本の皆さんにしてあげられる唯一のことなのです」と言ってくれました。

もうひとつの動きは、逆に文化芸術によって被災者を積極的に慰めようという運動の盛り上がりと、これからの東北の復興において文化芸術の果たす役割が大きいという議論の高まりです。前者は、かなり早い段階から、避難所や学校などで、とりあえず生きていくに必要な食料や寝る場所は確保できたが、その後の生活や職の見通しが立たず、また津波や家族を失ったトラウマが次第に表面化して気の滅入る毎日が続いている人たちの中から、音楽が聴きたい、落語を聴きたいという声が聞こえてきたことに始まります。悲しみにくれる周囲の避難者に遠慮していた方々が、遂にたまりかねてこうした希望を声にしたのです。これに呼応するアーティストがたくさん現れ、大きな運動に発展し

ました。
　また注目すべきは、東北には多くの祭りや伝統芸能がありますが、こうした先祖から引き継いだ地元の行事が、被災して傷ついた人々を慰め、コミュニティの連帯感を復活させたことです。有名な例が、福島県相馬市等の「相馬野馬追」です。毎年7月末の3日間、8つの市町村が共同で行うこの伝統的行事は、その場所の一部が原発の警戒区域にかかることから、開催が危ぶまれましたが、地元の強い希望で、警戒区域以外の地域のみで部分的に実行しました。また宮城県女川町の竹浦地区では、3つの避難所に分かれて暮らさざるを得なかった被災者が、津波で流され、損傷した用具を復元、修理して、伝統の獅子舞を行うことで、連帯感を取戻し、元気を回復することができました。
　こうした情報が流れた結果、災害からの復興過程において、住宅やインフラと同様に、有形無形の文化財の復旧が重要であることを、早くから地元が認識していたことが明らかとなりました。そしてこれはメディアに広く報道され、菅前総理の下に作られた「復興構想会議」が6月に提出した報告書に、復興の過程で文化芸術が果たす役割の重要性が明記されることになりました。

3. 進行中の事業
文化庁が震災直後から始めたのが、「文化財レスキュー事業」です。これは阪神・淡路大震災の教訓に基づいてつくった制度で、国宝、重要文化財など、国の指定する動産の文化財、つまり美術工芸品などを中心に、被災した文化財をとりあえず調査し、救出し、必要な応急措置をとるものです。瓦礫に埋もれたり、水に浸かっている文化財を見つけてとり出し、損傷状態を調査し、それ以上悪化しないように補修措置をとり、それらを安全なところに保管して、来たるべき本格的修復・復元に備えるというものです。これらは放置しておくだけで、瓦礫と一緒に撤去されてしまったり、水の影響で状態が悪化します。この作業には、地元の協力と共に、膨大な数の人材とそれぞれの分野での専門知識、そしてそれを有する人材が必要です。それは文化庁だけで対応できるものではありません。そこで文化財の知見と人材をもつ全国の美術館・博物館、研究所、大学の協力を依頼し、オールジャパンで取り組む体制としてつくったものです。また一旦救出して応急措置をとった文化財を、長期間保管する場所を確保することも重要です。何故なら折角応急措置をとった

貴重な文化財を、海外から現地に入る美術品専門の盗賊団から守ることも重要だからです。阪神・淡路大震災のときも、翌日には近隣からこうした盗賊団が現地に入ったそうです。まだ混乱の極みで、誰が誰だか分からない状況で、また誰でもボランティアで助けに来たと言えば通る状況で、彼らは目的を達成できるのです。そこで鍵が掛かり、温度や湿度の管理ができる博物館などの収蔵庫に、応急措置をした文化財を預けておくことが必要なのです。しかしこれも各館の空きスペースの問題や、コスト負担の問題もあり、いつまでも彼らを頼ってはいけません。3月1日現在で、延べ4,829人がこのオペレーションに参加しました。その過程で、国指定の文化財に限らず、地方自治体の指定したものなど、見つけた文化財はすべて対象にしたことは当然です。またこれにならって建造物等の不動産についても、「文化財ドクター派遣事業」を立ち上げ、これまでに11県198市町村に調査員を派遣しました。またこれら2つの事業については、不足する財源確保のために、公益財団法人文化財保護・芸術研究助成財団を窓口にして民間から寄付を集め、内外から計2億円以上の資金を集めることができました。

これらの被災した文化財の修理・修復のため、文化庁は2011年度の当初予算に加え、補正予算として32億円を獲得しました。2012年度予算としては19億円を計上しています。財政難にも関わらずそれなりの金額が確保できたことは、文化財の修理・修復が、復興の重要な柱であることが広く社会に認識されている証拠です。

現地の復興と文化財の保護という点で問題になるのが、道路や宅地の復旧開発、住宅の高台への移転などにあたって、松島など国の特別史跡に指定されている土地などの景観維持の義務と、新たな土地の発掘調査の義務です。これらの義務を厳格に維持することは、現地の復興の足かせになりかねません。他方で人命最優先とはいえ、無秩序な乱開発は、大事な景観や地中に埋もれている重要な遺跡を損ない、将来に禍根を残すことにつながり兼ねません。そこで文化庁は、開発のニーズや緊急性と、文化財保護の重要性のバランスをとるべく、地元との間に協議体をつくったり、発掘調査の範囲を限定し、またその調査費を例外的に国の全額補助の対象にしました。

また公立の文化施設についても、その復旧のための財政的助成を行っています。同時に被災地での文化芸術活動そのものを復活することで、被災者の精神的な支えを築くことを目的として、いくつかの新たな事業を始めました。その

ひとつが、子供たちに文化芸術を体験させるものです。被災地の学校や避難所で厳しい生活を余儀なくされ、また災害のトラウマに悩む子供たちが、健やかに勉強し、生活していけるように、県や政令指定都市が実行委員会をつくり、地元ごとの具体的な希望を募り、それに呼応するアーティストたちを派遣するシステムです。昨年9月から具体的な派遣を開始し、これまでに458件の実施が決まっています。

さらに、より広く地元の様々な文化芸術活動へのニーズをくみ上げ、それに応えていくために、文化庁が核となりつつ、アーティスト、芸術団体、企業ネットワーク、財団などによって構成されるコンソーシアムをつくり、4月1日に正式に立ち上がります。一方で被災地の文化芸術活動のニーズが多様であると同時に、他方でアーティストのオファーも多様です。そうした情報の全体像を一元的に把握することは極めて難しく、きめ細かいマッチングをすることが非常に困難です。そこで様々な支援を行っている関係者・団体が、現地の事情に関する知識や経験を持ちより、情報交換や連帯を話し合う緩やかなネットワークをつくることにしたのです。この仕組みは、今回の復興の後も、他の地域での災害その他の際にも応用することができると期待しています。

4.今後の計画

今後は、これまでのさまざまな取り組みを継続・発展しつつ、文化財の本格的修理・修復が始まることが予想されます。また文化芸術活動の振興の面でも、ハード、ソフトの両面で種々の企画が検討されています。その中には、新しい街づくりの過程に、アーティストの意見や提案を活かすために、現地にアーティスト・イン・レジデンスをつくり、内外のアーティストを一定期間住まわせる仕組みや、東北の文化芸術祭を開設するなど、意欲的な提案も見られます。また動く劇場をつくって、東北地域を巡回させるなどのアイデアもあるようです。こうした企画において重要なことは、これからの街づくりが、そこに住むひとびとにとって単に安全、効率的で便利なものであるだけでなく、心がなごみ、楽しく、幸せに暮らせるものになるように進められることです。それによって町に魅力が生まれ、大都会に行った若い人たちが帰ってくるだけでなく、他の地域からも集まってくるようになれば、それが復興にとって大きな力となるからです。

Seiichi Kondo
Commissioner, Agency for Cultural Affairs

1. The activities of the Agency for Cultural Affairs until now
The activities of the Agency for Cultural Affairs directly after the disaster divide into the following seven types:
(1) Grasping and inspecting the state of damage to cultural properties and cultural halls, and the effects on performances, and so on.
(2) Salvation and emergency measures for cultural properties and facilities affected by the disaster, and full renovation and restoration.
(3) Flexible operation of regulations on buried cultural properties and designated historic sites.
(4) Securing the necessary budget for repairs and restoration, and calling for donations domestically and abroad.
(5) Providing a range of cultural events, performances and experiences to encourage the afflicted areas, and constructing a system for connecting the needs of the devastated areas with willing artists and groups.
(6) Measures for mitigating so-called harmful rumors.
(7) Calling for a refrain from excessive self-restraint.

First of all, we conducted inspections of cultural properties such as temples and shrines, and arts and crafts, and the cultural facilities in the afflicted areas where these are stored or exhibited, including art museums, museums, and music halls. Fundamentally, we requested the local governments to do this and then report to us on the conclusions of their on-site inspections. In areas severely devastated, the priority of the local governments was to address humanitarian concerns, such as the search and rescue of survivors, recovering dead bodies, giving immediate care to victims, and securing lifelines; consideration needed to be given in order not to interfere with this. Also for the dispatching of specialists by the central government, it would not be possible to conduct effective inspections safely without local reception and support systems in place. Here the lessons from the Great Hanshin-Awaji Earthquake were fully harnessed. The reports from the local authorities started from an early stage. Partial reports on the state of afflicted cultural properties arrived from certain authorities as early as the day after the earthquake, and the numbers increased day by day. Naturally, reports were delayed from Fukushima where people were not able to enter certain areas due to the nuclear accident. Even so, in early 2012 when the nuclear power plant was under control to a certain degree, a team was immediately sent to important cave sites and was able to confirm partial damage.

There were surveys carried out on 744 National Treasures, Important Cultural Properties, Special Historic Sites and other examples of officially designated cultural heritage in Tokyo and eighteen other prefectures, including three severely devastated by the disaster (Iwate, Miyagi and Fukushima). Though this far exceeded the 173 from the Great Hanshin-Awaji Earthquake, fortunately there was damage to National Treasures in just five cases, and these were only modest.

Further, damaged cultural facilities numbered 290 in Tokyo and fifteen other prefectures, of which the damage was mostly hall ceilings that had fallen in, damage to stage equipment, broken walls or windows, or plumbing or electrical system failures. As a result, many performances were canceled or postponed for reasons of safety.

2. The response in the everyday life of the population and society, and from artists

This calamity had a large impact on the lifestyle of the population. The first was that it gave "meaning" to the triple hardships of the earthquake, tsunami and nuclear accident for everyone. Questions such as "What happened?" and "What went wrong?" sprung up. According to a certain philosopher, when problems occur, questions such as "How can this be resolved?" proliferate, yet in this case, there were many primitive questions.

But on the other hand, along with the many who noted the overconfidence of science and technology, and the deficiency of the crisis-management system, there was also much debate about civilization, such as the loss of the reverence towards nature that the Japanese had had from long ago (that is, the arrogance of humanity that considers it can control nature through science and technology), and the negative aspects of modern western civilization (promoting materialism, efficiency, and striving to achieve personal ambitions) that had come to the fore.

Faced with a calamity like this, there were many who questioned what they could do, or who felt powerless and irritated that they could not do anything, and this could often be seen among artists and groups. Many asked highly anguished questions such as "What can art do at a time like this?" or "Hasn't this demonstrated that art doesn't contribute to society?"

This led to two contradictory tendencies. One was a national mood of self-restraint. Having lost so many precious lives and with so many people in mourning and suffering, it became prevalent to ask whether it was right for those of us who survived and cannot do anything to just continue on with our fun lives, and so a situation ensued for some months where music events, theater, Rakugo,[1] fine art exhibitions and so on had to be canceled. The days went by without revealing any catalyst for life to return to normal, and the heartache continued for the artists and artistic groups. Despite no one having commanded it, a feeling spread among the Japanese that music and dance must be restrained. (This social climate also diminished consumption and had a bad effect on the economy, though at the same time, greatly contributed to frugality in power consumption during the summer, and thus the feared power cuts during times of peak demand could be avoided.)

In addition to this, overseas artists and art collectors anguished over how the effects of the Fukushima power plant accident successively canceled performances and exhibitions in Japan at the last moment, which took a great financial toll on music venues and art museums.

Concerned about this, I made an announcement on April 12th that the excessive self-restraint regarding cultural and artistic activities was stagnating society more than was necessary and, being counterproductive to the social strength required for reconstruction, it should be halted. Along with sending this by fax to cultural and artistic groups, it was also published on the official website of the Agency for Cultural Affairs. This drew many favorable responses. And by inviting diplomats in Tokyo to charity concerts and Kabuki performances, they relayed to their own countries that Japan's arts were healthy. I also visited the dressing rooms of artists who came to Japan while this was all happening to perform, and held a reception party to welcome the

1. A traditional form of Japanese entertainment, performed by a solo storyteller who relates a comical narrative.

performers who had come from overseas for the La Folle Journée in Tokyo in May. I was moved by how one soprano singer even brought her eight-month child with her in spite of the misgivings of those around her and performed the lead role in an opera as planned. When I went to her dressing room to give my thanks, she appeared with her child, a nanny, and her own mother, telling me: "Coming to Japan to sing at a time like this is the only thing I can do for the Japanese people."

The other tendency was, on the contrary, the enthusiastic campaign to console the victims of the disaster through culture and the arts, and the growing discussion over the size of the future role to be performed in Tohoku reconstruction by culture and the arts. The former started from quite an early stage at the evacuation centers and schools, where, though the food necessary for surviving and a place to sleep had been secured, the prospects for a life and occupation after this were not promising. People were depressed on a daily level by the trauma of the tsunami and those they had lost, and among them there were many who wanted to listen to music or to Rakugo. Those who had been sparing the feelings of the saddened refugees around them became unable to bear it and voiced these wishes. Many artists responded to this and it became a large movement.

It is also notable here that in Tohoku there were many festivals and traditional performing arts, and it was these local festivals and events inherited from their ancestors that healed the people damaged by the disaster, and that reanimated a sense of community. A famous example is the Soma-Nomaoi in Soma City and other places in Fukushima Prefecture. Every year for three days at the end of July, eight cities, towns and villages jointly hold this traditional festival, but a part of the site was now in the nuclear power plant no-go zone, and the event was in danger of not being held, but thanks to the strong wishes of the locals, it was partially carried out only in the areas outside the exclusion zone. In Takenoura, an area in the town of Onagawa in Miyagi Prefecture, the victims of the disaster were divided and forced to live in three evacuation centers, but by restoring and repairing the tools washed away or damaged by the tsunami, they were able to hold the traditional lion dance and recover their sense of community and vitality.

As a result of the circulation of this information, it became apparent early on that the local people had recognized the importance for the restoration of tangible and intangible cultural properties in the process of reconstruction from the disaster, in the same way as they recognized the need to restore residences and infrastructures. It was also widely reported in the media, and the report made by former Prime Minister Naoto Kan's Reconstruction Design Council in June specified the importance of the role played by culture and the arts in the reconstruction process.

3. Projects currently in progress

The Agency for Cultural Affairs started the Cultural Heritage Rescue Project straight after the disaster. This system was made based on the lessons from the Great Hanshin-Awaji Earthquake, and it surveyed and rescued the cultural properties hit by the disaster, especially arts and crafts—the heritage designated nationally such as National Treasures and Important Cultural Properties—and carried out emergency repairs as necessary. It found and removed cultural properties buried under rubble and submerged in water, and inspected the state of damage and performed reparatory measures to prevent further damage, and then stored them in safekeeping in a secure place in preparation for full restoration. If simply left as they were, they would be removed with the rubble or their condition would worsen due to the effects of water. For this work, an enormous number of manpower is required, along with the cooperation of the local people, as well as specialist knowledge and experts in each field. It is not something that the Agency for Cultural Affairs can do just by itself. It requested the cooperation of art museums, museums, research institutes, and universities from around the country with knowledge and manpower about cultural heritage, forming a truly national system. It was also vital to secure places where the cultural properties salvaged and given emergency care could be stored for a long period. This is because it was also important to protect the valuable cultural properties that had been rescued from art thieves who might appear at the sites from overseas. At the time of the Great Hanshin-Awaji Earthquake, thieves from neighboring countries apparently arrived on the sites the day after the disaster. In the height of the confusion where it is not clear who is who, and in a situation when anyone can get away with saying they had come to volunteer and help out, such people would be able to achieve their goals. Therefore it was necessary to deposit the rescued cultural properties in an archive, such as a museum, where they could be locked away, and the temperature and climate maintained. However, each facility had its own issues of space and the costs to be incurred, and so we could not depend on them indefinitely. As of March 1st, 2012, a total of 4,829 persons had participated in the operation of this project. In the course of this, it was natural that we did this for all the cultural properties we found, not only the nationally designated cultural properties but also those designated by the regional government bodies.

Learning from this, we also established the Cultural Properties Doctor Dispatch Project for architecture and real estate, sending investigators to 198 cities, towns and villages in eleven prefectures. For these two projects, we also used the Foundation for Cultural Heritage and Art Research as the interface for collecting donations from the private sector in order to secure the funds we were lacking, collecting a total of over ¥200 million from Japan and overseas.

The Agency for Cultural Affairs acquired an additional budget of ¥3.2 billion for the restoration and repairs of cultural properties damaged in the disaster, on top of the initial budget for the 2011 fiscal year. For the 2012 fiscal year budget, the Agency was allocated ¥1.9 billion. In spite of the financial difficulties, that we were able to secure a sum of this kind was proof that the repair and restoration of cultural properties was widely recognized in society as an important pillar of the reconstruction. Where reconstruction and the preservation of cultural heritage become problematic is in the obligation to preserve scenery of landscape in designated Special Historic Sites such as Matsushima and during the excavation of new land ahead of the redevelopment of roads and residential land, and when relocating to residences on higher ground. Rigorously preserving these duties shackles reconstruction. While human life is indeed given the greatest priority, disordered overdevelopment can also lead to harm to precious scenery or important ruins buried in the earth, and graver problems in the future. The Agency for Cultural Affairs had to balance the need for development and the urgency of the situation with the importance of preserving cultural heritage, and it created a consultative body with the local people, limiting the parameters of excavations, and covering the costs of excavations by a full state subsidiary.

We are also subsidizing national cultural facilities for the restorations. Simultaneously, some other new projects have been started aiming to construct spiritual support for the victims of the disaster by revitalizing cultural and artistic activities at the disaster zones. One such project was culture and arts experiences for children. In order for children forced into harsh lives at the schools or evacuation centers in the disaster areas and suffering from the trauma of the catastrophe to be able to live and study healthily, prefectures and government ordinance cities set up planning committees, soliciting the concrete wishes of each locale and then dispatching artists to respond to these. Since it started in September 2012, there have been 458 events held until now.

A consortium was also created with the Agency for Cultural Affairs at its nucleus and made up of artists, artistic groups, corporate networks, and foundations, formally established on April 1st to respond more widely to the diverse local needs for cultural and artistic activities. While these needs for cultural and artistic activities in the areas afflicted by the disaster are very varied, at the same time so too are the offers that come from the artists. Achieving an overall understanding of all this information is extremely difficult, and it is a great challenge to match up the offers and needs precisely. We decided that the relevant people and group involved in providing various kinds of support should create a loose network for exchanging information and discussing cooperation, gathering together expertize and experience on local contexts. We hope that this system can also be applied after the Tohoku reconstruction to other areas when they are hit by a disaster.

4. Future plans

In the future, we anticipate that the various frameworks we have been building until now will continue to develop, and that full renovation and restoration of cultural properties will begin. For the promotion of cultural and artistic activities, a range of projects both hard and soft are under consideration. We can see ambitious proposals here, such as artist-in-residency programs for Japanese and overseas artists to live for a period in the local area so that the opinions and suggestions of artists can be utilized in the process of new town development, as well as setting up cultural and artistic festivals in Tohoku. There are also proposals to create mobile theaters and tour the Tohoku region. What is important here is that the town and city development that takes place from now is not simply something that is safe, efficient and convenient for the people living in the area, but that it can evolve into something that allows them to live with comfort, enjoyment and happiness. If due to this, a town becomes attractive and not only do younger people who went to the big cities return home but people from other areas also move in to the town, then it will become a great force for reconstruction.

橘 正紀

「東京マグニチュード 8.0」監督
株式会社キネマシトラス 取締役

3.11が起きた時、うちのスタジオではちょうどパイロットフィルムとかアニメーションの制作中でした。このスタジオとはもう一つ別にスタジオを借りていまして、その建物がかなり古い建物なんです。

過去にも地震の経験をしているので、最初は地震を楽観的に考えていた印象がありました。でもやはり外に避難した方がいいと思ったのですが、近くには雑居ビルが多くあったり車の通りのある道路だったりと、逃げ場所がないところだったんです。だから都心では、大きい地震が来たからすぐに逃げようと言っても、逃げる場所がないなっていう印象でした。かなりの揺れを経験して、驚きと不安があったのですが、テレビのニュースで初めて事の重大さを知りました。東京の人間は阪神淡路大震災や中越地震を知っていますが、どこか他人事だったんですね。でも今回、東北という200キロ近く離れた所だったんですが、地震の影響で交通網が麻痺して、都心の人間は初めて大地震の影響を経験したと思うんです。ただ、皆落ち着いていましたね。地震当日は交通が麻痺して大分渋滞があったんですが、皆歩いて帰ったり、自転車で帰ったりしていました。

我々も「東京マグニチュード8.0」を作った時、インフラが破壊され、電線が切れて電気が来なくなるとか、道路が壊れて救急車両が来れなくなるという、ある程度の想定はしていたんです。でも原子力発電所が地震で壊れて、しかも放射能の問題を引き起こすとは考えていませんでした。原発が危ないって言われていたけれど、日本人がまさか起こるとは思っていなかった事故でした。そこから世界が一変したという感じでした。

3.11後の状況の情報を、僕はずっとインターネットで収集しました。自分で情報を集めていかないと判断が出来ない時代が来てしまったという印象を持ちました。神戸の地震の時は建物を建て直せばよかったんですけど、今回のは津波が起きて東北地方に甚大な被害をもたらし、しかも福島の原発の問題まであって、まだ解決されてない。この問題を解決するための決定的な回答

を得られないことは、日本が今まで経験した事のない状況であり、そしてとてもナーバスな問題です。

アニメ業界にもクライム・ムービーだとかディザスター・ムービーみたいなものがあって、まだどこまでエンターテイメントでやっていいのか難しい所です。

まだ仮設住宅に住んでいる人達がいたり、家族を亡くした人や生活がきちんとできない人達がいて、我々はその人達に対する配慮をしなくてはいけない。だから我々の業界、新しい作品で反応するにはまだ早いです。現時点、テレビのアニメーションは、見ている人に対して配慮しつつ、エンターテイメントを損なわないような感じで作っています。

もちろん、表現にはみんな気をつけていますが、アニメに関しては、やはり娯楽作品だから。見る人達が悲しかった事とか、ちょっと現実を忘れて楽しんでもらえるように我々は努力しようと。アニメがトラウマのようなものを取り入れて、人々のトラウマを消化させるところまではまだ立ち直ってないと思います。やはり、社会や一般の人達が問題を共通認識としてもって、初めてエンターテイメントとして紹介できるんですね。だからまだ、過去を反省するにしても早いと感じます。

阪神淡路大震災は建物が壊れただけだったから、瓦礫をとって建て直せばよかったんですが、福島の場合はそうじゃない。今もまだ復興がままならないっていう現実がある。阪神淡路大震災の直後は、非常に活動的に地震に対してどう取り組むべきかという本がいっぱい出たんですよ。我々も「東京マグニチュード8.0」を作る時に、地震が起きた時にどういうふうにすべきかという資料をたくさん見ました。

大きい地震を経験して、我々はそれを教訓にしなければならないということで、非常に前向きにそういう本がたくさん出版されたり、今回の地震の前に「252 生存者あり」(2008)という映画が日本テレビで作られたりしました。「252」とは日本のハイパーレスキューの中での暗号で「要救助者あり」という意味なんです。我々も地震に対してどういうふうに行動すべきかを考えてもらうアニメを作りました。だから日本を直撃した地震に関して、あの時点までは積極的に取り組んでいました。

東日本大震災直後我々は、ワンシーンで地震が出てくる「英雄伝説 空の軌跡 THE ANIMATION」という作品を作らなければなりませんでした。原作にあったシーンだから入れざるを得なかったんで、あまり大きく取り上げず、さらっと表現する配慮をしました。自由に思いや今の緊張を表現するよりも、見る

東京マグニチュード
8.0 - フィルムコミック
*TOKYO MAGNITUDE
8.0* (film comic)
©Tokyo Magnitude
8.0 Committee

人達にとって楽しめる内容にするほうがいいんじゃないかと思います。SFの世界で一時期、核エネルギーは人類の未来を切り開くかもしれないっていうので「鉄腕アトム」がありました。その後になると、原子力は危ないっていうのでクリーンなエネルギーが出てきました。最近SFを見る人達の知識が多くなってきて、リアリティーのある設定を求められるシーンが多くなっています。エネルギーの問題で例えば、日本は地熱発電を作れるから実際現実のエネルギーの替わりになるのではないかと、引用することが出来るのではないかと思います。この前テレビで見たのですが、アイスランドは火山地帯なので、地熱発電を利用しているらしいんですね。その発電に日本の発電機が使われていて、そういう情報をアニメの中に入れて紹介したりという手助けが出来るのではないかという気はします。

3.11後、「東京マグニチュード8.0」の反響は非常に大きかったですね。このアニメには、家族の絆とか、地震が起きた時どういうふうに対応すべきかを入れてあるんですね。つまり、日常がある幸せというものを知って欲しいというのをテーマにおいていたんです。ディザスター・ムービーにしては治安が悪くなって人が暴れるというシーンが出てこないっていう話をよく聞くんですが、荒廃した世界よりも、人間のモラルとか性善説を信じて、助け合って生きていくことを考えて欲しいっていうのが「東京マグニチュード8.0」のテーマなんですね。地

震が起きたときに家族や人に対してどういうふうに行動するべきかを考えさせられたという意見を頂いて、我々の伝えたい部分を感じてもらえたのがうれしかったです。

3.11を経験した後で、このような作品を作るのは非常に難しいと思っています。地震が起きた後で、とてもデリケートな問題なのですが、見ているファンの方々や防災関係の人から再放送をという声が届いています。ただこのアニメは阪神淡路大震災から復興しきった状態、十数年経ったから出来たんです。今、「東京マグニチュード8.0」を再放送しようというのは、大多数が見る中で、まだ正解を導き出せないまま今も3.11の悲劇が続いていて、生活をしている人達の気持ちに対する配慮が欠けることになるかもしれないのです。

3.11のあとに知ったんですけど、「風が吹くとき」(1987)というアニメーションがあって、おそらくチェルノブイリの事故直後か早い時期に作られた映画なんですね。それは一組の老夫婦が公に出た情報を信じて家に残り、徐々に被爆し、ゆるやかに死んでいくという、非常に社会的なフィルムです。これは、いま日本が直面している問題なのですが、まだ日本にとってはデリケートでナーバスな問題なのです。

アニメ業界や映画業界ではSF作品を通して、社会に対する不満や、もっとこうあるべきだというポジティブな意見を出してきました。放射能の核実験や水爆実験の問題があった時にゴジラが生まれて、公害の問題があってヘドラが生まれました。サンライズのガンダムシリーズも動力が原子炉で、それを破壊してしまったら居住区まで汚染されてしまうという。だからこれらの例は実際に起こった事を使って、一般の人達の意見を通してメッセージを表現しているのです。

ゴジラやガンダムなどの社会問題をテーマにしたものとは別に、新たに3.11の問題を反省するようなアニメを作るには、まだ何年もかかると思います。おそらく、海外に向けてこの3.11について考えてもらうアニメを作る方が簡単だと思います。アニメ業界は風俗・通俗文化や流行り廃りに流されていくものなのですが、作品の内容や見ている人達に向けて配慮をするようにしています。テレビのアニメーションというのは楽しみたいから見るものなので、楽しんでもらおうという気持ちでちゃんと作る、そういう気遣いの方が大切だなって思います。なので、3.11をテーマにアニメを作るには、まだ時間がかかると思います。

Masaki Tachibana
Director, Tokyo Magnitude 8.0
Director, Kinema Citrus

When 3.11 happened, I was working on an animation pilot at our studio. The studio is another one we rent and the building is quite old. I've experienced earthquakes in the past, so at first I was optimistic. And then I thought I'd better evacuate outside, but there were lots of multi-tenant buildings nearby, plus a road with traffic, so I didn't have anywhere to go. It really felt like in a big city, even if you say you should escape straightway when an earthquake happens, there is actually nowhere to go. I was surprised and uneasy when I experienced the large tremors, but it was when I watched the TV news that I then knew just how big it was. People in Tokyo know about the Great Hanshin-Awaji Earthquake and the Niigata Chuetsu earthquake, but they were someone else's problem. This time, though it was a place nearly 200km away, the transportation network was paralysed due to the influence of the earthquake, and I think that people in the city center experienced the impact of a large quake for the first time. And yet everyone was very calm. On that day, transportation was paralysed and traffic was in gridlock, but everyone walked or cycled home.

When we made *Tokyo Magnitude 8.0*,[1] to a certain extent we envisaged the infrastructure being destroyed, electricity lines being cut, the power going out, roads being damaged and ambulances unable to get to places. But we never considered a nuclear power station being destroyed by an earthquake, moreover it triggering the problem of radiation leakage. "Nuclear power is dangerous" was something that was often said, but this was an accident that the Japanese didn't think would really happen. It felt like the world completely changed afterwards.

I was constantly collecting information online about the situation after 3.11. I had this impression that now was the time when unless I gathered information myself, I wouldn't be able to tell anything. When there was the Kobe earthquake it was just a case of reconstructing the buildings, but this time there was a tsunami and it caused massive damage across

[1]. An anime series that ran for eleven episodes in 2009 on Fuji TV.

Tohoku, as well as there being the problems at Fukushima, which still haven't been resolved. It was a situation Japan had never experienced till now, one of not being able to obtain the decisive answer for how to resolve the problems, not to mention that it was very nerve-wracking.

In the anime industry, there are genres like crime and disaster movies, but there is then this difficult question of how far you can go with entertainment.

There are still people living in temporary housing and people who have lost their families or cannot live properly, and we have to be considerate of them. That's why it's still too soon for our industry to respond with a new anime. At the present moment, TV animation is being mindful of the people who are watching, while also still providing entertainment.

Of course, people are being careful about how they present things, but actually, anime is just entertainment. We endeavor to make things where the people watching can enjoy themselves and forget about reality, such as how they are sad about something. Things haven't yet recovered enough for anime to be able to incorporate traumatic things and assimilate people's traumas. After these problems have been recognized and shared by society and ordinary people, they can then become entertainment for the first time. That's why it still feels early to reflect on the past.

In the Great Hanshin-Awaji Earthquake, it was just the buildings that were destroyed, so we could take away the rubble and then rebuild. But with Fukushima it's different. Even now the reconstruction isn't going fast enough. Immediately after the Great Hanshin-Awaji Earthquake, a ton of books came out which looked at how to actively tackle earthquakes. When we made *Tokyo Magnitude 8.0*, we also looked at lots of resources about what to do if an earthquake happened.

Having experienced this big earthquake, many books were published that were very positive about learning lessons from it, and before the 2011 earthquake Nippon Television made a film called *252: Signal of Life* (2008). "252" is a code sent out to rescue services in Japan and means that people are in need of rescue. We had also made an anime that asked people to think about how they should behave in an earthquake. So by March 11th, 2011, a lot of media had dealt with an earthquake hitting Japan.

Immediately after the Tohoku earthquake, we had to make the anime film adaptation of *The Legend of Heroes: Trails in the Sky*, in which there is a scene with an earthquake. The scene was in the original so we had to include it, but we didn't make such a big thing out of the way we presented it. Rather than expressing ideas freely on the current tension, we thought content where the viewer could have fun was better. At one time science fiction like *Astro Boy*[2] was saying that nuclear energy would open the way to the future for humanity. And then after that, people said that nuclear power was dangerous and green energy came along. Sci-fi audiences have grown very smart in recent years and so there is a demand for scenes with more realistic settings. With the energy issue, for example, in anime we could draw on how it might be possible to replace current energy in Japan by building geothermal power generation. I saw on television the other day how Iceland is apparently using geothermal power generation, as it is volcanic. Japanese generators are being used for this, and I feel it would be helpful if we could introduce this to audiences by including the information in anime.

After 3.11, we got an incredible amount of feedback about *Tokyo Magnitude 8.0*. The anime series asks how the bonds in a family should respond if an earthquake happened. Our theme was getting audiences to understand the happiness of everyday life. We are often told that for a disaster movie, there aren't any scenes where law and order breaks down and people are going wild. But rather than destruction, we believe in humanity's morality, that people are fundamentally good, and making people think about how to live and help each other out is the theme of *Tokyo Magnitude 8.0*. People said that it made them think about how they should act towards their families and other people if an earthquake happened, and I'm so happy that viewers felt what we were trying to say. But having experienced 3.11, making this kind of work would now be extremely difficult. After the earthquake it was a very sensitive issue, and we were urged to broadcast it again by fans and people involved in disaster prevention. But this series was made only once ten years had passed after the Great Hanshin-Awaji Earthquake, and after the reconstruction was over. If we were to re-broadcast *Tokyo Magnitude 8.0* now, among the viewers there would be people for whom the tragedy of 3.11 is continuing, for whom a solution to their problems has yet to be found, and that would probably be lacking in consideration for the feelings of the people living today.

2. Classic Japanese manga by Osamu Tezuka and adapted in 1963 into the first major TV anime series.

3. A 1986 animated film adaptation of the celebrated graphic novel by Raymond Briggs (1982) about a nuclear attack on Britain by the USSR. Released in Japan in 1987.

4. A monster that appeared in the film *Godzilla vs. Hedorah* (1971) and who feeds on toxic waste.

I learned about it after 3.11, but there is an animation film called *When the Wind Blows*,[3] which seems to have been made soon after the Chernobyl accident. It's a film very much about society, depicting an elderly couple who trust the information released to the public and remain in their home, and little by little are contaminated by nuclear fallout and gradually die. This is a very political film. This is the problem directly facing Japan today, but it is still a very sensitive and scary one.

The anime and film industry has used sci-fi to express discontent or proactive opinions about what society should be doing. When there was the issue of radiation from the nuclear and hydrogen bomb tests, then we had Godzilla, and the pollution problem gave us Hedorah.[4] In Sunrise's *Gundam* series, the power for the characters comes from a nuclear reactor and when it is damaged, residential areas are polluted. So we see in these examples how they use things that actually happened to express a message through the views of ordinary people. Aside from these social themes dealt with by Godzilla and *Gundam*, I think it will still take many years to make an anime that reflects on the problems of 3.11. It would probably be easier to make an anime about it for overseas audiences. The anime industry is influenced by popular culture and the latest trends, so it is considerate of content and the viewer. TV anime is something we watch because it seems fun, so people think that what is important is making something for people to enjoy. This is why I feel that it will still take time before we can make an anime about 3.11.

タニノクロウ
劇作家・演出家・元精神科医

今現在は、基本的に医療活動はやっていないんです。2010年まで精神科医として働いていたのですが、辞めました。一方私は、劇作家、演出家としても今年で11年経ちます。震災直後は、この二つの職業をもつことに対して複雑な思いを抱えていました。

3月11日から数日後、私は静岡で行われる「ふじのくに⇄せかい演劇祭」に参加するため東京から静岡に行きました。公演は6月4、5日だったんですけど、現地滞在製作でしたので、その約3ヶ月間は準備のために静岡にずっと滞在してました。

我々の「庭劇団ペニノ」がその演劇祭に出るのは、2年近く前から決まっていたんです。私たちの拠点は東京です。滞在したSPAC（Shizuoka Performing Arts Center）の舞台芸術公園は色んな劇場や施設があったり、作品を準備するために必要なすべての道具や機材がある場所で、その様な場所で滞在製作ができるということは贅沢で理想的でした。そこで我々が発表したのが「エクスターズ」という作品です。

「エクスターズ」ふじのくに⇄せかい演劇祭2011@静岡・舞台芸術公園 野外劇場「有度」
Extase (World Theatre Festival Shizuoka under Mt. Fuji 2011) at Open Air Theatre UDO, Shizuoka Performing Arts Park
撮影：静岡県舞台芸術センター
Photo: Shizuoka Performing Arts Center

静岡に行き、その場所の空気を感じてから創作を始めようと思っていたので、「エクスターズ」は3.11後から製作に取りかかりました。とても、影響を受けました。でも、その作品の演出部分に震災の影響があったかどうか自覚はありません。これは非常に説明が難しいところなのですが、簡単に申し上げますと、戯曲と演出は別の自分が働いているという事です。善の戯曲に悪の演出を付ける事で作品が豊かなものになる事もあるという事です。

私はこの時点では被災地に行っていません。メディアを通してしか現状を分かってませんでした。私が実際被災地に行ったのは、演劇祭が終わってからなんです。演劇祭後は毎週末、今現在まで、医療活動の場合もあればそうでない場合もあるんですが、被災地に通っています。

話を戻しますと、この3.11後の作品「エクスターズ」は、私が被災地を見て作ったものではないということになります。ここが重要なところです。

この作品は野外劇場で行われました。私はいつも舞台美術を最初に決めてから始めるのですが、山奥の見渡す限りの大自然、その景観に自然の暴力性を感じずにはいられず、10m以上ある壁をセットとして作って、客席から見える森の木々たちを全て隠してしまったんです。野外劇でやる場合、やっぱりその醍醐味でもある自然を含めた借景を利用するのが定石なんですけども、私はそれを全部隠しちゃった。もう、自然なんか見たくないって。自然と対抗したセットでした。これが僕の震災に対する最初の反応だと思います。被災地に行きその光景を見た後であれば、また別の反応が起きたでしょう。普段のままでいる事は難しかったでしょうから。

私の希望で、出演者のほとんどを70歳を越えるおばあちゃん達にしました。静岡の県民劇団に入っている人たちです。しかし彼女たちは舞台経験の少ない人、またはほぼ無い人たちでした。野外劇も初めてでしたが、このようなご年配の方々を迎えてというのも初めてでした。

一流の俳優や演出家が集う国際演劇祭でこのような事をするのは、はっきり言えば掟破りのようなものです。しかし、2日間の2ステージということでしたので、私は鍛えられたプロの俳優を使うよりも、何かもっと、短い生、なす術無くそろそろ終わる生といいますか、弱い人間を舞台に上げたかった。

台詞は無くってすべて歌です。もちろんそれだけの年齢の方達に台詞は覚えられません。歌は、例えば「ふるさと」や「庭の千草」、「サラスポンダ」のような、いわゆる唱歌とか民謡を皆で歌いました。私はあのような悲劇の中、遠くに暮

らす母の事を思い出しました。そして母にどのような余生を過ごしてほしいかを考える事を発想の起点にしました。母が友人や子供たちと過ごす、死までの穏やかなひとときです。

舞台セットは大きな架空の老人ホームといった感じでしょうか、その中のプレイルームのような場所。滑り台や登り棒、ブランコに鉄棒など遊具がたくさん置いてあります。そして、ピアノにカラオケ用としてのレコードプレーヤーとマイク。もちろんおばあちゃんたちは遊具で遊ぶ事は出来ません。観賞用です。音楽がかかり、踊りたくても踊れません。彼女たちが出来る事は歌う事だけです。それと、歌い疲れたらテレビを見てトイレに行くくらい。観客は俳優が当たり前に出来ることを何も出来ない彼女たちの姿を舞台上に観ます。そして彼女たちが記憶の中に辛うじて覚えている歌の歌声を聞きます。伴奏も時に間違え、歌詞も間違えます。ハーモニーも崩れて行きます。それでも彼女たちはありったけのエネルギーを出しました。上手く動きたい、上手く歌いたい、美しく可愛く見られたい。でも上手には出来ません。しかし、彼女たちは「楽しさ」ということを、言葉を越えて観るものの胸に響かせてみせました。

当時、観客の誰もが、震災に対する心の傷を負って生きていました。

例えば10メートルの舞台セットの壁に対して、特に最前列に座った人は強く反応していました。舞台の壁と津波を比べてしまうこと、高さを想像し恐怖することは、そのとき自然なことでした。

しかしその壁は、野外劇だという舞台効果をさらに大きくするためにとても重要だったと思います。常に自然のにおいだとか鳥の鳴き声、動物の鳴き声も聞こえて、車の音も、そして急に強い風が吹いたりして、劇場は谷底に位置してたんで。野外劇だけど自然の借景を遮蔽することによって、お客さんの想像をより広げつつ、見ることができない自然、だけれどもそれを感覚で感じるようなものになり、自然との共生、共存を感じさせるものになりました。それは心地よいものであるということ。

作品を作る段階でとても重要なことがありました。この作品のセットの壁には膨大な量の木の板を使っています。この資材は福島、東北地方から来る予定だったんですが、流通の問題があったり、通信がきちんと動かなかったり、静岡でもなかなか資材が手に入らなかった時期でした。なので、関係者の中にも「たった2回の公演でこんなにたくさんの資材を使っていいの?」という人もいました。使う方も慎重にならざるを得ない状況でもあったし、でもその必要性を理

解し、最終的には皆賛成しました。資材はフェスティバルのオープニングの公演で使ったので、その後の公演にも再利用できたし、その板の大部分は知的障害者の施設に送って、壁画用の壁として再利用できました。だから、実際は色んな形で再利用できました。

将来、医療行為を再開すると思います。というのも、被災地にいる医師が減ってしまったからです。日本は全国的に医師不足ですが、今回の状況でさらに深刻になります。ですから再開しなければいけません。私は演劇を作ることを選んだんですが、被災地に何度も行くと、医療活動がとても重要だと感じます。私は4年間、仙台で非常勤で勤務していたので、東北には知り合いが多くいます。震災から3ヶ月後、被災地に何度も行って、向こうの心のケアに携わりました。多くの人たちは津波の到達したところから数センチ、数メートルで助かった人達です。津波が到達した所は何も無くなっている、反対に到達していない所にいた人は助かり、そしてその多くの助かった人たちが津波に飲まれていく人達を間際で目視している。これ以上の過酷な体験ってあるでしょうか？

手を伸ばしたり、手をつかんだことも出来ただろうし、でも届かなかったり、手を握っていたとしても波の力が強くて手を離してしまったり。このような体験をした方達を診るというのは困難です。医師たちも経験したことも想像した事もない状況ですから。しかし、それに立ち向かわなくてはいけません。

なので、私はこれから、演出家と医師としての自分が、お互い強く影響しあうであろうと思っています。これはかつて無い事で、混乱が予想されます。そしてそれは演劇作品を作る者としていい結果を生まないかもしれませんね。その可能性は高いと思いますが、そんなことはどうだって良いことです。

そして、原発の問題があります。原発の問題はこの先長い期間続き、忘れたくても忘れられないことです。いや、そういう次元じゃない。少なくとも今生きている人たちが死ぬまでには解決しません。そもそもそんな短期間で放射能汚染は消えません。原発の問題はとても根深く、長い間話し続けられるでしょう。「ついに」と言って良いと思いますが、政府と国民との直接的な対話が生まれると思います。政治がそう動かざるを得ません。そして偽物の民主政治が無くなるでしょう。被災地だけではなく、日本の新しい社会を作るために。

Kuro Tanino

Playwright, theater director, former psychiatrist

I no longer work in the medical field. I worked as a psychiatrist until 2010, but I have now quit. It has been eleven years since I started my career as a playwright and theater director. I have had mixed feelings about having these two careers since the disaster.

A few days after March 11th, I went from Tokyo to Shizuoka to participate in World Theatre Festival Shizuoka under Mt. Fuji. While the performance of my theater company was scheduled for June 4th and 5th, I was in Shizuoka for three months prior to the show to prepare for the work that we were creating on site there.

My company Niwa Gekidan Penino accepted the offer to take part in the festival around two years before. We are based in Tokyo. Along with its many theaters and facilities, Shizuoka Performing Arts Center (SPAC) is also equipped with every tool necessary for creating a new production, so staying and producing our work in that environment was a real luxury and very ideal. We premiered *Extase* at the festival.

Hoping to reflect what we felt in Shizuoka in our creative process, we started working on *Extase* after 3.11. The disaster had a huge impact on me but I'm not sure if it influenced my directing work. It's hard to explain but to put it simply, the playwright in me and the director in me are not the same personality. Adding "evil" direction to a play of "virtue" can create a rich work of art.

At that time, I still had not been to the disaster areas, so my understanding of the disaster only came from the media. I visited the regions hits by the disaster only after the festival was over. Since then, I have been visiting Tohoku regularly every weekend for both medical and non-medical activities.

To go back to the production in Shizuoka, it is important to note that I created it without actually going to the disaster areas.

Extase was premiered in an open-air theater. I normally design the set before anything else. Looking at the grandeur stretching as far as you could see, I could not help but feel the violence of nature. We built a set of walls ten meters high, covering every forest tree visible to audiences because I didn't want to see nature anymore. The stage design was counteracting nature; this was my first reaction to the disaster. My response would have been different if I had gone to the devastated areas and seen the destruction prior to starting work on the production because then I probably would not have been able to keep things as normal.

I wanted the actors to be old women over 70 years old who belong to a citizens' theater company in Shizuoka. They had very little or no prior experience of stage acting. This was the first time that I had staged an open-air theater performance as well as worked with elderly people.

Doing these things at an international festival where top actors and directors gather was frankly against the "rules." But given that we were only giving two performances over two days, I wanted to put people on the stage whose lives, so to speak, were coming to an end, working with fragile people, rather than professional actors.

There was no dialogue, only songs, because older people cannot memorize lines. They sang folk songs together, such as *Furusato* (Hometown), *Niwano chigusa* (The Last Rose of Summer), and *Sarasponda*. In the aftermath of 3.11, I was thinking about my mother who lives far away and how I wanted her to live the rest of her life, and this was a starting point for conceiving the play. I imagined her spending a very peaceful time with her friends and children until she dies.

The stage set looked like a recreation room inside an imaginary, large nursing home. On the stage there was a slide, a climbing pole, swing, and horizontal bar, as well as a piano and record player with a microphone for karaoke. Of course, the old women could not use the playground equipment. They could only watch them. They could not dance to music even if they had wanted to. All they could do was sing and watch TV once they were tired of singing, and go to the bathroom. Audiences saw how these ladies could not do anything professional actors are supposed to do on stage, and heard them singing songs they barely managed to remember. The piano accompaniment was off and the lyrics were wrong, while the harmony collapsed. The old women used up all the energy they had hoping to move nicely, sing well, and look beautiful, despite that they could not do any of this. They nevertheless moved audiences to an extent that went beyond "fun."

At that time the audience was living with the scars of the disaster. Audiences sitting in the front row reacted very strongly to the ten-meter walls of the stage set. It was natural for audiences to compare the walls with a tsunami wave and feel fear at the height.

But erecting the walls was crucial to emphasizing the effect of the open-air theater. Audiences could smell nature, hear the birds and animals singing, and the sounds of cars. Located in the floor of a valley, the walls of the stage set helped audiences expand their imagination while making them *feel* nature rather than see it visually. I think the set could make audiences feel the importance of a symbiotic relationship with nature and how comfortable that relationship is.

There was a significant moment in the process of making the production. We used a massive quantity of wooden panels for building the walls. These panels were supposed to come from Fukushima and the Tohoku region. But it was hard to get them delivered to Shizuoka because of problems in circulation and communication. Some people even asked me: "Is it reasonable to use this many wooden panels for only two performances?" The circumstances did make me very circumspect about how I wanted to use them, but in the end everyone agreed with me and understood the necessity for them. The panels used for the opening performance were reused for subsequent performances, and were actually reused in a variety of forms, most of them being sent to a facility for the mentally disabled to be used for wall paintings.

I think I will restart medical practice at some point in the future. The number of doctors in the disaster areas has been decreasing. The shortage of doctors in Japan will be even more severe after the disaster. That's the reason I want to restart my practice. I chose theater over medicine, but going to the disaster areas, I'm always reminded of how important medical activities are. I have a lot of acquaintances in Tohoku because I worked there as a part-time doctor for four years. I went to Tohoku three months after the disaster and treated people who were traumatized. Survivors can be people who were merely a few centimeters or meters from where the tsunami reached. While nothing is left of the areas the tsunami swallowed, those who were in the places where tsunami did not hit were saved. The survivors witnessed people being taken away by tsunami. Surely there can be no harsher experience than this?

The survivors might have been able to stretch out their arms and grab the hands of the others, but their arms might not have reached far enough or the strong wave might have separated their hands from the victims'. Examining the patients with these experiences is very difficult because their experiences are something doctors have never imagined or gone through. But we have to confront this.

I think from now, how I am both a theater director as well as a doctor will strongly influence each of my selves. This has never happened before and could be confusing. Moreover, this might not mean a good result for my theater work. The stakes are high, but it doesn't matter.

We also have the issue of nuclear power. This problem will continue to exist for a long time and people cannot forget this even if they want to. No, that's not it. The problem won't be solved at least until those of us alive today have all died, because radioactive contamination won't go away in such a short period. It is very serious and deep-rooted, and the problem is going to be discussed for a long time to come. And I think the word "finally" is right here. There will finally be direct dialogue between the government and Japanese citizens. Politics was forced into doing this. The fake democracy will surely disappear. And this is not only for rebuilding the disaster areas but also a new society in Japan.

Chim↑Pom
アート集団

3.11以前から僕ら、日本は現状維持的傾向社会の感じがあったような気がしてました。でもこれは、とりあえず幸福な社会状態だったから問題視されていなかったわけで、みんなそれなりに楽に生きていけたと思う。

地震と一緒に津波が起こった時、たくさんのことが変わって、みんな何が出来るか考えたと思うんですね。僕らも、人として、アーティスト集団として、何が出来るか考えました。3.11以降、日本を襲ったもの、裏にある本質を実証したくって、すぐに何かしなきゃいけないと思ったんですね。起こった事に対してすぐにリアクションをすることが大事だった。その、ボランティアとか募金活動じゃなくてね。でも、日本はその時自粛モードで展覧会だめ、パーティーだめとかですべておさえていた状態でした。

Chim↑Pomとして自分たちの役割を感じて、体をもって、その瞬間を生きていたという表現を未来に残したかったんです。だからその思いをアートに変えたんです。リアクションを起こすにあたり、グループとしては変わらなかったけど、覚悟と決心がつきました。のちのち、きっと3.11後、日本のアート界は何をしたのかと聞かれると思うんですね。この惨事に対して何もやらなかったとか無力だったと言われるかもしれない。だから、3.11に対するリアクションをChim↑Pomとしてやらなくてはいけないし、批判を受けてもやるべきだったと思ったんです。

地震が起きたときメンバーはバラバラにいて、連絡はメールで、地震から3日目には現地に行かなくちゃいけないと思いました。でも、当時、現地には行くのは難しくて、救急とか救命を現地ではしていたんですね。だからいつ行くかというタイミングを1ヶ月位以内で考えました。4月1日から遠藤一郎さんと一緒に展覧会をする企画をして、テーマは「never give up」。これを日本人に言いたかったんです。この言葉は広島の被爆者団体が使っていたのね。この言葉は重要、被災地と広島をつなぎたかった。展覧会の1週間位前から被災地に行きました。行く所、作品、ボランティアとか移動中の車の中でいっぺん

気合い100連発
2011
KI-AI 100 (2011)
©Chim↑Pom
Courtesy of MUJIN-TO Production, Tokyo

LEVEL 7 feat.『明日の神話』
LEVEL 7 feat. Myth of Tomorrow (2011)
©Chim↑Pom
Courtesy of MUJIN-TO Production, Tokyo

REAL TIMES (2011)
©Chim↑Pom
Courtesy of MUJIN-TO Production, Tokyo

Chim↑Pom | 179

に決め、それと物資も積んでボランティアもする。でも、現地に入ったら、作品を作り発表をしたほうがいいと思いました。

東京でも震災の影響は感じました。というのも東京は真っ暗だったし、計画停電もあったしね。5月の展覧会までは、僕らはそんな生活の中で作品を作っていた。その展覧会が始まったら、今のこのタイミングでアートをするってことについての批判もあったし、でも大事だと思ってくれた人もいっぱいいて、賛否両論が巻き起こった。で、僕らの展覧会は普通のギャラリーの展覧会では珍しくて、大阪に巡回したりとか、そこから海外の色んなメディアが象徴的な出来事として取り上げたりとかそういうことが相次いだのね。今でもメンバーの一人は福島にいるんだけどね。まだ終わってる感じがしないっていうか、何か気持ちの中で言うと、現地でボランティア的なプロジェクトをしたアートをやるというふうには考えてないんです。だから福島の原発の方に食い込んだ、その時の状況を表現するのが僕らとしては大事だった。それで「REAL TIMES」っていう作品が出来たんです。他にも作った理由はあるんですけどね。3.11後、福島エリアは見捨てられたんです。原発事故が起きてから、原発30キロ圏内の避難区域に誰も入ろうとする人がいなかったの。テレビを見ても30km離れたところからの映像しかなくって、報道されるのは東京電力と政府の発表だけだったし。みんなガチガチになって、自由に動ける人がいない、同じ人間が原発で働いているのに、取材が入っていかない。そのとき結局メディアが機能しなかったんだよね。ぶつかっていこうみたいな奴がいなかった。だから、原発の内部とか30キロ圏内で何が起こってるのか全然わからなかったの。で、僕ら、福島で起こってることは、現地の問題とか国内の問題だけじゃないって思ったわけ。これは世界的な問題だって。だから、将来、この時代を歴史的に振り返れるように、象徴的な作品を作ることが大切だった。原発の周りの地区は何にも動いてなかった、警察はいなかったし、監視もなかった。だから誰かが何かやっても、警察は機能してなかったんです。誰もそこに近づこうとは考えてなかった。過去にも防護服を使ってアート表現をした作家はいましたけど、みんな大御所になっているんだけど、その人たちがすぐに動けるとは思えなかったから、やっぱり家庭もあるだろうし、やんなきゃいけない大きなプロジェクトがあるだろうし。

日本の若い年代の人は、これからの日本を変えていくっていう意識はあると思う。僕ら若いアーティスト達っていうのはお金はないけど、今起こっていることに

体を活かしてアートをするしかないし、すぐにリアクションできると思う。こういう動くっていうこと、今起こってることに対してリアクションしたり現状を伝えたりって、やっぱり文化の力だと思うんですよね。文化がやるしかない。それで福島の原発の所まで間近に行った作品が「REAL TIMES」。タイトルはリアルタイムっていう意味と、モダンタイムズ的な感じのリアルな時代っていう事と、あとJapan TimesとかNew York Timesみたいな報道の意味が含まれてあったの。福島でも色々とやったけど、福島の原子力が使えなくて東京の電力供給の問題があったとき、現地に行きながらも、自分たちが生きている東京でも作品を作らなきゃいけないと思った。

渋谷駅でやった「LEVEL7 feat.明日の神話」という作品は、広島と長崎の原爆、第五福竜丸が被爆した際の水爆の炸裂の瞬間をテーマにした「明日の神話」という岡本太郎作の巨大壁画が渋谷駅構内にあるんだけど、日本でもっとも有名な絵ともいえるもので、もともと設置する予定だったホテルの壁の形にあわせて作られたものだから、左右の下が欠けた形で完成されてるわけ。その空白部分に岡本太郎のタッチで描かれた福島原発が爆発する瞬間の絵をゲリラで付け加えた作品。つまり「日本の被爆のクロニクル」を現実が更新したってことを可視化した。「福島」の「今」っていう身近な視線だけじゃなくて、「東京」で「歴史」っていう俯瞰した目線の作品を作ることで、人類へのメッセージになると考えたんです。ツイッターで話題になってマスコミが騒ぎ出して、大きな騒動になった。僕らは、今は日本は混乱期になっていると思っていて、それを象徴するような活動をしているのかもしれない。アートがエクストリームな現実を映し出しているからこそ、僕らの表現が過激になっているんだと思います。

Chim↑Pom
Art collective

Before 3.11, Japanese society seemed always hesitant about changing, but that characteristic wasn't considered problematic because society at large was pretty happy and people could live without hardships.

When the earthquake and tsunami hit the country, so many things changed and everyone thought about what they could do. We also thought about what we could do as human beings and an artist collective. After 3.11 we wanted to investigate the core of what happened and to do something immediately. Reacting to what happened right away was important, but not through volunteering or donating money. But in Japan, exhibitions or parties weren't allowed due to the self-censorship society was imposing upon itself.

We wanted to feel our role as Chim↑Pom and to leave behind creative expression that captured the moment alive now. We transformed this feeling into art. Although the disaster did not change us as a group, we kind of had to make up our minds. In the future people will ask how Japanese art responded in the aftermath of 3.11, and they might say that we did not act on it or that we were powerless. We as Chim↑Pom had to respond to 3.11 even if that meant we were criticized.

When the earthquake hit Japan, we were scattered around, corresponding with each other via email. Three days after the disaster, we thought we had to go to the disaster area, but getting there was extremely difficult because emergency aid services were given priority then. We were figuring out the timing of when to go within the frame of a month. We planned to organize an exhibition with artist Ichiro Endo entitled *Never give up!* from April 1st, which was the message we wanted to deliver to the Japanese people. Used by Hiroshima atomic bomb victim groups, this phrase is extremely important for connecting the disaster areas with Hiroshima. We ended up going to Tohoku one week before the exhibition. Deciding everything from where to visit to the artwork and volunteering in the car, we also packed the vehicle with emergency materials to do volunteering. But our idea was that once we were in Tohoku we should concentrate on creating work.

We felt the impact of the disaster even in Tokyo. Tokyo was completely dark and there were planned power outages. We were making art under these conditions until May. Once the exhibition started, some people criticized us for doing art in this extraordinary environment while a lot of others recognized the importance of art. So there was support as well as opposition. Unusually for a gallery exhibition, the show ended up touring to Osaka and many international media outlets covered it as a symbolic incident. One of the members of Chim↑Pom still remains in Fukushima and we don't feel like it's over.

Our honest feeling is that we have no intention of doing a kind of art project similar to volunteering. It was more important for us to create work that represents the Fukushima catastrophe. And as a result, we made *REAL TIMES*. There are many other reasons why we created this work. Since 3.11, the Fukushima area has been abandoned. No one was willing to enter the 30km mandatory evacuation zone since the catastrophe happened. We could only watch TV footage shot outside the zone as well as the information released by TEPCO (Tokyo Electric Power Company) and the government. Everyone was so restricted as no one could move around freely. Despite that there were people like us working inside the plant, no news outlets were entering it to report on it. The Japanese media was not functioning at all. No one was courageous enough to confront the reality. We did not know anything about what was happening inside the plant or within the 30km mandatory zone. We thought what was happening in Fukushima was not a local or domestic issue but an international issue. So with this in mind we had to make a symbolic artwork that enables us to look back at history. Nothing was moving around the Fukushima power plant. There were no police or surveillance. The police force was not functioning even if someone did something. No one was trying to get close to the zone. For example, in the past there was an artist who made work with a protective suit, but everyone is now well known and has difficulty responding quickly given that they have families to protect and projects to complete.

I think the Japanese younger generation intends to change future society. Even if young artists including us have no money, we just have to make art using our bodies and to react to what is happening right away. I think the power of culture lies in moving, in reacting to what is happening right now and conveying reality. Only culture can do this.

Our attempt of getting near the Fukushima nuclear power plant is entitled *REAL TIMES*, which means literary "real time" as well "realistic era" in the sense of Charlie Chaplin's *Modern Times*. It also means the press, like The Japan Times or The New York Times. So we did a lot of projects in Fukushima but thinking about the power shortage in Tokyo caused by the Fukushima disaster, we thought we also had to make work in Tokyo where we live while continuing to visit Fukushima. We created a work inside Shibuya Station called *LEVEL 7 feat. Myth of Tomorrow*. There is a large mural called *The Myth of Tomorrow* by Taro Okamoto[1] inside Shibuya Station depicting the atomic bombs dropped in Hiroshima and Nagasaki, and the hydrogen explosion that exposed the Daigo Fukuryu Maru[2] to radiation. This mural could be said to be the most famous Japanese painting. *The Myth of Tomorrow* was originally created to fit the wall of a hotel, so there are spaces missing in the lower left and right corners. In the empty space, we added, guerilla-style, an image in Taro Okamoto's style depicting the moment when the Fukushima plant exploded. We wanted to visualize how the Japanese chronicle of radiation has been renewed. We thought by creating work not just with a proximate perspective of Fukushima and today but with the perspectives of history and Tokyo, this work could be a message for mankind.

The response on Twitter was crazy and the mass media went wild about it, so it became a real hullabaloo. We think Japan is in this very confused era and our work simply represents that. Since art represents an extreme reality, our work has become radical as well.

1. Taro Okamoto (1911–1996), a famed Japanese sculptor and painter.

2. A Japanese fishing vessel that was exposed to fallout from a US hydrogen bomb test in 1954.

津田大介
ジャーナリスト/メディア・アクティビスト

地震が起きたとき、自分は中野でシンポジウムに出ていました。今まで生きてきた中で一番大きな地震でしたし、とにかく長い揺れでした。シンポジウムのホールは最新の免震構造の出来たばっかりの建物だったので大丈夫だったのですが、メリーゴーランドのように大きく揺れました。僕はすぐに大変なことが起きているって感じたんです。

ホールから出てみると、外の工事現場のクレーンが大きく揺れてました。日本は約15年ほど前、震度7クラスの阪神淡路大震災を経験している。これ位の大きさの地震が、もし、震源地が東京でなかったら、震源地は阪神淡路大震災クラスの大変な事態が発生しているのではと直感しました。

地震からほんの数分後、僕はすぐにネットを開き、ツイッターを見ました。ツイッターを見たらNHKの速報で「宮城震度7」と出てきて、僕がしたことは、ツイッターの検索機能で宮城と東北地方はどうなっているんだろうと思って、その地方に住んでいる人の書き込みを探したんですが、「すごい揺れた」みたいな書き込みすらなかったので、通信環境が駄目になっているのではないかと思いました。

まずは、家族に連絡をしなきゃと思って電話しようと思ったんですが、電話もメールも繋がらなくって。ただ、ツイッター、ネットだけは繋がっていたので、そのメッセージ機能で家族に連絡をしたら、程なく安否の確認が取れました。で、同時にその日に入っていた予定がキャンセルというかたちで、ツイッターで連絡を取り、そうしているうちにニコニコ生放送[1]の地震に関する特番から出演依頼を受けたんです。家族の安否の確認が取れていたのでその仕事を受けることにして、中野から原宿のドワンゴのスタジオまで車で向かいました。普通であれば車で40分位のところ、大渋滞だったので約4時間かかったんですよね。車の中で、僕はほとんどの時間、どんな情報があるのかを把握するためにずっとツイッターを見ていました。その時のツイッターで流れている情報は混乱しているんですよね。東京も電車が止まったため、多くの帰

1. http://live.nicovideo.jp/

宅困難者が出ました。

そんな時、東京都の猪瀬直樹副知事がツイートをしていて、「東京には多くの帰宅困難者がでているので、その方々のために東京都の施設を開放するので、必要な方はそこに泊まってください」みたいな書き込みをしたんですね。それを見て、これは副知事が言ったんで、公式な情報だっていうのでそれを僕はリツイートしたんですよね。そうしたら結構それがすごい数の感謝のツイートが返ってきたんです。僕、当時11万人位のフォロワーがいたんです。

その時、情報が混乱している時に、確定している正しい情報を飛ばすことによって、誰かの役に立つと思ったんです。なので、その4時間、車の中で明確で正しい情報を伝えるために混乱している情報の整理を始めました。

その後の3日間はニコニコの特番に出演しました。その3日間はほとんど寝ずに、起きているときは情報収集をしているか番組に出演しているかでした。当時は番組やイベントに出演したりっていうのがすごく多くて、いろんなあらゆる予定が2週間ぐらいキャンセルになったんですよね。で、その先も何が起こるかわからない状況になってたんです。それで、これがきっかけで、3日間の仕事の後、すぐに被災地で取材できるわけじゃない自分が出来る事って何だろうって思って、それは情報と徹底的に向き合うことじゃないかって思ったんですよね。自分自身がソーシャルメディアの中でリアルタイムで流れる情報のハブのような存在になれないかと思ったんです。で、そしてその時から、1ヶ月、僕はツイッターのより明確で正しい情報の選別と整理に専念しました。

もちろん僕はジャーナリストでもあるので、被災地に行って現地を見たいという思いもあったんですよね。たくさんの人が現地を取材しに行ったり、マスコミもレポートしに現地に行ってました。でも僕自身は被災地での取材経験もなかったし、動くためのガソリンもなかったので、現地にすぐ行っても出来る事は少ないなっていうのもあったっていうことと、情報の整理っていうのが自分の仕事かなって思って、それであれば、おそらくもっと効果的に貢献できると思ったんです。それとまだその時、ツイッターの情報と向き合っていた人が誰もいなかったので。で、それをするには一人では出来ないと思ったんで、ツイッターに詳しいアシスタントが必要だと思って、ツイッターに詳しい人に手伝ってもらえるように電話をして、そこから先は、不眠不休で働きました。

僕が起きてるときはテレビのニュースの情報を集め、そしてその情報を整理し、リツイートし続けました。あと、すべての記者会見を追いかけようと思って、官房

長官のであったり、東京電力、原子力安全保安院の記者会見を追いました。記者会見で明らかになった全部の情報を24時間ずっと、すぐにリツイートして、僕が休みを取っているときはアシスタントに代わりを頼み、記者会見が始まるときには起こしてくれと頼んで、とにかく情報の隙間を作らないようにしました。だから、公式な情報と非公式なツイッターで流れている情報を約3週間追い続けるってことをずっとやっていましたね。でその時期、震災に関する仕事以外はすべて断っていました。この仕事を断るってことは、自分の中では福島の原発が終息するまで続けたいと思っていたんですね。最初は1週間の予定が2週間になり、そして3週間たってこの仕事は終わることがないって気付いたんですね。それと同じ時期、ニコニコ生放送が震災1ヶ月後に震災の特番を特に被害の大きかった宮城の気仙沼で特番をやりたいので、一緒に同行取材をしてもらえないかっていう連絡が入りました。

それまで、パソコンの前で自分の仕事を自分なりに現地の方の役に立って欲しいと思ってやってきたので、どれだけ役に立っているんだろうみたいなものがあって、現地に行きたいとずっと思っていたんですね。そういった考えに忸怩たるものはあったんですけど、本当に自分が役に立っていたのか分からなかったので、その依頼を受け、震災1ヵ月後、被害のひどかった気仙沼に入り、その後陸前高田へ行き、被災地の取材をしました。僕もテレビやネットを見ながら情報を集め、情報の整理をしていたんですが、1ヵ月後の現地の状況は

2011年4月 宮城県
気仙沼市八日町2丁目
Youkamachi
2-chome, Kesennuma
City, Miyagi
Prefecture (April,
2011)
©Daisuke Tsuda

津田大介 | 187

本当に壊滅的でテレビや新聞では伝わってない圧倒される現実がそこにはあった。「メディア見てても全然わかんないじゃん」みたいなガツンという衝撃を受けました。そのとき僕が考えたのは「自分にはツイッターというメディアと発信力がある」ということでした。「ツイッターを使って東北エリアの情報を直接発信していかなくてはならない」と思ったんですよね。

この1ヶ月後に被災地に行ったという経験は自分の中ではすごく鮮烈に残り、定期的に現地に行って取材をしようと決めたんです。その後、月に1、2回は東北地方に行くようにしています。これは、僕の中での意識が一番変わったことでもあり、自覚することでもあったんですね。このときまでは、メディアを作り、情報を流すことを考えていたんですが、被災地に行き、現地の人たちがどんなに大変でどんなに多くの問題を抱えているかっていうのを知り、でもそういった情報はテレビやラジオでは十分に伝えきれない、そして時間が経つにつれ、こういう情報をマスコミは取り上げなくなっていく。でも、実際問題はすごい現実がまだあるんですよ。

これらの問題はマスコミからだんだんと忘れられてしまうこと、僕たちみたいなフリージャーナリストが取材し続け、それを発信していくことが重要だと考えています。情報を受信し、再発信しながら社会の意識を再び動かすことに努めたいですね。これは自分の中での一生のテーマというか一生の仕事になったなっていう、今までもなんとなくは思っていたんですけど、今はっきりと自分の中で枠ができたかなって。

僕がやった情報のオープン・ソースはどこでも、誰でもツイッターで情報を発信し、入手できます。震災前は約11万人のフォロワーが、今は約20万人に増えました。

他のクリエイティブ産業、例えば映画、漫画、アニメ、デザイン、建築など3.11後、創作活動が止まったと感じましたね。何人かのミュージシャンは音楽は無力と考えたり。でも、5月ごろ、皆が復興に向かってがんばって行こう、少しずつ希望を取り戻し始めた時、それを後押ししたのが音楽だったので、自分の感覚としては文化、芸術、娯楽（エンターテイメント）がたくさんの新しい意味を持つ時代が到来しつつあると感じます。それはクリエーターも同じ感覚をもっていると思うんですよね。

同時に3.11以降の表現というのが昔のような享楽的なものではなくなると思っています。それらが消えて、社会的な文脈から切り離せなくなると感じていて、例

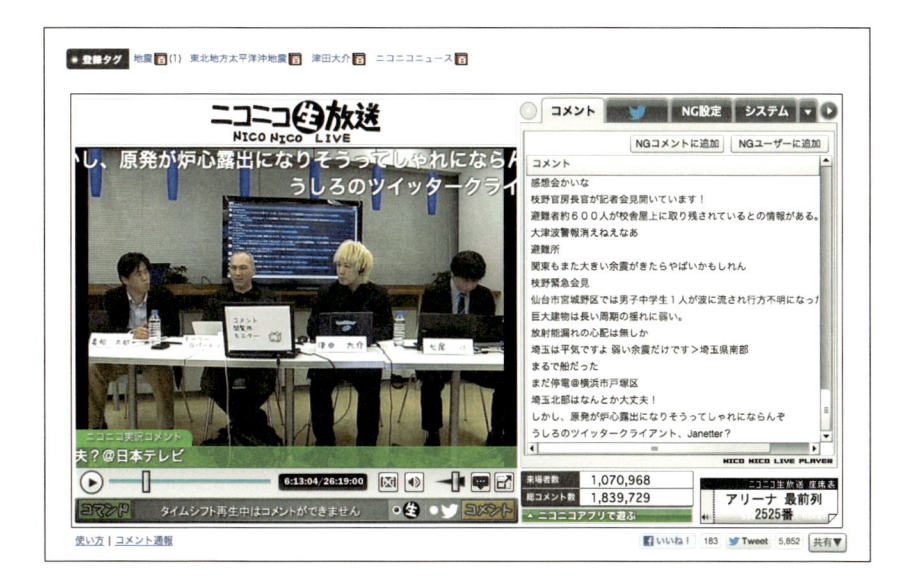

震災時のニコ生
Niconico Live,
broadcast on the day
of the earthquake
disaster
©niwango, inc

えば日本のミュージシャンはヨーロッパやアメリカに比べ、政治的な内容に取り組まなかったというか、あえて避けてきた部分があったと思うんです。多分これからは、そういうことを避けて作品を作っても、聞く側がリアリティーを感じられないようなそんな空気になり、多分このことがミュージシャンの意識を変えるのではと思います。この感覚は、他のクリエイティブ産業にもいえることだと思います。

Daisuke Tsuda
Journalist, media activist

When the earthquake hit, I was participating in a symposium in Nakano. It was the biggest earthquake I have experienced in my life. The quake lasted for a long time. The symposium venue, a brand new building with seismic isolation structure, wasn't damaged, but the building was shaking like a merry-go-round. I immediately felt that something very serious was happening.

When I came out of the building, a crane at a construction site was shaking strongly. Japan experienced the Great Hanshin-Awaji Earthquake, level 7 on the Japanese seismic intensity scale, about fifteen years ago. The epicenter wasn't Tokyo, though, so I felt that the epicenter wherever it was must have been experiencing something very serious akin to the Great Hanshin-Awaji Earthquake.

A few minutes after the earthquake, I immediately went online and checked Twitter. On Twitter I saw an NHK news flash: "Miyagi, level 7 seismic intensity scale." I searched for tweets from people in Miyagi or Tohoku, but there wasn't even one tweet saying "it was really shaking," which got me thinking that the communication network must have been completely destroyed.

I wanted to contact my family first but neither phone lines or phone email were working. But the Internet connection was fine so I confirmed my family's safety through Twitter. Simultaneously I also canceled my work scheduled for that day through Twitter. In the meantime, I was asked to be on a Niconico Live[1] show, a special program about the earthquake. Knowing my family was safe, I took the job and headed from Nakano by car to Dwango's office in Harajuku. While it normally takes 40 minutes by car to get there, it took four hours because of heavy traffic. I was checking Twitter inside the car to get a grip on what was happening. The information circulating on Twitter was very confusing at that time. There were many people who could not get home because the trains had stopped running in Tokyo.

1. http://live.nicovideo.jp

At one point, Naoki Inose, the Vice Governor of Tokyo, tweeted something like "Tokyo's public institutions are open for staying overnight for those who cannot get home." When I saw his tweet, I retweeted it because the tweet was official information from the Vice Governor. I had about 110,000 followers at that time and received a lot of tweets thanking me.

What I realized at that time was that I can be of help to others by circulating accurate information when information is confusing. During those four hours of the car ride, I started to sort out the confusing information to relay what was clear and accurate.

I was on the Niconico special programs over the following three days. I barely slept for three days and when I was awake, I was either collecting information or appearing on the show. My work at that time was mainly taking part in events or media programs, most of which had been canceled. I was uncertain about my future work schedule. That made me think about what I could do as someone who could not go to Tohoku to report about it right away. I thought that what I could do was exhaustively confront all the information and exist as a real-time information hub on social media. From that time on, I concentrated for a month on selecting and sorting out the clear and accurate information on Twitter.

I am also a journalist so I had the urge to go to Tohoku and see what was happening with my own eyes. But many journalists including mass media outlets were already there to report news. Without prior journalistic experiences in Tohoku or gasoline for driving around, I thought my actions there would be limited. I thought I could make a better contribution through organizing information. Plus, no one was seriously tackling the information on Twitter. I knew I could not do it alone, so I contacted an assistant with extensive knowledge of Twitter. I worked tirelessly from that time on.

While I was awake, I gathered TV news sources, organized them, and retweeted them. I also wanted to follow all press conferences by the Chief Cabinet Secretary, TEPCO, and the Nuclear and Industrial Safety Agency. Right away I tweeted every single piece of information revealed in a press conference for 24 hours. When I was asleep, I asked my assistant to take my turn. Trying not to leave a gap between information, I asked my assistant to wake me up when a conference started. For three weeks I endlessly followed both official and unofficial information circulating on Twitter. I turned down every job offer unrelated to the disaster. I did not want to do any unrelated work until the Fukushima nuclear problem ceased to exist. But first, it was a week, then two weeks, and finally when it reached three weeks, I ultimately realized that this work would not be finished within three weeks. Around the same time, Niconico Live approached me with their plan to create a special program in Kesennuma, Miyagi Prefecture, one of the worst hit areas, and they asked me to go there with the crew to gather information.

While until then I had hoped my computer work would somehow help those who were affected, I wasn't sure if it did, so I had always wanted to go to the disaster area. I was a bit ashamed of thinking this way, but I really didn't know if my work was in any way helpful. I accepted the offer and went to Kesennuma, one of the hardest-hit areas, and Rikuzentakata to report on them one month on from the earthquake. Although I had been collecting and organizing information from TV and the Internet, the reality there was so catastrophic that it was nothing like what I had seen on TV or in the newspapers. It was a complete shock to me; it felt like the media had not reported this at all. I thought, with Twitter and its power to deliver information, I have to start relaying the information about this reality in Tohoku directly.

This experience of visiting the disaster zone one month after the catastrophe had a strong impact in me and I decided to make regular visits to there. I have been going to Tohoku once or twice a month since then. Until then I used to think about creating a media outlet and releasing information, but going to Tohoku and knowing how people were struggling and facing very serious problems drastically changed my understanding, and made me aware of how the media works. TV and radio did not sufficiently report these stories. And as time goes by, the mass media gradually stops reporting these stories while the overwhelming reality remains the same.

While mass media starts to forget about them, it is important for freelance journalists like myself to keep covering Tohoku. I want to re-activate society's awareness through receiving information and relaying it on. This has become a core theme of my work or let's say, my life's work. I used to think about it unconsciously, but now I have a definite frame.

Anyone, anywhere can acquire the information I collect in this open source way. My Twitter followers have now increased to 200,000 from the 110,000 I had before the disaster happened.

I felt that the other creative industries such as cinema, manga, animation, design, and architecture stopped their creative activities after March 11th. Some musicians thought music was powerless in a case like this. But around May when everyone was starting to work together for reconstruction and getting hope back, it was music that gave people a boost. I personally think that a new era is arriving in which culture, art and entertainment have many new meanings. I think many creators share a similar feeling.

I think the post-3.11 arts and creativity will no longer be hedonistic. This old type of work will disappear and a new type of work with social context will emerge. For example, I think, compared to their European and American counterparts, until now Japanese musicians have always avoided tackling political issues. But from now on listeners won't feel it's real if music avoids the social and political context. And this will change the consciousness of musicians and can also be applied to other creative industries.

中村政人

3331 Arts Chiyoda 総括ディレクター

3331 Arts Chiyodaは創造性とアート制作を実践するアートセンターです。「3331」とは、おめでたい席で感謝の意を表す江戸時代からの風習「江戸一本締め」の手拍子のリズムを表しています。東京都千代田区にある旧練成中学校を活動拠点としており、この建物は地域の防災拠点でもあります。僕らは、改修時にこの建物の正面入り口と隣接する公園をウッドデッキでつなげました（大きいバルコニーのようで建物の1階部分と公園を結んでいる）。2011年に東日本大震災が起こったとき、館内にいた人達は皆、建物から公園に避難しました。千代田区の職員の到着に時間がかかったため、僕らはすぐに道に溢れている人達や家に帰れない人達を支援する側にまわりました。地震後の最初の晩、僕らの施設は近隣地区の避難所になりました。僕らは毛布を渡し、帰宅難民の人達と一緒にその晩を過ごしました。3.11以前より、アートと文化を促進するために地域の人たちとつくっていたネットワークは、震災時には避難者をサポートするネットワークに代わり、防災的な意識は日ごろから必要だと実感した大切な瞬間でした。

3.11の後、僕らはアーティスト集団として何をやるべきかを考え、数日後には

3331屋外
Outside 3331 Arts Chiyoda
©2010-2014 3331 Arts Chiyoda

体育館でのチャリティーイベントの計画を立てました。また被災地である東北にも行き、多くの被災者の生きる力・作る力のすごさを実感しました。被災地で彼らと出会った経験は、支援活動を行う上で貴重なものとなりました。被災者自身の立ち上がる意志に対し、僕らはぶれてはいけないと思っていますし、それらをつないでいきたいと考えています。

そして僕らは、アーティスト、建築家、コミュニティ・デザイナー、また岩手、宮城、福島、東京の現地コーディネーターから構成される「わわプロジェクト」を立ち上げることを考えました。これは色々なチャンスを作るためのプラットホームです。「わわ」とは「私は」を意味し、多くの「私」が大きな「わ=街」を作ることを願い、名づけました。活動に関する情報を載せるサイトには英語版もあり、また定期的に新聞も発行し、被災地で生活している人たちに配布しています。

さらに、被災地では何が起こり、被災者は何を考えているかということを被災地のリーダー達が語る、英語字幕付きのビデオを上映する展覧会を2011年の韓国・光州ビエンナーレに出品しました。このビデオにはそれぞれに募金箱が置かれており、誰でも募金できます。例えば、このインタビューに出演している一人である芳賀さんは、被災後「復活の薪」を売り始めました。「復活の薪」とは、瓦礫のなかから木を集め、それを米袋に入れて500円で販売します。この発案は彼が被災地のコミュニティの方々と一緒に決めたものです。彼と一緒に働く人は働いた分だけお金をもらう、このように被災に対して直接リアクションする方法を彼らは見つけました。職を失った漁師さんたちが山で薪を集めるという労働・雇用を生み出しました。彼の次の目標は山で新しい学校を作ることです。

別のインタビュー映像では、2つの神社を失った岩手県山田町の宮司さんが語っています。山田町はお祭りが盛んな地域で、震災でお神輿など流されてしまった中、いくつかを修復し、お祭りを復活させました。やっぱりこういう「お祭り」という神事は何百年も続いていて、それぞれの場所に思いが宿ってるんですね。場というのはそこに住む人達のアイデンティティですが唯一の物ではない。

日本は政教分離で、国は神社に一切援助しないんです。僕らのインタビュー企画で何十万かは集まってます。

この展示は、ソウル、台北、東京でも行いました。

わわプロジェクトは「コマンドN」というNPO団体が運営しており、そこで企

中村政人 | 195

画事業を行っているスタッフたちはアーティストです。「コマンドN」はアーティストとオーディエンスが積極的に関わるためのコンテンポラリー・アート・プロジェクトを企画します。名前はマッキントッシュのショートカットキー「command+N」が由来で、「新規」＝「常に新しいことに向かう」を意味します。こういうタイプの組織は、将来、被災地での企画事業を行う場合に有効だと考えています。現地を支援する組織としては、国が組織する社会福祉協議会もありますが、現地のコミュニティに対してアクティブなつながりが弱いのです。しかし、逆の例もあります。岩手県の遠野では、地元のボランティアグループが社会福祉協議会の建物を借りて活動をしています。公共の組織が所有する建物を使い、地元の人たちが作ったボランティア団体のネットワークを利用する。被災地の人達の要望に即座に応えるためには理想的な形だと思います。

3331 メインギャラリー
Main gallery at 3331
Arts Chiyoda
©2010-2014 3331
Arts Chiyoda

3331 Arts Chiyodaで活動しているアーティスト達も東北地方に赴いています。例えば、日比野克彦さんは「HEART MARK VIEWING」という活動をしています。被災地の人たちにハートマークのパッチワークを作ったり、募金活動のために展覧会などを行っています。

他にも開発好明さんが他のアーティスト仲間と一緒に日本の南から東北地方のある北へと移動しながら行う展覧会をしていました。そして、岩間賢さんの宮城県石巻市桃浦地区を支援する「ユイノハマ プロジェクト」には僕も参加していて、瓦礫の処理をしに行きました。桃浦地区は約95%が津波に

流された小さい町で、数多くの子供たちも犠牲となっています。さらに仮設住宅もなく、住む場所もありませんでした。そのため、地元の漁業組合の組合長さんや支援者が寝泊りできる場所を考え、新しく仮設住宅を建設しました。この地域には学校だけが残っていますが、学校自体は廃校になってしまう可能性があるため、校長先生と考えているのは、よりサスティナブルな建物としての活用です。つまり、この町から出て行った人たちが戻ってくるきっかけを作るようなもの。例えば、サマーキャンプで自然を学んだり、被災地でその痛みや辛さを同時に学んでいくというのを考えています。

支援プロジェクト：わわプロジェクト
WAWA Project
©2011-2013 WAWA Project

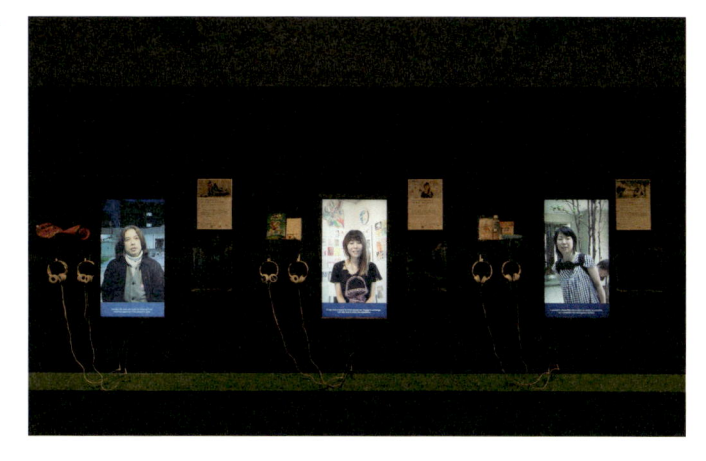

震災から何ヶ月も経ち、被災地に何度も行き、僕らはよりサスティナブルな生き方を見つける必要性を感じています。この言葉は最近日本でもカタカナで使われるようになってきましたが、より思慮深く自然と向き合う必要性を説明するのに有効だと思います。例えば、岩手県吉里の芳賀さんは、山と海を繋ぐことで新しい自然観を生みだし、その自然と共生する質素な生活を提案しています。芳賀さんの「純粋」で「切実」な活動が多くの市民を勇気づけ、具体的な復興のビジョンを支え始めています。このサスティナブルな自然観は、新しく再生される社会の基本理念となりえるものです。日本は第二次世界大戦を含めて色々な災害を乗り越え、新しい社会を作ってきました。でも、3.11の被害をうけた自然豊かな地域と都市圏とでは、大きな違いがあると思います。両地域とも産業と自然の資源の利用により発展しました。しかし今、自然が私たちに与えてくれる恩恵に対し、より尊敬の念を持って生活していく方法を見つける必要があると思います。この「尊敬」は、日本の次代の発展にとっても、現在、

中村政人 | 197

すさまじい発展を遂げるアジア諸国にとっても刺激になるのではないかと考えています。

例えば、秋田県に根子村という所があります。この村は山々に囲まれいて、約200軒の家があります。この農村には根子番楽という歌舞伎に似たものがあります。この番楽は村の人達が自分たちのためにやっているんですね。自然の恵みに対しての感謝と鍬入れされた畑も含め自然の美しさを称えるために行うものです。日常の生活スタイルや自分達の無形文化を継承する意識が精神的にも自然環境と豊かに循環している。自分自身に「純粋」であり、自然環境に「切実」な生き方がここでは実現しています。この高度なサスティナブルコミュニティがここでは、当たり前のように存在している。これはとても大切だなと思います。この小さな村で自然と共生する豊かな生活観があるというのは非常に大事です。これはどの国でもあることだとは思うのですが、僕ら日本人は何かを忘れてしまっているのではないでしょうか。戦後の発展により、現在多くの知識とテクノロジーを使うことが出来ますが、自然に対する行動、そして社会的な行動の意味を見直されなければならない時期に来ていると思います。

Masato Nakamura
General Director, 3331 Arts Chiyoda

3331 Arts Chiyoda is an art center for creativity and producing art. The name "3331" represents the Edo Ippon Tejime handclap. It is traditionally used for showing appreciation to others.
Based at the former Rensei Junior High School, 3331 Arts Chiyoda functions also as the area's disaster prevention center. While renovating the center's building, we connected our main entrance to the adjoining park with a wood deck. It now looks like a big balcony linking the ground floor of the building and the park. When the 2011 Tohoku earthquake and tsunami happened, everyone inside the center evacuated to the park. As it took a while for Chiyoda ward officials to arrive, we started assisting people crowding in the streets and those who could not get home. The center became the area's shelter for the first night after the earthquake. We handed over blankets and stayed overnight with those unable to go home. The network we had built with the neighboring community for promoting art and culture before 3.11 became the network for supporting evacuees. It was an important moment for us to realize that we need day-to-day awareness of disaster prevention. After 3.11, we thought about what we could do as an artist group and after a few days we planned a charity event. We also went to the disaster areas in Tohoku, and felt the vitality and creativity of the victims. The encounters with these people in Tohoku became critical for us to engage in activities that supported them. We have to be strong in supporting their will to recover and we want to create a network.
We decided to launch the WAWA Project comprised of artists, architects, community designers, and coordinators from Iwate, Miyagi, Fukushima, and Tokyo. It's a platform for creating different opportunities. We named it "WAWA" because it means "I am," which conveys our wish that a lot of "I" (*wa*) eventually creates a big "WA," which also means connection and circle in Japanese. The project has an English website and regularly publishes a newspaper that we distribute to people in the disaster areas.

We also submitted a series of videos with English subtitles to Gwangju Design Biennale 2011, in which leaders from the disaster areas talked about what happened in their respective regions and how the victims are thinking. A donation box is placed in front of each monitor so anyone can donate money. For example, one of the interviewees, Masahiro Haga started selling Revival Firewood. Revival Firewood is firewood collected from the debris from the disaster and is sold in a rice bag for ¥500. Haga conceived this idea together with other community members. All the income generated through sales is returned to those who work to collect the firewood. They found a way to directly respond to the disaster, including creating a new job collecting firewood for fishermen who had lost their jobs. His new goal is to establish a new school on a mountain. There is another interview with a chief priest of a Shinto shrine from Yamada in Iwate Prefecture. While Yamada is known for its festivals, some of the portable shrines used for festivals were washed away by the disaster. He restored some of them and revived festivals. A festival is a religious service; it has been around for centuries, and in it resides the identity of each locale. A physical place is not the only thing with which people living there identify.

In Japan there is a division of state and religion, so the government does not provide any financial aid to Shinto shrines but, due to this interview, the shrine has collected the equivalent of thousands of dollars. The exhibit was shown in Seoul, Taipei, and Tokyo.

WAWA Project is run by commandN, a non-profit organization, and the staff responsible for planning programs are artists. commandN plans contemporary art projects, platforms where artists and audiences actively engage with each other. Its name comes from the shortcut key on a Mac computer, "command + N " meaning "new" and "constantly going for new things." I think this type of organization will function effectively in the future when working in the disaster areas. There is the Japan National Council of Social Welfare, a national organization responsible for aid work in the disaster areas, but it does not have an active connection with local communities. There is a reverse example. In Tono in Iwate Prefecture, a local volunteering group rents and bases itself in a building owned by the Japan National Council of Social Welfare. While the local volunteering group uses the building of a public institution, the public institution uses the volunteering network the locals created. This represents an ideal model to meet the immediate needs of the disaster victims.

Artists based at 3331 Arts Chiyoda have also been to Tohoku areas. For example, Katsuhiko Hibino has been conducting a project, Heart Mark Viewing, in which he makes patchwork heart marks together with the victims, and organizes exhibitions for collecting donations.

Other examples include Yoshiaki Kaihatsu's traveling exhibition with fellow artists, moving from southern Japan up to Tohoku. Satoshi Iwama's Yuinohama Project supports the Momoura district in Ishinomaki City, Miyagi Prefecture. I am also part of the project and I went there to help clean up debris. Tsunami washed away 95% of the small town that is Momoura district and many local children also became victims of the disaster. There is no temporary housing or place to live in the district. The project helped to build a new temporary facility where a president of a local fisherman association and volunteers can stay overnight.

While the local elementary school remained, it faces potential closure in the future. Together with the school's principal, we are thinking about utilizing the school's building in a sustainable way, creating a place for those who left the district to come back and stay, like a summer camp for learning about nature as well as the hardships of the disaster.

Several months on from the disaster, as I have been to the affected areas a number of times, I feel the urge to find a more sustainable way of living. While we recently write "sustainability" in the script for denoting foreign words, the word is also useful for explaining the need to face nature in a more considerate way. For example, Masahiro Haga from Kirikiri in Iwate suggests a simple and modest lifestyle of coexisting with nature by connecting with the mountains and the sea. His "pure" and "compelling" activities have encouraged a lot of citizens and started to function as concrete visions for reconstruction. His sustainable vision for nature could be a foundational principal for regenerating society. Japan has always created a new society after overcoming disasters such as World War Two. However, I think there is a significant difference between the nature-rich areas damaged by 3.11 and urban areas, even though both areas were developed by maximizing natural resources and industrialization. Right now, we need to find a way of living that respects the benefits nature offers. This feeling of "respect" can be an important aspect not only for Japan's development of the next generation, but also for other rapidly developing Asian countries.

For example, there is a village called Neko in Akita Prefecture. Surrounded by mountains, it has around 200 households. Neko has a form of entertainment similar to Kabuki that is called Bangaku. Villagers perform Bangaku for themselves, appreciating nature's offerings as well as praising the beauty of nature, such as the practice of breaking the ground of a field. This spirit of inheriting the village's everyday lifestyle and intangible folk culture forms a rich cycle with nature. You find a kind of lifestyle that is true to yourself and compelled by nature. A high-level, sustainable community exists here, and this is very important to recognize. It is astonishing that a vision of living symbiotically with nature exists in this tiny village. As we can see in other countries, Japanese people have forgotten something important. Due to the postwar development, we have access to knowledge and technology. Yet we have now arrived at an era where we have to question our behavior towards nature and the meaning of our social behavior.

南條史生

森美術館 館長

六本木ヒルズの野外広場に出現した遠藤一郎の「未来へ号 RAINBOW JAPAN 2012」。
東北の被災地を含む日本全国を縦断して各地の人々と交流。
Endo Ichiro, *GO FOR FUTURE CAR RAINBOW JAPAN 2012*, that appeared on the outdoor plaza of Roppongi Hills. The artist interacted with people while driving the length of Japan, including the areas of Tohoku hit by the disaster.
©2012 六本木アートナイト実行委員会
©2012 Roppongi Art Night Committee

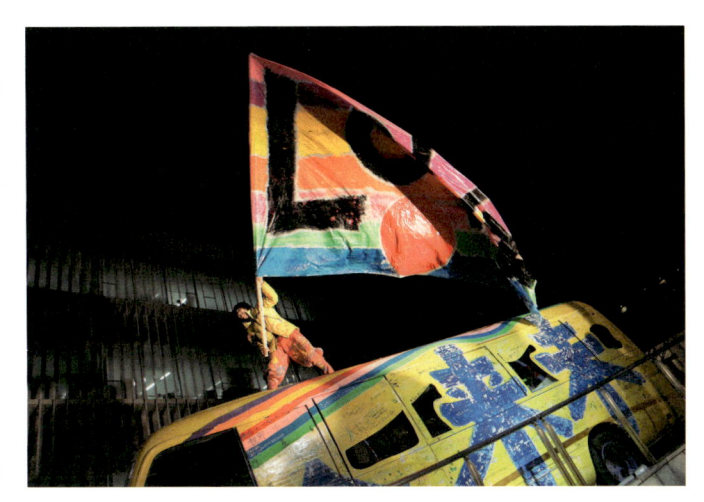

地震が起きた時、私は羽田空港に向かっていました。空港に到着すると、すべての便が欠航になったのですぐに現状の重大さが分かりました。オフィスが無事なのを確認し、電話が通じなかった両親の安否を知るために実家に向かいました。そして、無事だった両親と一緒にテレビを通して何が起きていたのかを知りました。

テレビで津波とその出来事から逃げることが出来ない沢山の人々を目にしました。津波は一瞬のうちに、多くの人々の命を奪いました。津波のシーンは繰り返し放送されていたので何回も見ましたが、その後、福島の惨事と放射能の問題がより大きく報道されるようになりました。これは津波よりもずっと長期間、広範囲に影響を与えるもっと大きな問題だとすぐにわかりました。長い期間福島の広い地域が封鎖されるでしょう。一年以上たった今になってもまだ、将来何が起こるのかを私たちは正確には知り得ません。

それと同時に人々が個人的な考え方をしなくなり、いろんな人と意見を分かち合い、協力し、心を開く人が増えました。従来の仕事のあり方や見栄に縛ら

れた自己中心的な考えがこの大惨事のあと、よりフレキシブルで、率直な考え方に代わりました。土地に関しても多くの人はより自由にあちこちにと動けるようになりたいと考えるようになりました。土地に縛られる必然性が薄れたのです。それに、技術の発展のおかげで人々の移動はより簡単になっています。パソコン一つあればどこでも仕事が出来る、という人たちも増えました。

別の言い方をすると、震災後多くの人がライフスタイルを見直し始め、生きる上での価値基準を変えようとしています。アート作品においては、まだ大きな変化は見られませんが、私からみて例えば遠藤一郎、開発好明、中村政人などのアーティストは、いろいろな方法で社会と一緒に作り出す、あるいは対話を生み出すアート活動に努めています。このようなタイプのアート活動はますます増えているように感じられます。アーティストたちは、被災地の人たちと共に活動するために現地を訪問し、活動しています。だからアーティストたちがしていることは、人と人との関係を発展させ、それらの関係がアート作品をつくるという原理に立っています。

社会全体にこのようなシェアリング（共有）し、互いに助け合うことの意義が顕著になってきていると思います。シェアリングは個人が何かを占有しようとすることとは正反対のことです。つまり皆で考え、みんなで作り、みんなで管理することが大事になったのです。例えば、個々人が異なった目的、時間、予算にもとづいて車という資産をシェアするカーシェアリングのように。

だから本当は政治も変わらなければなりません。今日では、インターネット上の情報を集約すれば、国民の声や政治的な方向性のほとんどを知ることが出来ます。そうなると政府の役割は最終的に、リスクコントロール、つまり警察と軍事力のコントロールにつきといっている人もいます。今の代議員制の政治では、政治家は本当は現実を把握できてはいないのではないでしょうか。直接みんなの意見を反映する方法があれば、多分その方が健全です。もし直接投票で方向性の対立が生じたら、そのときこそ政治は議論の場をもてばいいのです。将来、民主主義政治のシステムも、もっと新しい形に変わる必要があるのではないでしょうか。

被災地を以前のように復興させるという活動が行われていますが、津波の影響で現地の人口が減っているだけでなく、日本全体の人口もどんどん減少しています。ですから、将来、日本にどのような社会が訪れるのかを考えながら新しい町を再興することが重要ではないかと思います。情報システムやエネル

全長13メートルの巨大こけし「花子」。東北各地の伝統的な文様を纏って、東京ミッドタウンに設置された。
A massive 13-meter *kokeshi* doll at Tokyo Midtown Galleria. Wearing traditional patterns from the various parts of Tohoku, the *kokeshi* is called Hanako.
©2012 六本木アートナイト実行委員会
©2012 Roppongi Art Night Committee

ギーシステム、交通機関のシステムなどの新しいインフラを今こそ、これらの地域で実験してみるべきです。それが行われれば、その街は様々な意味で発展することになるでしょう。

これは現在のメタボリズムとは何かという考え方です。メタボリズムとは1960年代の日本に起きた建築運動の名称です。メタボリズムの運動は時代的に戦後の復興期だったので、社会インフラと土地の再開発とのつながりがありました。しかし、今もし、都市の新たな発展の可能性を論じるなら、新しいインフラや交通機関、情報システム、エネルギーシステムを考える必要があります。だから、政府は過去の単なる複製のような復興ではなく、新しい都市の可能性を指導し、実現し、支援する必要があると思います。それが、本当に未来へ向う復興のはずです。

アート分野においては、昨年、六本木アートナイトという六本木の街中で行う

一晩限りの展覧会を中止し、来年(2012年)行う計画をしています。私たちは今年参加する予定と同じアーティストに来年も参加してもらえるか聞きました。するとアーティストたちは私たちに、今年と同じ作品を出すことはできないと言いました。もうあの災害の情景を見た後では、同じものを作ることはできないというのです。まだ何をしていいのかはっきりと分からないというアーティストも何人かいます。

今、13mの大きなこけしを作っています。アートを通して被災地を支援しているアーティストを招待し、アートナイトで活動を発表してもらうことも計画しました。アートを通しての復興は、次の六本木アートナイトのメインテーマです。

この出来事の記憶として、何人かのアーティストは、津波が到達した地点沿いに桜の木を植えることを提案しました。別のアーティストたちは、被災を免れた建物を保存することを考えています。それは未来の世代に過去の経験を伝えることであり、アートに可能な役割の一つなのです。アートは、無力ですが、また大きな意味をもつだろうと信じています。

Fumio Nanjo
Director, Mori Art Museum

When the earthquake occurred, I was heading to Haneda Airport. I understood how severe the situation was because as soon as I arrived at the airport, all flights were canceled. After confirming that everything was all right at my office, I headed to my parents' house because I could not reach them by phone. I watched TV with them and then understood what really had happened.

On TV I saw the images of the tsunami and the victims who could not escape from it. In a moment the tsunami took the lives of thousands of people. I watched the images of the destructive tsunami, repeated over and over again on TV, but after a while the media then shifted its focus to the Fukushima catastrophe and the radiation. I instantly understood that the issues related to radioactivity would have a longer and wider impact on society than the tsunami. A vast area of Fukushima would be sealed off for a long time. A year on, we still don't have accurate information on what will happen to us in the future.

At the same time, an increasing number of people have opened up their minds and are sharing their opinions and cooperating with others, instead of focusing on an individualistic way of thinking. The selfish way of thinking only focusing on existing working models or displays of wealth has been replaced by flexible and genuine ways of thinking. When it comes to land, more and more people have also started to prefer mobility since the necessity of being tied to the land has become less relevant. And due to the technological development, human mobility has become more convenient: Growing numbers of people are now able to work anywhere as long as they have a laptop.

In another words, since the disaster many people have started to reconsider their lifestyles and change their sets of values. No obvious change has been seen in artworks, but artists like Ichiro Endo, Yoshiaki Kaihatsu, and Masato Nakamura are engaging in artistic activities that create dialogue collaboratively. I feel that this type of artwork will increase in the future. Artists have visited the disaster areas to work with victims. They are working under the principal that developing human relationships creates art.

I think a sense of sharing and helping each other has become more prominent in Japanese society at large. The idea of sharing is completely opposite to individual monopolization. It has become more important for people to think, create, and manage things together, like the example of car sharing, which enables people to share the piece of property that is a vehicle, as per different objectives, schedules, and budgets.

Politics too needs to change. Today you can grasp a whole spectrum of citizens' voices and political directions by collecting online information. This means that some people say that the ultimate role of the government is limited to controlling risks, such as what the police and military do. In our current system of representative politics the politicians do not have a grasp on reality. If there is a way to reflect the voices of people directly, that sounds healthier to me. And if conflict in direction rises from direct voting, that is when politics comes into play by providing a platform for discussion. I think the current democratic system needs to change in the future.

People seem to be working on reconstructing the disaster areas into how they were before. Given that not only the population of these areas but Japan's population in general is in decline, I think it is important to imagine a new vision for society during the process of rebuilding the towns. We should experiment with new infrastructures such as information, energy, and transportation systems in these areas. If this is done, the areas will develop in all kinds of ways.

We need to ask what is contemporary metabolism. Metabolism was a Japanese architecture movement active in the 1960's. Overlapping with the era of reconstruction after the war, the Metabolism movement was connected to the development of social infrastructure and urban redevelopment. If we talk about the possibility for new urban development, then we need to think about new transportation, information technology, and energy systems. Instead of copying the past, we need to explore, practice, and support new urban development, which will lead us to reconstruction that moves towards the future.

In terms of art, we had to cancel Roppongi Art Night,[1] the one-night-only art event in the Roppongi area. But we are planning to hold it in

1. A major public art event that began in 2009.

2012. We asked the artists we had planned to have participate in the 2011 event if they were willing to join us for the 2012 edition. The artists responded that they could not submit the same work. They said that after seeing the images of the disaster, they could no longer make the same work. Some artists said they still didn't know what to make.

We are currently making *kokeshi*[2] doll that is thirteen meters big. We also plan to invite artists who are supporting the disaster areas to showcase their activities. Reconstruction through art will be the main theme of the next Roppongi Art Night.

To remember the disaster, some artists proposed planting cherry blossoms along the line where the tsunami reached. Another artist is thinking of conserving a building that escaped the destruction of the disaster. Passing on past experiences to future generations is one of the possible roles for art. While art may be powerless, I believe it will have a great significance in the future.

2. Wooden dolls, originally a folk craft from the Tohoku region.

福原義春
株式会社資生堂 名誉会長

突然の災禍が被災地域におけるコミュニティと人々が共有する文化に甚大な影響を与えたことが判って、それらの復興と再活性化に取り組むことにしました。3.11は人々の生命観、価値観、ライフスタイルには最近の30年をとれば最大の影響があったといえるでしょう。人々は物質的・金銭的な思考から脱して精神的・人間的な基本に戻ることになりました。絆はその一つの象徴です。

この震災で日本全体として大きいダメージを受けました。しかし、災害に冷静に立ち向かう日本人の精神性の高さと深さが海外から好意をもって受け止められ、この状況からどのようなリカバリーとクリエイションをするかが注目されています。日本人は一人ひとりが「日本人とは何か」「コミュニティとは何か」「どのようにして生きていくのか」と深く考えざるを得ない状況になりました。私はそのことは、日本がグローバルな世界の中で普遍的な日本の価値を発見し、さらに新たな価値を創造することにつながっていくのではないかと考えています。そして東北特有の粘り強い人間性と、地域コミュニティの絆の強さは、時間はかかっても震災のダメージを克服し、日本全体に活力を与える新しい文化を創造してくれるものと信じています。

世界には数え切れないほどの文化の定義がありますが、私自身は「文化とは、より良く生きようとする人間の創造的行為、目に見える過程が文化である。そして、時代ごとの文化を背景にした成果物が芸術である」と言い続けてきました。人間は、より良く生きようと願い、努力することによって「ただ生存するだけの動物」ではなくなる。とすれば、文化こそ人間を人間たらしめる要素なのではないでしょうか。したがって、生きていくための安心・安全が満たされたあとには、より良く生きたいという願いが人間に生じるのは当然のことです。そして、より良く生きたいと願う人間の創造的行為が文化であるならば、文化は人々の心に前向きの活力を与えることで、昨日の絶望を今日の欲望に変え、今日の欲望を明日への希望に変えてくれると信じています。被災地に限ったことでは

ありませんが、打ちひしがれた人にこそ、明日への希望が必要であり、そこから生まれた日本文化は、新たな物語と世界的な普遍性をもった日本ブランドの創造にもつながると信じています。そして今後も3.11以降の価値観に沿った活動を更に積極化したいと考えています。

Yoshiharu Fukuhara
Honorary Chairman, Shiseido

When it was revealed that the sudden disaster had a huge impact both on the communities and the culture shared by locals in the disaster areas, I was determined to work on rebuilding and revitalizing these communities. It has had a greater impact on people's views on life, values, and lifestyle than anything in the last 30 years. Casting off materialistic and monetary ways of thinking, people are returning to spiritual and human fundamentals. The emphasis on *kizuna* (ties, bonds) symbolizes this.

Japan as a whole experienced the destructive damage as a result of the earthquake. However, the height and profundity of the Japanese people's spirit in calmly dealing with the disaster was received favorably overseas, and there is much anticipation about how the Japanese are going to engage with the processes of recovery as well as creation. The disaster put all of us in a situation where we thought deeply about what it means to be Japanese, what "community" means, and how we are going to live. I expect these inquiries will lead us to discover the Japanese values that are also universal in this globalized world, and create a new set of values. Furthermore, I believe that the tenacious quality of the Tohoku people and the strong bonds in the regional communities will eventually contribute to overcoming the damage caused by the disaster, and create new culture that can energize the entire nation, even though the process may require a great deal of time.

Throughout the world there are numerous definitions of culture. As I have always said, culture means our creative endeavor to live better and its visible process. And the output of the culture in each era is the arts. The fact that humanity hopes and endeavors to live better distinguishes us from mere animals that simply exist. If this is true, culture is the decisive element that makes us human. It is, thus, natural that the idea to live better surges once our needs for security and safety are met. And if our creative endeavor to live better is considered to be "culture," culture provides positive energy for people, transforming yesterday's despair into today's hope, and today's desire into tomorrow's hope. This is not necessarily limited only to the disaster areas, but more than anybody it is those in despair who need hope for tomorrow, and the Japanese culture born out of it will create a new story as well as a new Japanese brand with universality. I would like to engage further in activities based on post-3.11 values.

藤原秀樹

面白法人 KAYAC 京都支社長
ART-Meter ディレクター

ART-Meterはアート・絵画の委託販売オンラインのギャラリーとして6年前に誕生し、約3,500人のアーティストが登録しています。一方、作品の登録数は今5万点位あります。どなたでも画家登録がART-Meterのウェブサイトからでき、作品を売ることができます。登録は直接インターネットからできます。そのため、画家活動をサポートするウェブサイトになり、ファインアーティストのためというよりも、アマチュアに向けて幅広く開かれています。3.11の影響は、私たちのART-Meterのギャラリーの中でも感じました。実際震災後すぐ、サイトから作品を登録する数が通常より減りました。3.11、僕は鎌倉にいました。とても大きな地震で、テレビではその起こった事のショッキングなシーンを報道していました。自分でも経験したことのないことでした。それは多くの画家の方も僕と同じようにショッキングだったようで、彼らの内の多数は作品を制作し続けることができなかったです。だから、そのショックは多くの画家の方の制作を止めました。完全に止まったわけではないですけど、アーティストの登録も通常より減ったということですね。

3.11以前、僕は関東地方で働いていましたが、震災後僕たちは京都にオフィスを開けました。そのため、関東地方と関西地方の地震に対する感覚の違いに気づくことができました。関西地方は、あの地震に関して東日本と比較して甚大な被害を経験しておらず、主にテレビの放送を通じて地震を経験しました。最初、僕は西日本にいるアーティストは地震の影響をそれほど受けていないのかと思っていました。マスメディアを通しての間接的なことで、彼ら自身は体験していないですし。でも実際、日本でも地震の起こらなかった場所に住んでいるアーティストの作風の変化に気づきました。例えば、アーティストの北村さんはART-Meterでもっとも人気があり、評価され、作品もよく売れているアーティストのうちの一人です。北村さんは九州の大分に住んでいて、3.11以後、彼も作風に変化がありました。ですから3.11は、東日本以外に住んでいるアーティストの作風が変わったり、作品を表現し続けることが困難な状況

に置かれたりと、影響を与えたと思います。

3.11以後、これとは別の変化に気づきました。それは毎日僕たちの所にアーティスト達から、復興のために何か役に立つことができないかと、たくさんの意見が届くようになりました。アーティスト達自身が何かできるのではないかと。彼らはアマチュアに近いアーティストで、彼らのアクションは社会的に大きな影響を与えることができないと知っていますが、「皆でやれば何かできるんじゃないか？」というメッセージが届くようになりました。そこで僕たちは震災にあった地方を手助けしようと、募金活動を始めることを考えました。その企画は4月1日から始めて4月30日までやりました。通常のART-Meterですと、作品を販売するとき売り上げをアーティストとART-Meterでシェアしています。画家が55％、ART-Meterが45％です。しかしチャリティーイベントにあたり、売り上げのすべて寄付するためにアーティストの方々に自分の作品を寄付したい人はいますかと募集しました。はっきりとした作品数は覚えていないのですが、とにかく数千点の作品が、寄付したいとアーティスト達からの申し出で集まりました。まず、ART-Meterのサイト上で行い、あと代官山のHILLSIDE TERRACEさんがギャラリースペースを無料で貸してくれたので、そこでもイベントを開催しました。このイベントのおかげで、多くの画家さんと彼らの作品、それを買ってくださったたくさんのお客様、そしてツイッターでこの活動を広めてくださった多くの方々を集めることができました。何かこう、一つの運動が社会に広まっていく感覚はありました。この現象について話が少しそれるんですが、地震が起きたとき電話が繋がらなくなったんですよ。ただし、その時にインターネットは繋がっていて、連絡を取ったり、ニュースを知らせたり、最新情報を把握するのにみんなツイッターとかFacebookのような、いわゆるソーシャル・ネットワークを使っていました。このことはとても重要な社会現象だと思います。僕もソーシャルメディアを使っていて、皆がより近く、より一つになった感覚がありました。

話をイベントに戻すと、200点位の作品を売ることができ、1ヶ月のチャリティーの売り上げは50万円になりました。そんなに大きい額ではないのですが、それはART-Meterのポリシーとアマチュアの画家さん達にも販売する場を持たせるようにするという目的のため、作品の販売価格はとても安いんです。平均すると1点3,000円位じゃないかな、だからチャリティーで集まった金額は大きくないんですけど、でも多くの人がこの企画に参加したかったことを象徴していま

す。だから、この活動は、画家さん達がすぐに自分たちに出来る事として熱心に取り組んで下さり、そして多くの画家さんはチャリティーのために作品を作り、販売しながら3.11に対して自分たちの出来ることをしたいという気持ちを感じたと思います。さらにギャラリーを無償で貸して頂いたり、ソーシャルメディアを使って広めてくださったりという事はとても意味のある結果だったと思います。

北村直登
Naoto Kitamura
© ART-Meter

もう地震から何ヶ月もたった今、一部の画家さん達の中には大きく作風が変わっても、何ができるかを考え、作品を再び制作し始めていることがわかります。例えば北村さんは作風に変化が見られました。3.11以前は動物の躍動感を鮮やかな色彩で描いていましたが、震災後は彼の作品で初めて風景画を取り入れました。青色を多く使った絵や、以前の作品よりもっと鮮烈な人物画を描いています。そして、その青い空間は癒しなのか、祈りなのかを表現しているように見えます。この絵は北村さんが震災後に描いた作品です。50号の大作を観衆の前でライブペインティングしました。あと、町の絵を描いているアーティストさんがいます。artnoteさんといいます。このアーティストさんは震災後しばらく作品を作ることができなかったんですが、東北の復興後の町の絵であるというふうに考え直して、もう一回描き始めたとおっしゃっています。
ですから画家それぞれ、3.11に対する考え方や受け止め方は違うと思うんですけども、こういう難しい時期だからこそ、自分のアートの役割を考え直すきっかけになったと思います。僕、カヤック（ART-Meterの運営会社）に入る前はカイカイキキ（現代美術家の村上隆氏が率いる企業）で働いていて、そこはファイ

ンアートを扱っていました。本当のアートの王道でした。反対にART-Meterはファインアートとは別の、アマチュアよりのサービスをしています。これによって僕は、アマチュアのアーティストがプロのコレクターではない一般の方に作品を提供したりという、もっと広い意味でのクリエイティブ産業の全体像を見られる立場になりました。この視点はとても重要で、なぜならインターネットの到来で、インターネットを通して、プロではない買い手がこのクリエイティブ産業の多くを占める可能性が出てきました。それによってロングテール理論（2006年アンダーソンにより提唱）の時代がやって来たと思います。このコミュニケーションの手段は3.11以後、よりいっそう重要なこととなりました。それはインターネットから届く情報を信用し、それを活用する人の数が増えたからです。具体的には、緊急時、防災時にインターネットを活用する方法というのを官公庁から相談を受けています。この必要性は、官公庁の方が明らかに3.11後、インターネットの重要性を見直したといいました。

僕らは東北地方のアーティストさんたちが、彼らの制作活動を再開するにあたり困っているかもしれないと思い、宮城県、岩手県、福島県、青森県で活動するアーティスト達の作品を目に付きやすく、作品制作を促せるようにし、また日本赤十字への募金活動も続けるため、2012年3月9日から3月31日まで「応援しよう！東北で活躍する画家」と題して特集を組みました。そして僕らはチャリティーイベントで、画家も買い手も応援する人も、一つになったという経験を今もしています。それは物事を新しく作り出して再生していけるようにアートがとても役に立つ、一つの手段に成り得ると僕らは考えます。

Artnote
Artnote
©ART-Meter

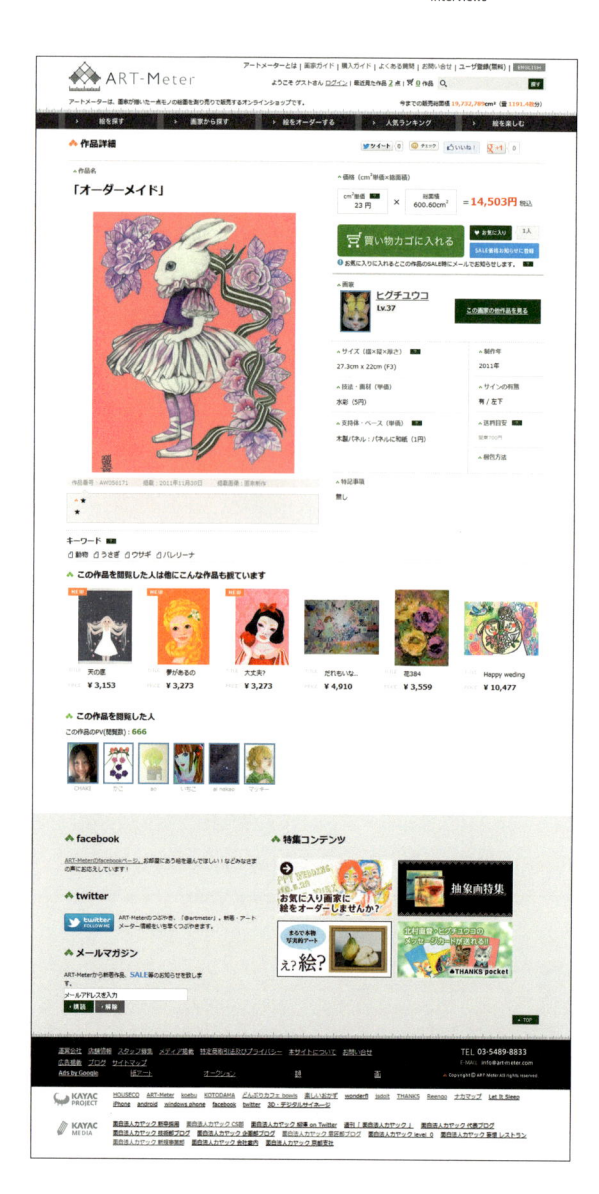

ART-Meterのオフィシャルサイト
ART-Meter website
©ART-Meter

Hideki Fujiwara
President, Kyoto branch of KAYAC Inc.
Director, ART-Meter

ART-Meter was founded six years ago as an online art and painting gallery based on a consignment system. We have about 3,500 registered artists and 50,000 registered artworks. Anyone can register as an artist on ART-Meter and sell their work. The website is open more to amateurs than fine art artists, and supports artistic activities. We felt the impact of 3.11 within the ART-Meter community. For example, right after the disaster, the number of registered artwork declined.

I was in Kamakura on March 11th, watching the shocking coverage of the disaster on TV. I had never experienced this in my life. Many painters also felt shock like I did and that they could not continue painting. It didn't completely stop but the artist registration did decrease. I was working in the Kanto area before 3.11 but we opened an office in Kyoto in the aftermath of 3.11, which made us aware of the difference in perception of the disaster between people in the Kansai and Kanto areas. People in Kansai experienced the earthquake through their TVs without being affected directly. So at first I thought artists living in west Japan did not feel the impact of the disaster because their experience of the earthquake came mostly from the media. Yet I actually noticed changes even in the artwork by artists who live far away from the disaster areas. For example, take Naoto Kitamura, one of the most popular, acclaimed, and bankable artists on ART-Meter, and who lives in Oita Prefecture in Kyushu. His painting style has also changed in the aftermath of 3.11. The disaster in this sense influenced artists in west Japan at large, affecting artistic styles and imposing very difficult circumstances on artists about how to continue producing art.

I also noticed another change in the post-3.11 era. A lot of artists contacted us every day wondering if they could do something to help the reconstruction efforts. Being amateur artists and knowing their actions have little influence on society, they nevertheless sent us messages about being able to make a difference by doing something together. In response we ran a fund-raising campaign from April 1st until April 30th. In general, when we sell artworks, ART-Meter shares the sales with the artist. ART-Meter gets 45% and the artist gets 55%. But for this fund-raising campaign we put out an open call asking artists if they were interested in donating artwork without their share as all the sales were going to be donated. I don't remember the exact number but we got several thousand artworks. We first did the fund-raising on the ART-Meter website and then organized an event at Hillside Gallery in Daikanyama, Tokyo, which offered us use of the space for free. Thanks to this event, we brought together a lot of artists, their artworks, customers, and those who helped us to spread the word on Twitter. I experienced the process of a movement that spreads widely through society. It's a bit off topic, but when the disaster happened, the phone service wasn't working but the Internet was fine. Everyone was using social media such as Twitter and Facebook to communicate with each other and get the latest information. This is a very important social phenomenon. I myself also used social media and it gave me a sense of becoming one with others.

Going back to the charity event, we sold about 200 pieces and our sales over the month amounted to ¥500,000. This is not a lot of money but considering our mission was to provide a platform for amateur painters to sell their work, the prices were set very cheap to begin with. On average, a single artwork only cost about ¥3,000. So although the money we raised wasn't so much, the event symbolizes the participation of many artists. A lot of artists engaged passionately with the campaign, creating work especially for it and selling it because they hoped to do what they could to help. The gallery was also kind enough to offer its space for free and many people spread the word about it via social media. The result was very meaningful.

Several months have now passed since the disaster and some artists, though their painting styles have greatly changed, are still thinking about what they can do and have started producing work again. For example, I saw a change in Kitamura's style. Whereas before 3.11 he painted vibrant animals in vivid colors, he tried landscape painting for the first time after the earthquake. Another notable change is that he uses blue color a lot now and paints human portraits that are more pronounced compared to his previous work. The blue spaces on the canvases seem to represent healing or prayer. Kitamura did a live painting of this particular large painting—a size 50—in front of an audience after the disaster. Another artist, artnote, who paints towns, couldn't produce any work for a while after the disaster. But after he reconsidered the towns he draws as representing the reconstructed towns in the disaster areas, he then started to paint again.

While each artist has a different take on 3.11, I think precisely because it was such a difficult period, it gave them the opportunity to think about the role of the artist. Before working for KAYAC, the parent company of ART-Meter, I used to work for Kaikai Kiki, which is run by artist Takashi Murakami and deals in fine art. While Kaikai Kiki is proper contemporary art, ART-Meter provides a service dedicated to amateur artists, helping them sell their work to ordinary citizens. My working experience at ART-Meter enables me to see the creative industries from a broader perspective. This perspective is vital because the arrival of the Internet opens up possibilities for non-professional buyers to dominate the creative industries. I think the era of long tail distribution as advocated by Chris Anderson has finally arrived. This new online communication became even more important after 3.11 because the numbers of people who trust and utilize the Internet have drastically increased. To put it in concrete terms, public agencies contacted our company for consultations on the possible uses of the Internet in times of emergency and for disaster prevention. People from the agencies said that they had re-evaluated the importance of the Internet after 3.11.

To respond to the concern that Tohoku-based artists might be having difficulty restarting their artistic work, and also to continue our fund-raising efforts for the Japanese Red Cross, we created a feature page on our website from March 9th till March 31st, 2012. It was called "Support Tohoku-based artists!" and visualized the work of artists based in Miyagi, Iwate, Fukushima, and Aomori. We still experience the same excitement we had when we organized the charity campaign, a feeling of solidarity with artists, collectors, and supporters. We believe that art can be very helpful for recreating and regenerating things.

古谷誠章

早稲田大学教授
建築家

3.11から数ヵ月が経ち日本社会は変わりつつあって、人々の考え方も変わったと思います。一番大きかったのはそれまでの価値観だったと思います。できるだけコストを切り詰めようというコスト至上主義の考え方がありました。でも今では人が手間暇をかけること、新しいアイデアに知恵を絞って、新しい価値を生み出すことに重きを置かないといけないと考えます。

エネルギーを考えた場合にも、これまでは原子力発電が他の方式よりコストが安いから使うと説明されてきた。つまり目的はコスト削減であり、安全性や廃棄物処理を含めた総合的な観点ではなく、どちらかと言えば経済性で判断されてきたんですね。その陰でいろいろなものが見過ごされてきたわけです。

また、被災地の多くの人たちは漁業や農業の産業で働いていました。彼らも常々このコスト至上主義に翻弄されてきた。今、僕たちはその感覚をもとに戻し、人々の生活の質を改善させるいい機会を与えられたと思います。この被害を受けた土地を飛躍的に経済発展させるような復興はなかなか難しいと思いますが、大量生産や価格競争に苛まれないような、丁寧に獲られた魚、丁寧に栽培された野菜、人々の生活と直接つながった漁業や農業の新しい意味を作ることが出来ると思います。

アーティストやデザイナーは、この新しい生活のスタイルを作り出すことの手伝いが出来ると思います。何も無いところから手間や知恵をつくして何かを作り出すという喜びや幸せを作り出すんです。こういう手助けをするにはアーティストやデザイナーのような人がいいと思うんですね。

僕は今から30年近く前に、岩手県の田野畑村で体育館や集会ホールを設計しました。今でもそこは村人たちのコミュニティセンターになっていますが、大震災直後には人々の避難所になっていました。すぐさま4月には、避難生活を少しでも快適なものとするために、間仕切りや身の回りの棚やちゃぶ台等を作りにいきましたが、それはいわば緊急時のための支援です。しかし未来の世代のために役に立つ方策も考える必要があるんです。三陸地方はか

復興村営住宅の平面形イメージ：各住戸の前には自家菜園や漁具の手入れの場所があり、住民同士が日常的に交流する場所ともなる。(2011.12.6)
Planar image of hamlet housing reconstruction. There is a place for taking care of fishing equipment and a garden in front of each residential unit, which is also a place where residents might interact with each other on a daily basis (December 6th, 2011).
©Nobuaki Furuya

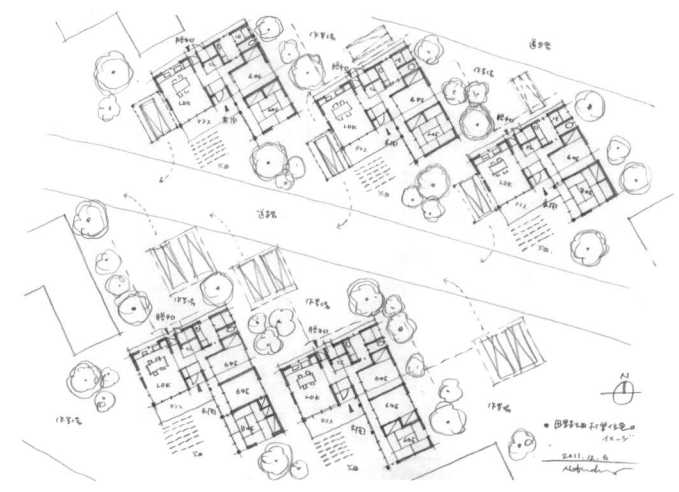

って、明治39年（1906年）と昭和8年（1933年）の大津波を経験をしています。つまりこのコミュニティは過去に昔の世代が津波の経験をしており、お年寄りだけではなく若者たちにもそれが伝承されていて、3.11に大津波が港に押し寄せた時、彼らはどのように対処しなければいけなかったのかを知っていました。「津波てんでんこ」という言い伝えです。そういう経験や知恵の継承が、防波堤を超えるような大津波にも有効で役に立ったわけですよね。

僕が過去に研究した事例では、インド洋大津波の震源地バンダ・アチェに近いシムル島と呼ばれる島では、100年以上前に津波被害を経験し、その経験がいまだに島の人々に伝承されていました。2004年の地震の後、海水が引き潮になったのを見て、彼らは津波が来ると分かっていました。この住民によって共有された知恵が彼ら全員を海岸から高台に避難させ、一人の犠牲者も出さなかったのです。

つまり声を大にして私が言いたいのは、防波堤などのハードウェアも地域や住民を守るためにとても重要ですが、地域の人々の知識や知恵もまたそれ以上に大きな役割を果たすという事なんです。

コミュニティの記憶を保つために、こうした知恵を眼に見える形で世代を超えて語り継ぐ必要があるんです。そんな時、デザイナーやアーティスト達は時代を超えて共有の記憶になるもの生み出すために土地の人々と協働することができます。過去の災害というネガティブな記憶でも、それを題材として人々に親しまれ将来のためにポジティブに役に立てるようなものにするのです。

建築家は建築を通して、人々の暮らしを幸せにする役割を果たすことが出来るはずです。建築はある意味で人々の記憶のメモリーデバイスなんです。人々は住んでいる家の中でそれを感じることが出来ます。こういう記憶をまた次の世代につなげることや、生き生きと毎日の暮らしを営み、それを伝えていくようなことに役に立ちたいなと思っています。

避難所に設置した更衣用のブース、女性の更衣や子どもの勉強、風邪等を引いた人の就寝用に使える。(2011.5.4)
Booths placed in a refugee center as changing rooms, and study rooms for children, and spaces for sleeping for people who have caught a cold (May 4th, 2011)
©Nobuaki Furuya

復興村営住宅のモデル:高台移転の村営住宅のデザイン、一部には店舗付きの住戸もあり、人々のたまり場にもなる。(2011.12.25)
Model of hamlet housing reconstruction. Residential upland relocation with some residential units fitted with retail spaces, but also with areas for people to come together. (December 25th, 2011).
©Nobuaki Furuya

Nobuaki Furuya
Professor, Waseda University
Architect

A few months have now passed since 3.11 and I think Japanese society is changing, as well as the way people think. What changed the most were the existing values we had based on cost optimization. I think we need to focus on creating new values while putting time and care into exploring new ideas.

Concerning the energy policy, for example, we were told that the government used nuclear energy because it costs less than other energies. So here too, economic efficiency and cutting costs were top priority without considering comprehensive perspectives such as safety and waste management. Driven by cost efficiency, our society has overlooked many aspects like this.

Many people in the disaster areas used to work in the fishing and farming industries. They too were at the mercy of cost optimization. I think we have gained the opportunity to get our decency back and improve people's quality of life. I think it will be difficult to create dramatic economic development in the region. But what we can do is regenerate the fishing and farming industries to promote quality fishing and vegetable crops, industries not wracked by mass production or price wars, but rather more connected to our everyday life.

Artists and designers can help to create this new lifestyle. By making something from scratch with care and wisdom, they create joy and happiness. I think artists and designers are the perfect people for this type of helping.

About 30 years ago, I designed a gymnastic hall and assembly hall in Tanohata in Iwate Prefecture. While it still functions as a community center for locals, it was also used as a shelter in the immediate aftermath of 3.11. I went to the center in April to create partitions, shelves and low tables, aiming to make the life in the shelter more comfortable. What I did was emergency aid, so to speak, and now we need to think about strategies useful for future generations. The Sanriku region has experienced two big tsunamis in the past, one in 1906 and another in 1933. The past generations of Tanohata community have experienced tsunamis, which have been passed on not only to the older people but also to the young generation. When the 3.11 tsunami arrived at the harbor, people knew what to do. "*Tsunami tendenko*," a slogan widely shared among local population, is a good example. It means that when a tsunami arrives, each individual should escape to a hill and each person is responsible for protecting his or her own life. This inheritance of experiences and knowledge was remarkably effective and useful in 2011, when the tsunami was higher than the seawall.

One of my past case studies shows that Simeulue island, near Banda Aceh, a seismic center of 2004 Indian Ocean earthquake and tsunami, experienced tsunami destruction over 100 years ago, and that experience is still shared by the villagers to this day. When the earthquake happened in 2004, locals knew that a tsunami would come by looking at the low tide. The knowledge shared by local populations enabled them to evacuate to a hill and no one died.

What I want to express here is that while hardware such as a seawall is important for protecting a community and its inhabitants, shared knowledge and wisdom play an even greater role.

To retain the memories of a community, we have to pass down wisdom in a visual form across the generations. Designers and artists can work together with local people to create memories to be shared by people timelessly. They can use even negative memories, such as past disasters, as a resource for creating something that people find familiar and helpful in the future.

I think architects can play a role in making people's lives happier through architecture. In a way, architecture is a memory device. People can sense this in the house they live in. And I want to serve in this passing along of the memories of vibrant everyday life.

山口真樹子
公益財団法人 東京都歴史文化財団
東京文化発信プロジェクト室 企画担当ディレクター

2008年より国際交流基金ケルン日本文化会館にて、主に舞台芸術の分野における国際文化交流の仕事に就いていました。その後帰国、2011年春より東京都歴史文化財団東京文化発信プロジェクト室の仕事を始めました。2011年3月11日の地震発生時は屋外にいました。あまりに揺れが大きく、また長く続いたので、とっさに1970年代の映画「日本沈没」[1]を思い出しました。当時テレビで放映していた作品で、子供の私にはとてもショッキングな映像だったことを覚えています。3月11日のあの地震は、立っていられないほどの激しい揺れで、気分が悪くなるくらいでした。いやな予感がしました。その後も頻繁に余震が起き、怖くて外出できなくなりました。最新の状況を把握するために、インターネット、ツイッター、facebook、テレビ、ラジオから離れられない毎日が続きました。同時に、「たとえ明日世界が滅びようとも、私は今日、リンゴの木を植える。」という言葉が現実感をもって胸に迫ることがよくありました。

東京文化発信プロジェクト室では、「世界的な文化創造都市・東京」を国内外にアピールするとともに、国内外の関係者が東京に集うプログラムや事業を展開しネットワークを強化するため、平成23年度よりネットワーキング事業を開始しました。具体的には、10月に開催する東京クリエイティブ・ウィークの期間中に、国際会議と国際招聘プログラムを実施するというものです。震災が起きたことにより状況も変わり、国際会議についてはより具体的なテーマやコンセプトを求め、「新しい社会をデザインし、新たなつながりをつくるために」と「3.11以後の文化の力」をテーマに、未来の社会の姿を考えるFUTURE SKETCH 東京会議（2011年10月28日・29日）を開催しました。海外からゲストスピーカーも迎え、新しい創造的社会形成について議論を展開した結果、コミュニティ間のネットワークの重要性、新しいリーダー像、コミュニケーションのためのチャンネル維持の重要性、さらには、草の根市民社会のネットワーク形成、アジアにおける芸術文化を核とするネットワーク形成など、具体的な課題提起や提案がなされました。

[1]. 森谷司郎監督により1973年に公開された日本映画。

ネットワーキング事業のもうひとつの柱である国際招聘プログラムの内容も、震災後の日本の芸術文化をめぐる状況に触れることを中心に企画しました。国際招聘プログラムは、若手の芸術文化関係者を東京に招き、様々な文化事業を視察し、日本の関係者との交流を深め、ネットワークにつなげていくプログラムです。震災直後は状況が不安定で、プログラムの実現が困難なのではないかと思った時期もありました。最終的には13か国から参加者があり、10日間に及ぶ充実した滞在プログラムを実施し、関係者とのネットワーク形成や、ブルガリア、イタリアの雑誌やウェブマガジンへのアーティストインタビューの掲載など、様々なフィードバックや成果を得ることができました。

国際会議の企画を進めていた当時、アートや文化がこの状況について何が出来るのか、明確な答えは出ていませんでした。震災を目にして人間の無力さを思い知らされましたが、一方で人が生きていく上で、文化や芸術が大きな意味をもつことが改めてわかってきたと思います。

東京に住むことが唯一の選択肢ではないと考える人も出てきました。地方へ移住し、人生において何が一番大切なのかを改めて考えながら、新しい土地で活動を始めたアーティストもいます。芸術や文化には、これまで自明とされてきた社会の前提や常識を問い直し、新しい発想やものの見方を提案し、社会の変化や変革を可能にする力があると考えています。今後も海外の関係者とのネットワークを拡充し、意見交換を重ね交流を深めながら、この点について考えていきたいと思います。

FUTURE SKETCH 東京会議（2011年10月28日・29日）
Future Sketch: Tokyo Conference (October 28-29th, 2011)
©Culture and Social Innovation: Tokyo Conference, Tokyo Culture Creation Project Office

国際招聘プログラム
International Visitors Program
Future Sketch: Tokyo Conference (October 28-29th, 2011)
©Culture and Social Innovation: Tokyo Conference, Tokyo Culture Creation Project Office

Makiko Yamaguchi
Tokyo Metropolitan Foundation for History and Culture
Director of Programming, Tokyo Culture Creation Project

From 2008, I worked for the Japan Cultural Institute in Cologne (the Japan Foundation) in Germany, responsible mainly for international exchange in performing arts. I then came back to Japan and since 2011 have been working for the Tokyo Metropolitan Foundation for History and Culture's Tokyo Culture Creation Project.

When the earthquake occurred on March 11th, 2011, I was outside. The quake was so big and long, it instantly reminded me of *Japan Sinks*[1], a movie from the 1970's. It had been broadcast on TV and I remember as a child being very shocked by it. The 3.11 earthquake caused tremors so strong that it was hard to remain standing up and it made me feel sick. I had a bad sense of foreboding. The frequent aftershocks made me scared of going outside. To understand the latest situation, days went by where I intensely monitored the Internet, Twitter, and Facebook. At the same time, something Martin Luther once said really struck me as very true: "If I knew the world would perish tomorrow, I would still plant my apple tree today."

In 2011 Tokyo Culture Creation Project started a networking project and program to gather both international and domestic cultural professionals with the aim of promoting "Tokyo as a global culture creation city." More precisely, it planned to organize an international conference and international visitors' program during Tokyo Creative Week in October. The disaster changed the circumstances so we wanted to set up a more detailed theme and concept for the conference. With "draw the future with the power of our culture" as its theme, we organized FUTURE SKETCH: Tokyo Conference on October 28th and 29th, 2011 to imagine a future society. As a result of discussion on the formation of a new creative society with international guest lecturers, the following concrete issues were presented: The importance of networking among communities; a new vision of leadership; maintaining channels for communication; the formation of a network

1. A film directed by Shiro Moriya and released in 1973. It is based on the book by Sakyo Komatsu. Another major film adaptation was released in 2009.

linking with grass-roots civil society; and the formation of a network based on art and culture as a nucleus in Asia.

Another core pillar of the networking project was the international visitors' program we planned for participants to understand the situation for Japanese art and culture in the aftermath of 3.11. The international visitors' program invites young arts and cultural professionals from overseas, and provides them with opportunities to visit various cultural enterprises, interact with their Japanese counterparts, and strengthen networks. At one point I thought we would not be able to realize the program because of the uncertain social climate immediately after the earthquake. In the end, with participants from thirteen countries, we managed to run a ten-day comprehensive program and gain meaningful feedback and results, such as forming a network of cultural professionals, and publishing artist interviews in Bulgarian and Italian magazines as well as online magazines.

While planning the international conference, we did not have a clear answer for what art and culture could do in this devastating situation. This catastrophe reminded me of how powerless human beings are, but I also came to understand again how much meaning art and culture have for our lives.

Some people started to think that living in Tokyo is not the only option available. In fact, some artists moved away to regional Japan and started to work in new places while re-considering what is the most important thing in their lives. I think art and culture possess the power to question existing social ideas and common practices, and to propose new ideas and perspectives, and make social change possible. We want to keep on thinking about this in the future while extending our international network of cultural professionals and exchanging opinions with our peers.

山野真悟

NPO法人 黄金町エリアマネジメントセンター 事務局長

ロゴマーク
Logo of the HIYORI
ART CENTER in
Ishinomaki City
©2012 日和アートセンター
©2012 HIYORI ART
CENTER

3.11後の僕のリアクションは、どのようにすれば被災地に対して良い形での復興の手伝いが出来るかを考えることでした。震災から2ヶ月後、僕は2度ほど被災地に行きました。女川辺りはまだ壊滅的な状態でしたが、石巻ではすでにボランティアの人たちが活動していました。僕らは横浜の団体として何が出来るかを考えていましたが、出しゃばりで押し付けがましいことはしたくなかったので、まずは小さいことから出来る事を考えました。

この横浜の黄金町エリアは、数年前まで売買春の店舗がたくさんあったところで、今僕らのNPOはそこで活動しています。横浜市がこの地区の再生を考えた時、アイデアのひとつとして、アーティストがレジデンスとして利用出来るようなエリアをつくるという案がありました。その結果、僕たちのアートによるまちづくりが始まりました。

それで、石巻でも似たような形で何か出来ないかと考えたんです。アートの力で壊されたものを再生し、アーティストのためのレジデンスの施設をつくることをまず考えました。そして、もしそのレジデンスとして使っている間に地元の人がそれ

とは違う別の目的として利用したければ地元の人にお返しする。このような目的で配慮と押し付けがましくならないように気をつけながら、石巻市と地元商店街と向き合いました。石巻市は僕らの目的に理解を示し、良い返事をしてくれました。そうこうしているうちに、神奈川県がNPOと横浜市に助成してくれることが決定し、市と僕らのNPOと大学の先生たちが共同して被害にあった建物を2年間借りて、その修復費、そこで働いてくれる人の人件費などに充てる資金を得ることが出来ました。

当時被災した建物の多くが解体予定となっていたため、物件は容易には見つかりませんでした。11月に入ってようやく建物を貸してくれる人が現れました。僕らはその建物の持ち主から許可を得て、11月から修復作業をするために最初のアーティストを送り込みました。一番最初に送ったアーティストは鉄と木のエキスパートです。彼の最初の仕事は重労働と、このプロジェクトに興味を持ってくれる地元の人や地元の協力者を探すことでした。

本来こういう状況には技師や現場作業員を送り込むはずです。コストが高いと感じていてもそういう業者を送り込むのが普通です。でも逆に、アーティストから見た違う方法、しかも、コストがかからない方法があると思うんです。そして、技師や現場作業員はその現場に行ってすぐに状況を的確に判断して必要なことを言い、仕事をするけれど、アーティストの場合は、現場に着いたら地域社会や現地の人と相談をして、現地にとって何が必要なのかを聞いて、問題の対処にあたると思うんです。こういうタイプのアプローチに有効なアーティストたちがいると思います。

オープニングパーティーは増田拓史によるプロジェクト「石巻食堂」で、地域のお母さんがつくった家庭料理を味わった。
The opening party for the "Ishinomaki cafeteria" project by Hirofumi Masuda at the HIYORI ART CENTER, featuring home cooking by local women.
©2012 日和アートセンター
©2012 HIYORI ART CENTER

山野真悟 | 233

この視点はアート活動の「産業化」の可能性をもっていると思います。長い目で見れば、これは地域の「コア」つまり地域に根付く、ある種、時間をかけて町に広めるような生産、消費、利益をもたらす効果があると思います。僕らが横浜で行ったアイデアが石巻でも役に立てばいいですね。

リノベーション計画と施工を担当したアーティストの増田拓史
The artist Hirofumi Masuda, who was in charge of the construction and renovation project
©2012 日和アートセンター
©2012 HIYORI ART CENTER

Shingo Yamano
Secretary General, NPO Koganecho Management Center

My reaction to 3.11 was to think about how I could help the reconstruction efforts in the disaster areas. Two months after the disaster I went to the areas twice. In the Onagawa area the situation was still catastrophic, but in Ishinomaki volunteers were already working actively. We thought about what we could do as a group in Yokohama, but we didn't want to do anything presumptuous, so we first thought about a small action that we could start right away.

Our NPO (non-profit organization) is based in Yokohama's Koganecho area, where there were a lot of brothels until a few years ago. When Yokohama City was thinking about revitalizing the area, one of the ideas was to create a district where artists can stay as a part of an artist-in-residency program. The result was that we started our efforts of building the community through art.

At first, I thought about doing something similar in Ishinomaki, regenerating what was destroyed through the power of art and creating a residential facility for artists. If local people wanted to use the facility for a different purpose during the residency period, we would return it to the locals. Being very conscious not to be too self-assertive, we worked with Ishinomaki City and local stores. As Ishinomaki City understood our objective and responded favorably, Kanagawa Prefecture decided to fund Yokohama City as well as our NPO. Together with Yokohama City and some university teachers, our NPO rented a damaged building for two years, with the funding we received covering the renovation and labor costs for those who work at the residency.

It was not easy to find a suitable building because many buildings hit by the earthquake were scheduled for demolition. A landlord who was willing to rent out a building finally came along in November 2011. With permission from the landlord, we sent out the first artist to start renovating the building from November. The first artist we selected was an expert in iron and woodworking and his first job, besides doing heavy manual labor, was to look for local collaborators who might be interested in this project.

You are supposed to send engineers or construction workers to this type of environment. Though more expensive, sending specialized contractors seems to be the conventional choice. But I think from an artist's perspective there are different ways of doing things and less expensive ones too. As soon as engineers and construction workers arrive at a site, they understand the circumstances accurately, say what's necessary, and start working. An artist, though, upon arriving at a site, figures out possible actions after consulting with local people and listening to their needs. There are artists who are good at this type of approach.

This perspective has the potential to "industrialize" art activities. From a long-term point of view, this type of art brings about production, consumption, and benefits while taking root in a local area over a long period. I hope that our idea formed in Yokohama will be useful in Ishinomaki.

山本高之
アーティスト

3.11の地震があった時、僕は名古屋のハワイアンレストランにいました。地震はとても長く続きました。幸いなことに名古屋には被害がなく、震災から免れたということは地元のテレビのアナウンサーからもはっきり述べられていましたが、テレビもラジオもすぐにすべてのことは報道しませんでした。マスメディアのシステムがすべてを遅らせているように見えました。そこでインターネットを使って他の情報を探すなかで、福島の原子炉の爆発の映像も見つけました。画像やビデオ、情報などを選べたり自由にアクセスしたりすることのできるインターネットは、今の時代非常に重要なメディアであり、真実性の度合いを見極める必要があるとはいえ、今まで自分が得ていた情報とは別の情報源として、(とりわけ震災以後)大切なものになりました。

地震を契機として起こった一連の出来事は、バブル時代からの衰退よりさらに深さを増した、本当の意味でのどん底に達するような、今後の日本の衰退への第一歩のように見えました。

ファインアートのアートプロダクションの観点から見ると、アートに対する批評的な視点の欠如という3.11以前の状況が、クリアになって来ていると思います。アーティスト、特にヨーロッパやアメリカの海外から来るアーティストたちは文化的なエリートであり、豊富な知識をもつ彼らや美術評論家たちは、アートがどのようなものであるかを決定する、あるいはアートとそうでないものとを区別する資格をもつと自他ともに認識していました。このような状況の下、観客は彼らに認められたものは必然的にアート作品であるとみなしてきました。そういう事に対して僕は反対です。アーティストはある程度の知識を持っていますが、彼らにすべての判断をゆだねるべきではなく、観客が何がアートで何がアートでないかを決めるべきなのです。3.11以降、日本にはアーティストやアート作品、それとアート市場に対する作品の価値の概念が議論に付されている印象があります。評価や選別の責任を専門家だけに任せないために、観客自らの役割も議論の対象になっています。実際のところ、一定のアート作品を理解するため

に基礎的な知識は必要ですが、だからといってそれについて掘り下げた研究までは求められていません。けれども、いずれにしても評価や選別の責任は観客に返されるべきだと考えます。

震災が起きて、子供たちにとって役立つことを子供たちと一緒にしたいと思い、何ができるかを考えました。子供たちは幼い時の経験にとても敏感です。幼少時に僕と一緒に「何か」を経験した彼らが、大人になってからトラウマや問題を乗り越えられるようなコンディションになるように努めています。たとえば、震災後秋田県の大館で実施したプロジェクト「なまはげといきる」では、なまはげという東北地方の民俗行事に登場するモンスターと、福島の原発事故による放射能汚染とを関連付けることで、原発の危険性をより理解できるようにしました。このプロジェクトは2011年8月に秋田の新聞の社会面に「怖いなまはげとの共生」という見出しで取り上げられました。

他の例としては「CHILDREN PRIDE」があります。東京の小学生を対象として企画されたこのプロジェクトは、子供たちが日常生活を送るなかで抱く個人的な要求を、デモ行進によって表現するというものです。興味深いのは、デモの最中に行うコール・アンド・レスポンスを通じて、個々の願いをみんなでシェアすることが出来るということでした。その後、この企画は全国各地で継続的に行っています。

将来について考えることは、震災を機に、日本の社会構造が変わるであろうということです。そして、特に新しい世代についてですが、人々が他人にアートの評価や選別を任せないで、自分たち自身でそれを行う責任が持てるようになったら、アートは社会にとって重要な役割を持つことが出来るようになると思います。

「チルドレン・プライド」
2011
Children Pride
project (2011)
©2014 Takayuki
Yamamoto

きみのみらいをおしえます
子どもたちが自由な発想
で「新しい占い」の方法
を考案し、好きな工作
材料をつかってオリジナ
ルの「占いの部屋」をつく
ります。ワークショップ発
表会では、実際に「占い
師」としてお客さんを占い
ます。

"Telling your future"
workshop (2012)
Children devise a
method for a new
kind of fortune-
telling with free
thinking. The
children create their
homemade fortune-
telling booths with
their choice of
materials. During
the workshop the
children become
fortune-tellers and
inform the audience
what's in store for
them.
©2014 Takayuki
Yamamoto

Takayuki Yamamoto
Artist

When the 3.11 earthquake hit Japan, I was in a Hawaiian restaurant in Nagoya. The earthquake lasted for a very long time. Fortunately, I learned through local TV news that Nagoya wasn't significantly damaged. Both TV and radio did not report everything that happened and it seemed to me that the system of mass media intentionally delayed information. I was searching for different information online and found an image of the explosion at the Fukushima nuclear power plant. While it is important to examine the accuracy of online media, it has become essential especially after the disaster as an alternative source of information from the one we used to access in the past, allowing people to search freely for images and videos.

The series of incidents that happened in the aftermath of the disaster seems to me the first step towards Japan's serious decline, to an extent more severe and deeper than the recession that occurred after the bubble economy collapsed.

From the perspective of producing fine art, the situation that existed before 3.11 of a lack of criticality in art became even clearer.

Artists, especially those from Europe and America, are a cultural elite. With their rich knowledge, artists and art critics claim to have the credentials for determining the nature of art and distinguishing what is and what is not considered "art." Viewers under these circumstances inevitably presume what this cultural elite recognize to be art. I disagree with this. While artists do have a certain amount of knowledge, we should let viewers decide what is and what is not art rather than leaving the entire judgment to artists and critics. Since 3.11, there have been debates about the concepts of the artist and art, and the value of an artwork in the art market. Instead of leaving the responsibility of evaluating and selecting only to experts, the role of the art audience has also become a topic of discussion. It is true that you have to have basic knowledge to understand art but that does not mean viewers have to conduct in-depth research. I think the responsibility for evaluating and selecting art should be left up to art viewers.

I wanted to do something for and with children when I thought about what I could do in the aftermath of the disaster. Given that children are extremely sensitive to experiences when they are young, I wanted to make an effort to offer them experiences of doing "something" with me which in the future might help them overcome their trauma and problems. For example, Living with Namahage is a project I did in Odate in Akita Prefecture after the disaster. It connects *namahage*[1], a monster who appears in Tohoku's folk customs, with the radioactive contamination caused by the Fukushima nuclear power plant accident, and it hopes to help children understand the danger of nuclear energy. This project was featured in a local Akita newspaper with the headline "Coexisting with Scary *Namahage*."

Another example is Children Pride. Aimed at elementary school children in Tokyo, this project lets children express their personal and everyday demands through demonstrations. What was interesting was how children came to share their individual wishes through a process of call and response. I have continued to do Children Pride events in other Japanese cities.

What I think will happen is that the disaster will become the tipping point for the structure of Japanese society to change. For the next generation, I think art will play a critical role within society if people take on more responsibility for evaluating art, instead of letting others decide.

---

1. A type of demon or ogre that exists in Tohoku folklore. *Namahage* are portrayed by men with fierce red masks and straw capes in certain rituals in Akita in northern Japan.

Karamitsu Akamatsu
The new monster after 3.11

Rikuzen Takada: panoramic from the roof of the hospital

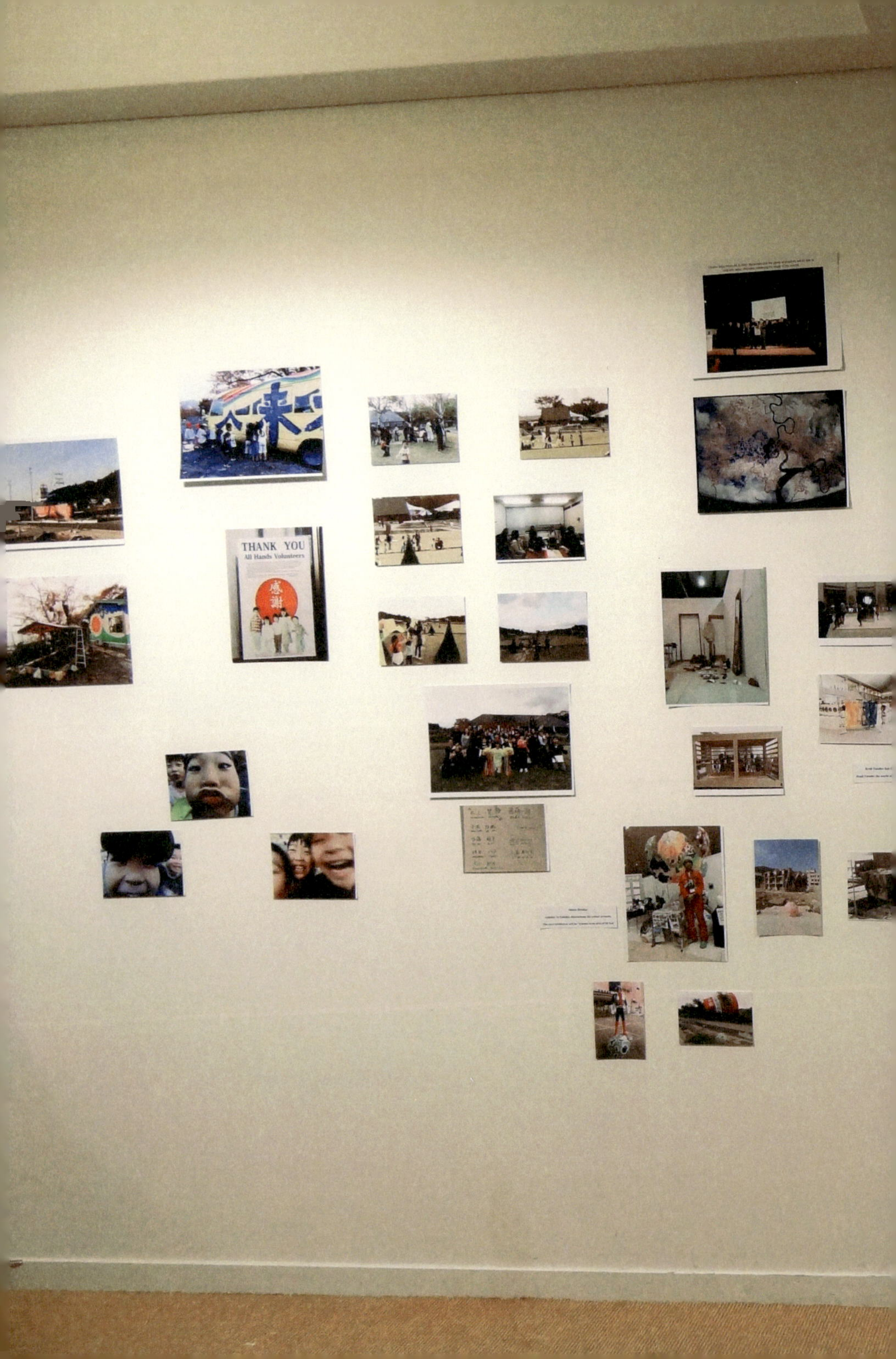
THANK YOU
All Hands Volunteers
感謝

THE ICONS OF THE THIRD MILLENIUM

Nuclear power plants are the form of physical heritage of the third millennium. All the physical heritage of humanity has almost always been and preserved by chance. In very few cases have been preserved by the will of humanity. Nuclear power plants are physical heritages that humanity must preserve, take care and scared for the next centuries.

Guido Fiorti

謝辞

本書の完成に関わってくれた全ての人に感謝の意を表したい。またリサーチ中に出会った全ての人が提供してくれた時間と、本プロジェクトへの関心にもお礼を述べたい。私をレジデント施設に受け入れ、本リサーチを遂行するために必要なサポートを提供してくれたトーキョーワンダーサイトに感謝する。特にディレクターの今村有策さんは、東京滞在中に私が人々に連絡し、イベント(2012年に開催された国際会議であるResArtistも含む)に出席するのを、強くサポートしてくれた。トーキョーワンダーサイトのスタッフの皆さんにも感謝の意を表明したい。特に青木真希子さん、浅野五月さん、深町浩祥さん、杉本ひと美さんには、滞在中とその後のサポートに対して感謝したい。私と同時期にレジデンスに滞在していたアーティストにもお礼を述べたい。彼らとはアイデアをぶつけ合い、当時起こっていたことに関し、意見や情報を交換できた。後藤和子さんや野田邦弘さん、文化経済学会には、学会の二十周年を祝うイベントであり、3.11後の文化の役割という問題を東北地域の文化従事者と議論する場に招待してくれたことに、お礼を述べたい。また、インタビューを引き受けてくれた人々にも、彼らの忍耐と、3.11前後の個人的な経験談を再構築するため辛い瞬間を再訪してくれたことに対し、深く感謝を表明したい。他の多くの方々にお礼を述べたい。この本に収められている声を聞いてくれる全ての人たちが、この酷い出来事に対して能動的なリアクションを起こした人々の声を、やすらぎと激励のあかしとして受け取ってくれれば幸いだ。また、ボローニャに住む、3.11後に連帯イベントを実現するために動いてくれた日本人とイタリア人にも感謝の意を表明したい。また東北芸術工科大学の近藤一弥教授と彼の学生(大山夏葵、白田祐季、高橋栞、粒木まり恵、津留拓也、半澤智朗、眞坂麗)にも、この出版物のデザインとその有用な助言についてお礼を述べたい。そして最後に、大岩希代子さんの貢献がなければこの出版は不可能であった。また日本語文章をインタビューの参加者に送るための準備を手伝ってくれた平文代さんにも再度お礼を述べたい。

2015年3月 グイド・フェリッリ

Guido Ferilli

Acknowledgments

I wish to thank all those who have collaborated in developing this testimony, and in general I wish to thank the availability and interest expressed by all those people whom I have encountered over the course of the entire research period.

Foremost, I would like to thank TWS for hosting me at its residency program and for having given me all the support needed to carry out the research and its director, Yusaku Imamura, for endlessly helping me contact people and attend events during my stay in Tokyo, including the international conference ResArtist, held in October 2012. I also wish to thank the staff of TWS, especially Makiko Aoki, Satsuki Asano, Hiroyoshi Fukamachi and Hitomi Sugimoto, for their support during the residency and in the subsequent months.

Many thanks to the artists who were present during my stay in the residency and with whom I was able to confront ideas and exchange opinions and information with regards to what was happening. I also wish to thank Kazuko Goto, Kunihiro Noda and the Japan Association for Cultural Economics for inviting me to their event, organized to celebrate the twentieth anniversary of the Association, and which also dealt with the issues of the role of culture after 3.11 and with cultural operators in the Tohoku area.

A profound thanks goes to the people who agreed to be interviewed, for their patience and willingness to revisit those terrible moments in order to reconstruct the narrative of their personal experience pre- and post-3.11.

I would like to thank all the Japanese and Italians living in Bologna who have worked to realize the events of solidarity following 3.11. I am indebted to Professor Kazuya Kondo and the students of his course at the Tohoku Design University (Natsuki Oyama, Yuki Shirata, Shiori Takahashi, Marie Tsubuki, Takuya Tsuru, Tomoro Hanzawa, Rei Masaka) for the design of the publication and their helpful advice. Last but not least, many, many thanks to Kiyoko Oiwa, without whose contribution this publication would not have been possible, and Fumiyo Taira for helping me prepare the Japanese version of the texts that I sent to the interviewees. There are truly many more people that I would like to thank. What I hope is that everyone who hears the voices in this book actively reacting to the terrible events of 3.11 will find them a sign of comfort and encouragement.

Guido Ferilli, March 2015

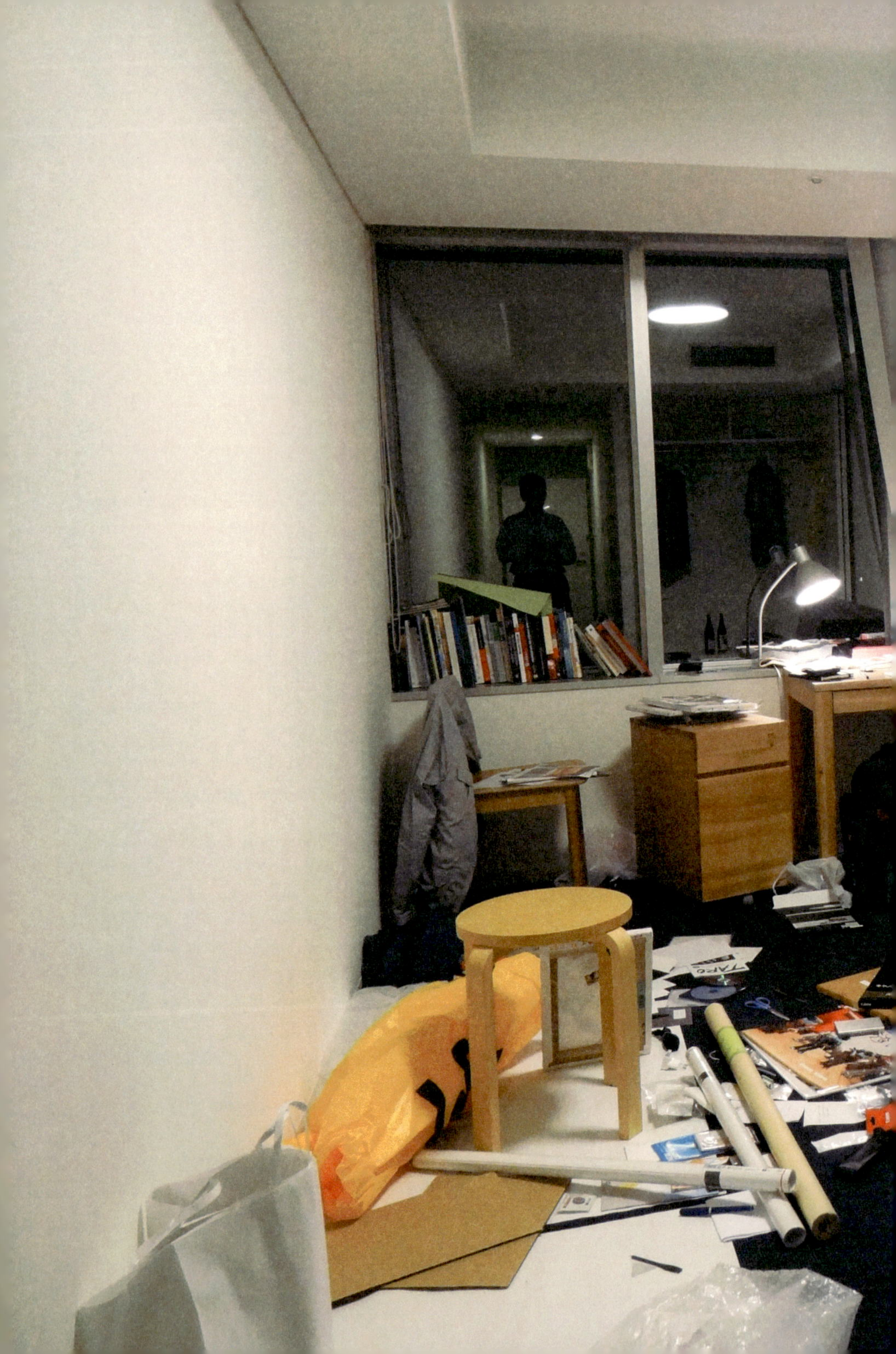

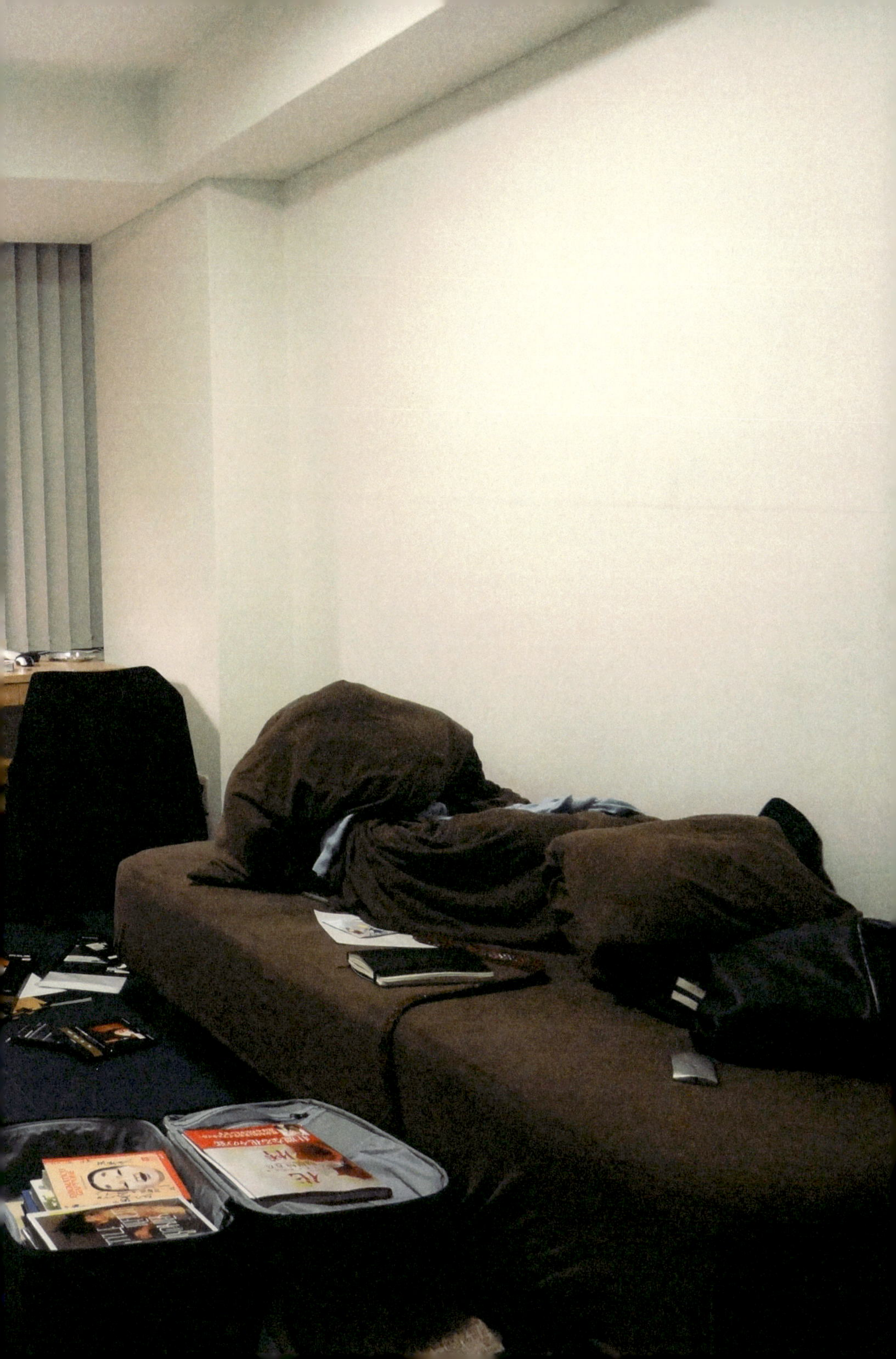

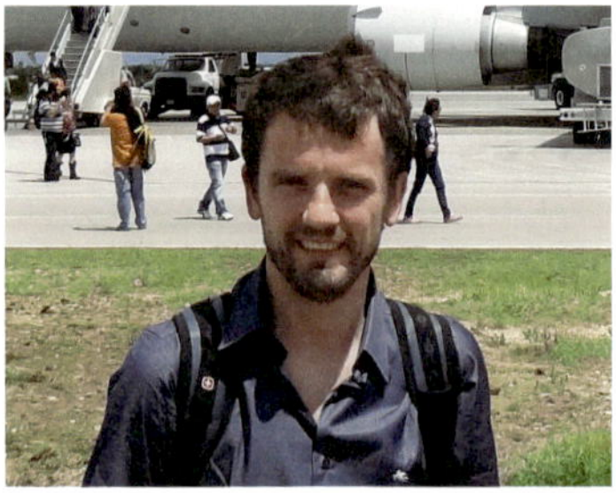

グイド・フェリッリ

1967年イタリア生まれ。ボローニャ大学で経済を学び、2009年エジンバラ・ネピア大学にて博士号取得。現在、IULM大学(ミラノ)助教。
1990年代終わり頃からイタリア国内(サルデーニャ州、ベネト州、ラツィオ州、ロンバルディア州、ペスカーラ、ラクイラ、モデナ、シエナ、ピストイアなどの都市)、国外(カルタヘナ〈コロンビア〉、ベロオリゾンチ〈ブラジル〉、チュニジア、スウェーデン)で文化経済、文化創造産業、地域開発についての数々のプロジェクトを研究・開発してきた。また、ゲスト・スピーカー、議長、講師、パネリストとして多くの国際会議でプレゼンテーションをしている。
「ヨーロッパ文化と経済のプラットフォーム」発展のための戦略グループ「A Soul for Europe」のメンバー、ベネチアのアルセナーレ再検証のための研究チームのメンバー。国立21世紀美術館(MAXXI、ローマ)のマネジメントや財務的持続研究に従事。DiCEプロジェクト(ベネト州の分化地区全域のシステム)のマネジメントを終えた後、ヨーロッパの創造産業、雇用について考える「Tool Quiz」の科学プロジェクト・マネージャーを務めた。現在はデジタル遺産について考える「SmartCulture」に携わる。
近年は、エクアドル世界遺産の官庁から国家遺産に関するプログラムやプロジェクトのセミナーに招待されている。また欧州委員会の先進的なプロジェクト「New Narrative for Europe」の研究にも携わっている。

Guido Ferilli

Guido Ferilli was born in 1967 in Italy. He graduated with a degree in economics from the University of Bologna and gained his PhD from Edinburgh Napier University in 2009. Currently he is Assistant Professor at IULM University (Milan).
Since the late 1990s he has researched and developed various projects in the Italian regions of Sardinia, Veneto, Lazio, Lombardy and in the cities of Pescara, L'Aquila, Modena, Siena, and Pistoia, as well as internationally in Colombia (Cartagena de Indias), Brazil (Belo Horizonte), Tunisia, and Sweden with regards to the fields of cultural economics, cultural and creative industries, and regional development. He has presented his work at many international conferences as guest speaker, chair, lecturer, and panelist. He is a member of the strategic group "A Soul for Europe", working towards the development of the European Culture and Economy Platform. He was also a member of the research group for the requalification of the Arsenal of Venice and the management and financial sustainability study for MAXXI (National Museum of XXI Century Arts), Rome. After overseeing the DiCE project (System Wide Cultural District of the Veneto Region), he became project manager for the scientific project partner of Tool Quiz, a European project on creative industries and employability, and is now involved in SmartCulture, a European project on digital heritage. Most recently he was invited by the Ministry of Heritage of Ecuador to give seminars on programs and projects related to national heritage. In recent years he has also been involved in the initiative New Narrative for Europe, promoted by the European Commission.

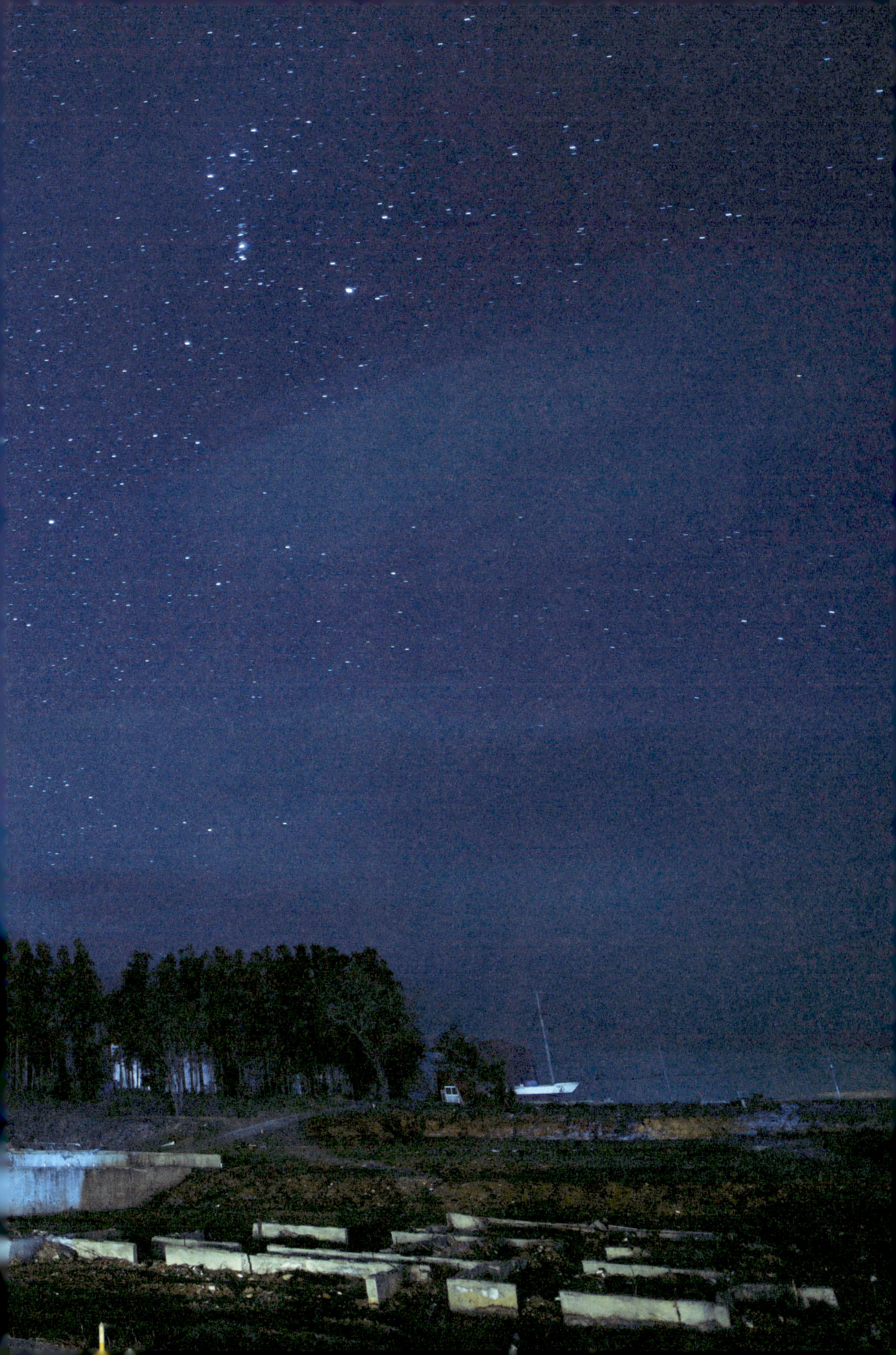

本書の印税は全額、東日本大震災 芸術・文化による復興支援ファンド「GBFund」に寄付させていただきます。
url: http://www.mecenat.or.jp/gbfund/

All royalties of this book go to GBFund – The Great East Japan Earthquake Restoration Fund,
url: https://www.mecenat.or.jp/en/post/gbfund/

写真提供：初沢亜利
(Cover, pp.6-7, pp.32-33, pp.252-253)

Photo courtesy: Ari Hatsuzawa
(Cover, pp.6-7, pp.32-33, pp.252-253)

3.11への文化からの応答
24人のクリエーター・文化人へのインタビュー

グイド・フェリッリ

発行日：
2016年5月1日 初版発行

デザイン：
近藤一弥
東北芸術工科大学近藤研究室

翻訳：
hanare x Social Kitchen

発行者：
姫野希美
発行所：
株式会社赤々舎
京都府京都市下京区堀川五条東入中金仏町
215-6 増田屋ビル
Tel.075-371-8025
http://www.akaaka.com

印刷：
株式会社オノウエ印刷
プリンティング・ディレクション：
花岡秀明
製本：
新日本製本株式会社

©2016 Guido Ferilli
©2016 AKAAKA Art Publishing, Inc.

ISBN 978-4-86541-033-4 C0070
本書の無断転写、転載、複製を禁じます。

Commitment to 3.11
Response to Disaster through Culture and Creativity in Japan

Guido Ferilli

First Edition:
May 1, 2016

Design:
Kazuya Kondo
Tohoku University of Art & Design, Prof.
Kondo Design Laboratory

Translation:
hanare x Social Kitchen

Publisher:
Kimi Himeno
Publishing house:
AKAAKA ART PUBLISHING, Inc.
Masudaya-Building, 215-6 Nakakanabutsu-cho,
Horikawa-Gojo Higashi-iru, Shimogyo-ku, Kyoto,
600-8332
http://www.akaaka.com

All rights reserved. No part of this publication may be
reproduced or transmitted in any form or by no means,
electronic or mechanical, including photocopying, recording or
by any information storage and retrieval system without prior
permission in writing from the publisher.

Printed in Japan